THE CHRONICLES OF FERNÃO LOPES

Tomb of King Pedro of Portugal (14th century). South transept, Monastery of Alcobaça, Portugal. The monarch had the tomb carved in his lifetime choosing to be represented wearing a Roman toga and holding the sword of Justice. An interesting detail is the dog at his feet, possibly his favourite, though certainly an indication of the king's love for hunting. (Image by courtesy of Direção-Geral do Património Cultural / Arquivo de Documentação Fotográfica (DGPC/ADF), Portugal)

First published 2023
Tamesis (Serie B: TEXTOS)

ISBN 978 1 85566 396 1

Tamesis is an imprint of Boydell & Brewer Ltd
PO Box 9, Woodbridge, Suffolk IP12 3DF, UK
and of Boydell & Brewer Inc.
668 Mt Hope Avenue, Rochester, NY 14620, USA
www.boydellandbrewer.com

The publisher has no responsibility for the continued existence or accuracy
of URLs for external or third-party internet websites referred to in this book,
and does not guarantee that any content on such websites is, or will remain,
accurate or appropriate

A CIP record for this title is available from the British Library

THE CHRONICLES OF FERNÃO LOPES

VOLUME 1

THE CHRONICLE OF KING PEDRO OF PORTUGAL

Edited by
Amélia P. Hutchinson
Juliet Perkins
Philip Krummrich
† Teresa Amado

Translated by
† R. C. Willis
Philip Krummrich
Juliet Perkins
Iona McCleery
Francisco Fernandes
† Shirley Clarke

Principal Consultant
Patricia Anne Odber de Baubeta

With an Introduction by
Chris Given-Wilson, † Nicholas G. Round and David Green

TAMESIS

To medievalists of all ages who preserve and share the knowledge and under-standing of times past to illuminate the future, especially the colleagues, collaborators and friends we sadly lost in the course of this project:

Teresa Amado
R. C. Willis
Shirley Clarke
Nicholas G. Round

CONTENTS

LIST OF ILLUSTRATIONS

The editors, contributors and publisher are grateful to all the institutions and persons listed for permission to reproduce the materials in which they hold copyright. Every effort has been made to trace the copyright holders; apologies are offered for any omission, and the publisher will be pleased to add any necessary acknowledgement in subsequent editions.

PREFACE

It is with great pleasure that, on behalf of the whole team participating in this project, we present *The Chronicles of Fernão Lopes*, the first complete English translation of a set of works of primary importance for the history of Western Europe at the end of the 14th century. On opening this first volume, it will not have escaped the reader's attention that this is the result of the collaborative initiative of a group of people and funding institutions. Without the support of every single one of them the present edition of Fernão Lopes's chronicles in English would not have been possible.

This publication also represents a long-deserved act of justice towards 'the father of Portuguese historiography', one of the major chroniclers of medieval Europe, and yet scarcely known outside his country of origin. The joy and satisfaction of making his oeuvre available to an international readership rest in the knowledge that it answers a need often expressed by colleagues wishing to reference Lopes's work, fundamentally for research but also for teaching courses in Medieval Studies in universities outside Portugal and Brazil. In fact, this is how the idea of the present translation project started.

It all began in 2005, when a group of Iberian medievalists attending a session moderated by Professor María Bullón-Fernández, at the International Medieval Congress, in Kalamazoo, became aware of my research on Lopes's chronicles, especially the characterisation of female personalities as part of his narrative strategy. These colleagues lamented the fact that, apart from an anthology dedicated to the presence of the English in Portugal, there was no full translation of Lopes's extant works, and speculated as to when one could be expected. None was being prepared at the time. What is more, publishers in the US had refused book proposals with studies on Fernão Lopes because, as his chronicles were not available in English, in their opinion, such a circumstance seriously curtailed the interest of their readership, unable to make use of the primary source in its original Portuguese. Action was therefore called for.

On my return from the congress, I consulted colleagues who, like me, had a keen interest in Medieval Studies combined with many years of experience in teaching and working on translation. Dr Patricia Anne Odber de Baubeta, former Head of Portuguese Studies at the University of Birmingham, UK, immediately supported the idea and soon we began to plan the ideal team for the task. To our delight, everyone we contacted accepted the challenge, including Teresa Amado, Professor at the Classical University of Lisbon, the internationally renowned expert on Fernão Lopes. Coincidentally, she too was planning her own translation project.

In the circumstances, the logical step was to bring everyone together into a single team, especially in view of the long and complex task before us. This became the group of six native anglophone translators, proudly named on the title page of the present volume, indefatigably guided by Teresa Amado's intimate knowledge of Lopes's work.

In the first years, my mission was to provide the necessary conditions for the translation project to go ahead, 'to let the translators translate', as I used to say jokingly. For the most part, this entailed administrative matters: applying for grants, writing reports, researching specialised terminology, developing an ancillary interactive website with a glossary to facilitate the translators' work, and preparing for the translating team's annual meetings sponsored by the Instituto Camões and the University of Birmingham. These occasions offered valuable opportunities to compare notes, solve problems, and, above all, to develop greater cohesiveness among the team and in the resulting work.

Similarly to team sports, it is the shared nature of the achievement that generates the greatest feeling of elation. Despite the long hours of work over the months preceding the meeting, and the intense discussions engaged upon, there reigned an atmosphere of celebration and energetic collaboration, as the progress made became evident. New objectives were agreed for the year ahead, and the teamwork forged ties of friendship, keeping the channels of informal consultation open to everyone. Dr Odber de Baubeta was instrumental in organising these annual meetings as our host at the University of Birmingham. Her expertise in the strategic planning of long-term projects associated with her continued assistance on translation issues has been invaluable.

There were two very fortunate circumstances from the outset of this project – an interested publisher and generous funding. Tamesis Books, an imprint of Boydell & Brewer, readily offered a contract thanks to Professor Alan Deyermond's recommendation as their advisory board member and internationally acknowledged scholar in medieval Hispanic literature. Elspeth Ferguson, Tamesis Commissioning Editor, with whom Teresa Amado had already established contact, was also unwavering in her encouragement. This backing from a reputable academic publisher contributed to the second fortunate circumstance – considerable grants, first from Direção-Geral do Livro dos Arquivos e das Bibliotecas, Portugal, and then from the National Endowment for the Humanities, US, followed by smaller sums from the University of Georgia's Willson Center for Humanities and Arts, US, the

Instituto Camões together with the University of Birmingham and The Anglo-Portuguese Society, in the UK, and the Luso-American Development Foundation, in Portugal.

Sadly, in the course of this 12-year project, we have lost four dear colleagues: Teresa Amado, our Portuguese expert, as mentioned above, and three British team members, Clive Willis, Emeritus Professor at the University of Manchester, Shirley Clarke, University of Birmingham, and Nicholas Round, Emeritus Professor, University of Sheffield, another outstanding scholar in medieval Hispanic literature. He is also a contributor to the introduction published in the present volume. Nevertheless, each time we suffered the loss of a team member, we became firmer in our resolve to complete the project.

Looking back, we realise that beyond reaching the goal originally set, we have achieved a few 'firsts'. Apart from being the first complete English translation of Fernão Lopes's chronicles, this is the first time they are being published in a single edition, together with the first comprehensive general index encompassing all chronicles. The general index will include all the names of the people mentioned in the chronicles, no matter how insignificant, and all the place names too. In the course of our work, we became aware of how important place names were for identifying events, people with similar names, and, of course, to follow itineraries. Despite the books on royal itineraries already available, in view of the itinerant nature of Peninsular medieval courts, for administrative or military reasons, we believe that the systematic indexing of the place names in these extensive chronicles will be most helpful to the reader. In time, we noticed that our guiding objective of producing a reliable translation of Lopes's chronicles had led to yet another: to transform the joint index into a useful research tool.

To readers not yet familiar with Lopes's work, we particularly recommend all the introductions to each chronicle in the present edition. They focus upon each respective period and its relevance in the history of Western Europe, as well as the issues and objectives inherent to the chronicler's work, from his concept of history to his craft in producing a document of historical, literary and cultural significance. We also recommend the introduction to Derek Lomax's and Robert Oakley's anthology of translated passages from the *Crónica de D. Fernando* and both parts of Lopes's *Crónica de D. João I*, published in the volume titled *Fernão Lopes. The English in Portugal 1367–1387* (Warminster: Aris & Phillips, 1988).

To some, the general bibliography in the fifth volume may seem unexpectedly long for a translation. The intention is to satisfy the curiosity and interests of a wide readership by suggesting more generic works side by side with academic studies and articles intended to encourage the reader in going beyond the information provided in the introductory studies to the present volumes.

Hopefully, many items in this bibliography will call the attention of international medievalists to issues of interest to their own research by pointing to
parallels with other European regions and circumstances. Fernão Lopes has
a keen eye for detail and perspectives often more attuned to the common
people, by comparison with other contemporary chroniclers, which can be of
considerable assistance to the modern scholar.

Ultimately, we wished to share with the reader most of the bibliography
our team consulted during a decade of labour as a token of our commitment
to attempting the most accurate translation we were capable of.

Many of our translators and collaborators are specialists in specific areas
of Medieval Studies, with several of their articles and monographs listed
in our general bibliography. They contain important studies on diplomacy,
administration, military affairs including medieval military orders, the navy,
the structure of a courtly society and, inescapably, Fernão Lopes's chronicles
as a literary masterpiece carefully constructed according to a well-defined
objective.

Lopes's works, however, also share concerns very much in line with our
own 21st century: the economy and its fluctuations in times of crisis, currency
devaluation, periods of inflation. He even offers specific examples of how these
problems impacted the purchasing power of ordinary mortals. His description
of the relative values of different coins and currencies is also fascinating.
Interspersed in the narrative, one can find interesting information on health,
food or lack thereof, its impact on the human body, as well as on how to
improvise food for an army on the move. Though passing unnoticed until
not long ago, much attention is given to women, their roles within different
social strata and impact on events and the world surrounding them. In fact,
Lopes's chronicles lend themselves to very promising comparative studies on
kingship and queenship.

All this, and no doubt much more still to be discovered, has been hiding
under the heavy layer of medieval Portuguese prose, hence our delight in
making it available to a wider readership in the world.

The translated text we bring to you in the present volume is based on
Giuliano Macchi's critical edition of Fernão Lopes's *Crónica de D. Pedro*
(Lisbon: Imprensa Nacional-Casa da Moeda, 2007). The preference for this
text in particular is due to the rigour achieved by its editor after exhaustive
consultation of the extant manuscript copies dating back to the 16th and 17th
centuries, as well as the first printed edition of 1735 by Rev. José Pereira Bayão.

Macchi had published an earlier critical edition of this chronicle in Rome,
in 1966. Unfortunately, he was unable to complete his second revised edition
for the Imprensa Nacional-Casa da Moeda (IN-CM) because he passed away
suddenly in 2003. Teresa Amado, leading authority on Fernão Lopes and

key member of our translation project, as mentioned above, knew Macchi's text intimately. She had been responsible for completing the preparation of his manuscript for publication; hence her recommendation to use it as the base for the present translation. Unfortunately, she passed away suddenly in 2013; thus, it was now our turn to complete the first English translation of Fernão Lopes's chronicles, the last great project Teresa Amado participated in, although without the benefit of her expertise. Her mark, however, and the lessons we learned with her, are patent.

With regard to the other chronicles, we followed a similar policy as there were good critical editions available, namely those published by the IN-CM: the *Crónica de D. Fernando*, also edited by Giuliano Macchi (published 2004) and the *Cronica del Rei Dom Joham I de boa memoria e dos Reis de Portugal o décimo, Parte primeira*, as a facsimile of Anselmo Braamcamp Freire's 1915 edition, published in 1977 with a preface by Luís F. Lindley Cintra. The *Parte segunda* was edited by William J. Entwistle and published also in 1977.

At the time our translation work was in progress, Teresa Amado was also coordinating a research group at the Centro de Estudos Comparatistas of Faculdade de Letras de Lisboa, working on a new critical edition of the *Crónica de D. João I, Primeira Parte*, intended as a joint publication of the Imprensa Nacional and the Centro de Estudos Comparatistas. Interestingly, she found that 'the exercise of translation into another language forced her to a new perception and discovery of the original meaning in the text, which literary analysis couldn't always transmit successfully', as Professor José Mattoso remarks in his '*In memoriam* de Teresa Amado'.[1] Sadly, she did not see this publication either, and the volume only came out in 2018; despite that, and understandably, there is a close relationship with our *Chronicle of King João I of Portugal, Part 1*, though it did not come out in time to be used as one of our primary sources. Cristina Sobral, Professor at the Universidade Clássica de Lisboa, completed that edition together with Amado's team of collaborators at the Centro de Estudos Comparatistas: Ariadne Nunes, Carlota Pimenta and Mário Costa; to all we are truly grateful.

Before closing, I must return to where I started: the team responsible for this translation. As already hinted above, there was a good balance between the expertise all members shared as translators and their different, though complementary, areas of specialisation. Clive Willis was an expert in Camões, the

---

[1]   Editor's translation of: 'O exercício da tradução para outra língua obrigou-a [a] uma nova percepção e descoberta do sentido do texto original que a análise literária nem sempre conseguia transmitir': José Mattoso, '*In memoriam* de Teresa Amado', *Medievalista*, 15 (2014), 8–11 <https://journals.openedition.org/medievalista/257> [Accessed 2 February 2022].

16th-century author of the Portuguese epic *Os Lusíadas*, but he also nurtured a special interest for the Peninsular Wars (1807–1814). Philip Krummrich, besides his own publications dedicated to poetry and travel, has several translations of works by Portuguese, Spanish, and Galician authors, from 18th-century António José da Silva's plays to Fernando Pessoa's quatrains and, more recently, works by the Galician novelist Teresa Moure. Juliet Perkins is a scholar in Portuguese 14th and 15th-century historical and philosophical writings, with an enviable background in the Classics, but who also publishes on 20th-century Portuguese authors such as Maria Judite de Carvalho, José Cardoso Pires, and Herberto Helder. Iona McCleery is a historian, with research interests in medieval Portugal, medicine, food, and eating, and an active member of the Leeds Institute for Medieval Studies. Shirley Clarke was a fine linguist mastering several Romance languages, including Portuguese; she taught at various schools, at the University of Birmingham, translated the 'Barca plays' by Gil Vicente, the 16th-century father of Portuguese theatre, and won first place in the Vida Hispanica Camões Translation Prize. Francisco Fernandes is also a linguist, a lecturer in Portuguese and in translation at the City University of London, as well as an excellent translator.

How was it possible to create a cohesive text when six translators were working simultaneously on different sections of the same chronicle? The answer is: with great dedication and collegiality, guidance from an expert in Lopes's chronicles, and multiple revisions, as explained below in the 'Translators' note'.

Finally, in answer to the disappointment of colleagues who in 2005 wondered why Lopes's chronicles had not been translated yet, there is a very good reason: only the use of digital technology and the internet could facilitate the constant revisions and circulation of drafts among a large group of specialists and collaborators scattered around the world.

Without wanting to be too presumptuous, we believe that this English edition of Lopes's chronicles will open new avenues to many areas of medieval studies. It will bring to a wider international community of scholars a rich new source until now inaccessible to them because it remained in its original medieval Portuguese.

We can only hope our readers will be as enthralled by Lopes's narrative as we were translating this important contribution to the study and understanding of one of the most tumultuous and decisive periods in Western Europe.

Amélia P. Hutchinson
Cascais, 30 October 2022

ACKNOWLEDGEMENTS

The Chronicles of Fernão Lopes is an undertaking that could only be fulfilled thanks to the vision and generosity of a considerable number of people and institutions. Their trust and commitment to this project for over a decade deserves our utmost gratitude.

Our indebtedness to the late Professor Alan Deyermond is immense, for recognising the importance of publishing a translation of Fernão Lopes's chronicles in English and for bringing our project to the attention of Boydell & Brewer with very positive words of endorsement. We are also most grateful to Elspeth Ferguson, former Tamesis Commissioning Editor, for encouraging our first steps in this undertaking, and to her successors, first Scott Mahler and then Megan Milan, who has seen this project to its completion.

The Direcção Geral do Livro, dos Arquivos e das Bibliotecas, Portugal, was the first institution to award the project a significant grant thanks to the support of Dr Assunção Mendonça at the Arquivo Nacional da Torre do Tombo, Lisbon. This institutional demonstration of trust was instrumental in attracting another very generous grant from the National Endowment for the Humanities (NEH), US. This enabled us to conceive and finance most of this translation project together with an auxiliary website containing interactive information on the content of the chronicles, as well as a glossary for the use of our translation team and, hopefully, for other translators working on similar texts. In time, this website expanded to become the Fernão Lopes Portal at present hosted by the Faculdade de Ciências Sociais e Humanas at the Universidade Nova de Lisboa (NOVA). Dr Lydia Medici, liaison officer at the NEH, will never be forgotten for her genuine engaged encouragement and invaluable assistance, becoming for us the human face of a most prestigious but exacting and complex organisation. We are equally grateful to the University of Georgia's Willson Center for Humanities and Arts, US, the University of Birmingham supported by the Instituto Camões and the Anglo-Portuguese Society, in the UK, and the Luso-American Development Foundation, in Portugal for the grants they awarded to this project.

For advice on applying for and managing a large project, we express heartfelt thanks to Dr Patrícia Anne Odber de Baubeta, former Head of the Department of Hispanic Studies, University of Birmingham, UK, and to

Professor Thom Whigham, University of Georgia (UGA), in the US, who shared with us his experience as a panellist in other prestigious grant-awarding institutions. He also reviewed our first draft of the *Chronicle of King Pedro of Portugal*. Professor Francis Lough, Head of the Department of Hispanic Studies, University of Birmingham, in 2010, saw to the initial launching of this project, and confirmed the university as the venue for its annual meetings. We are equally grateful to the Centro de Interpretação da Batalha de Aljubarrota (CIBA), namely Dr Barbara Cardoso, Mrs Sónia Veríssimo, and its director, Dr João Mareco, for their generous encouragement and support, including the venue for our last annual translators meeting.

Several Portuguese institutions, such as the Biblioteca Nacional, despite their limited budgets during the climate of financial austerity prevailing in 2010, offered their contribution in the form of logistic support. The Art Library of the Calouste Gulbenkian Foundation gave permission to post on the project's auxiliary website photographs of historical architectural interest from their digital collections. Speaking of photographs, in view of the saying that 'a picture is worth a thousand words', our gratitude goes also to the Torre do Tombo, Museu do Dinheiro, Direção Geral do Património Cultural, and the Directors of the Monastery of Batalha and the Monastery of Alcobaça, Dr Joaquim Ruivo and Dr Ana Pagará, respectively, for their assistance in obtaining the beautiful and meaningful images that have made the frontispiece of the volumes in the present edition.

We were most fortunate to enjoy the support and encouragement of a large group of eminent scholars, colleagues, and friends who generously shared with us their expertise, advice, and bibliography on many relevant areas of study fundamental for the comprehension and subsequent translation of Lopes's chronicles. In Portugal, Professor João Gouveia Monteiro, University of Coimbra, kindly and patiently assisted us on many issues related to military equipment and strategy, the organisation of a military society, the battlefield, in particular the Battle of Aljubarrota, and the aftermath of similar military conflicts. At the NOVA, Dr Miguel Gomes Martins was most helpful on matters related to siege engines; Dr Miguel Metelo Seixas assisted with issues of heraldry on banners and seals; Dr Mário Farelo was able to identify important members of the clergy only referred to in the chronicles by their Christian name; Dr Giulia Rossi Vairo kindly shared bibliography on titles and ranks in the Portuguese navy; and Dr Tiago Viúla de Faria, before authoring his insightful introduction to *The Chronicle of King João I, Part 2,* in volume 4 of the present edition, assisted us in deciphering the names and identifying several persons of English, French, or Gascon origin mentioned in Lopes's chronicles. Dr Viúla de Faria joined our translation team as a consultant in Anglo-Portuguese diplomatic relations in 2012. Since then, he has contributed to the Fernão Lopes Portal and had an important role in its migration from UGA, where it was originally developed, to NOVA. We also have a tremendous debt of gratitude to Professor Maria João Branco, former Director of the Instituto de Estudos Medievais, not only for her readiness to assist in any academic or administrative matter, but also, in particular, for offering a new home to the Fernão Lopes Portal at the NOVA, in Lisbon, the chronicler's city. Thanks to her, this digital tool will remain in open access online serving initially as a set of interactive footnotes to the *Chronicle of King Pedro of Portugal*. Further development of the portal to include the other chronicles is planned for the future given the much-appreciated support of her successor, Professor Maria de Lurdes Rosa.

Jorge Almeida, independent researcher and editor of a modernised Portuguese version of Fernão Lopes's chronicles, must also be recognised for his work in this field and for his generous advice on many difficult passages. I also thank Isabel de Pina Baleiras, with whom I share a fascination for Queen Leonor Teles, for the helpful exchange of correspondence we had on this extraordinary female personage.

In the UK, Dr Barry Taylor, the British Library, has been extremely generous, kindly sharing with us his advice and expertise on matters related to indexing, one of the most laborious tasks in this project, which entails several hundreds of entries and sub-entries. Dr Tobias Capwell, Wallace Collection Museum, on the other hand, has assisted us in providing answers on several questions related to medieval weapons and armoury, particularly on identifying what appeared to be a nomenclature problem as a very early example of systematic updating of military equipment at a national level. Regarding military affairs, we cannot thank enough Dr Axel Müller, Director of the International Medieval Congress, University of Leeds, for calling our attention to the regular use of firepower in late 14th-century Portugal. Professor Chris Given-Wilson, University of St Andrews, besides authoring the historiographical introduction to Fernão Lopes in the present volume, was also one of the first to encourage a translation of his chronicles. Dr David Green, Harlaxton College, also contributed enthusiastically to this volume with a very informative introduction to King Pedro's reign in the context of the contemporary European historical and political scene. A special note of remembrance and gratitude is due to the late Dr Luís de Sousa Rebelo, King's College London: a brilliant Lopesian scholar, an impressively kind person, and an inspiring PhD supervisor to some members of our team. His exemplary research approach and his advice in the first stages of our translation became important guidelines to follow. The same can be said of the late Professor Nicholas Round, University of Sheffield, author of the literary introduction to Lopes's narrative style and rhetorical strategy, also in the present volume. He was an outstanding Hispanist, a person of immense knowledge, and an admirable translator, whose interest and energy devoted to this project were remarkable. Even after a prolonged period of illness, as soon as he recovered enough, he threw himself into reviewing the translation draft of our four volumes, offering pertinent observations, footnotes, and suggesting much-improved alternative translations. Our first proofreader, Helen Oakley, Open University, UK, must also be remembered for her diligent patience reading a script still struggling to find 'Fernão Lopes's voice'. Her timely observations pointed out inconsistencies to be ironed out and allowed us to appreciate the text from the point of view of the reader not familiar with its context and contents.

Our thanks go also to many colleagues in the US, including Professor Rita Costa Gomes, Towson University, a strong 'instigator' of this project, consultant, contributor to the Fernão Lopes Portal, and author of the introduction to *The Chronicle of King Fernando of Portugal*, in volume 2 of the present edition. She was instrumental in identifying many Portuguese and Castilian personalities and clarifying specific Portuguese medieval concepts before we were able to decide how to translate them. Professor Josiah Blackmore, Harvard University, a rare American scholar publishing on Fernão Lopes, willingly accepted our invitation to write the introduction to *The Chronicle of King João I of Portugal, Part 1,* in volume 3, and reviewed our first efforts in translating *The Chronicle of King Pedro of Portugal*. We remember also the late Professor Noel Fallows, UGA, who assisted us with specialised bibliography and his expertise on military matters in medieval Castile. To Professor José Manuel Calderón Ortega, University of Alcalá, Spain, we are grateful for his prompt reply also recommending bibliography on the types of ships mostly used in medieval Castile.

A very special word of thanks and appreciation goes to Professor Teresa Amado's sister Luísa Amado and niece Joana Sousa Monteiro. Their generous assistance helped our project team, in some way, to overcome the great loss of our esteemed colleague and co-Director, by making available to us the last translation notes and corrections, which she did not have the opportunity to share when her life was suddenly cut short.

At this point, I will let Teresa Amado's own words thank a number of Portuguese colleagues whose names have remained in the anonymity created by the geographic distance that separated the members of our team. In the e-mail message below, dated August 2012, I assume Teresa is referring to colleagues at the University of Lisbon and at NOVA:

> Relativamente às grafias dos lugares, a verificação só em parte foi feita por mim. Está lá muito trabalho do Clive, que é óptimo sobretudo para nomes não portugueses, mas para esses também, e, nas outras traduções, está o trabalho precioso dos meus colegas geógrafos e historiadores que

tenho consultado para os casos bicudos. Agora é só aproveitar todo esse trabalho já feito.[1]

Needless to say, all members of our translation team were absolutely outstanding. Without their support, dedication, and the long hours of labour invested in addition to their usual personal and professional commitments, the present edition of *The Chronicles of Fernão Lopes* would never have become a reality. As project director, I am also deeply indebted to their respective families, and mine too, for having consented to 'co-habit' with Fernão Lopes for the last 12 years.

In closing, a final word of thanks to all colleagues and friends who, over the years, expectantly asked whether this translation had already been published. To us, the question in itself reflected interest and encouragement.

[1] Editor's translation: 'Concerning the spelling of place names, that has been done only partly by me. There's a lot of Clive's work invested there, which is great, especially for non-Portuguese names; but for those, as well as for other translations, there is the precious work of my colleagues in Geography and History, whom I have consulted on the thorniest cases. Now, it is just a matter of making use of all that work already done.'

Sponsors

NATIONAL ENDOWMENT FOR THE HUMANITIES

The Fernão Lopes Translation Project, including the publication of Fernão Lopes's chronicles for the first time in English, has been made possible in part by the National Endowment for the Humanities: Exploring the human endeavor

REPÚBLICA PORTUGUESA

CULTURA

DIREÇÃO-GERAL DO LIVRO, DOS ARQUIVOS E DAS BIBLIOTECAS

Funded by the Direção-Geral do Livro, Dos Arquivos e das Bibliotecas / Portugal

REPÚBLICA PORTUGUESA

CULTURA

BNP BIBLIOTECA NACIONAL DE PORTUGAL

THE ANGLO-PORTUGUESE SOCIETY

MOSTEIRO DA BATALHA

PATRIMÓNIO CULTURAL

Direção-Geral do Património Cultural

CAMÕES INSTITUTO DA COOPERAÇÃO E DA LÍNGUA

PORTUGAL

MINISTÉRIO DOS NEGÓCIOS ESTRANGEIROS

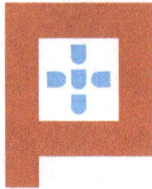

BATALHA DE ALJUBARROTA CENTRO DE INTERPRETAÇÃO

IEM INSTITUTO DE ESTUDOS MEDIEVAIS NOVA FCSH | FCT

FLAD LUSO-AMERICAN DEVELOPMENT FOUNDATION

Franklin College of Arts and Sciences UNIVERSITY OF GEORGIA

Willson Center for Humanities & Arts UNIVERSITY OF GEORGIA

THE WALLACE COLLECTION

TRANSLATORS' NOTE

It is with a sense of achievement and pride that we present the first full English translation of the chronicles of Fernão Lopes. A little more than 585 years after the death of Lopes's patron, King Duarte, the work of this unique historian will be available to non-speakers of Portuguese. We have worked throughout as a team, from rough drafts to final revisions, enjoying the advantage of mutual support between colleagues and the benefits of digital technology. The following note will cover some of the problems and solutions of the project, first concerning style and tone, secondly concerning terminology.

A long-dead writer of history deserves accuracy in translation. That has been our principal aim. Given that translators inevitably have individual voices, we have striven for consistency of style and tone in accordance with those of Lopes. It is worth noting that his chronicles present a range of styles and registers: from the very formal, echoing sources such as diplomatic and legal documents and official correspondence, to the idiomatic and anecdotal. Lopes was not only a reader but a listener. His oral sources were important: eyewitness accounts, local legends, and popular sayings feature in his chronicles. Like Livy, he had an ear for dialogue. This he frequently recreated to flesh out his characters, often to guide his presentation of them to suit his ideological ends, to lend vividness to a scene, to explore people's motives. By turns grave and ironic, courteous and scathing, impartial and partisan, his voice is as varied as his material. In attempting to convey faithfully this range of style, we have had to resist a number of temptations. We did not want the translation to sound archaic, nor did we want to modernise it beyond recognition. We encountered many seemingly dull passages, full of legal jargon and rhetorical flourishes, by comparison with thrilling battle scenes and enticing courtly intrigues. Our goal was to make such passages intelligible. We intended that papal decrees should sound like papal decrees, that descriptions of taxes, penalties, and ransoms should be duly sober but as clear as we could make them. In those passages where Lopes cites speech in a more popular register, we have given ourselves more leeway, trying to avoid anachronisms while allowing readers of the English version to taste the same contrast as is found in the Portuguese.

Lopes often writes very long sentences, far longer than a good stylist would be inclined to write nowadays. In our translation, we had to decide whether we had the freedom to divide at least some of those extensive sentences into more manageable chunks, in order to make the English text readable and thus smooth out any features that would puzzle or frustrate the intended readers. On the other hand, if Lopes's style is characterised by long, complex sentences, a translation will be more faithful and authentic if it maintains the general shape of the original. However, we have frequently broken up the many long paragraphs where modern English practice warranted it. We have been cautious about trying to improve the text and to resist the temptation to make Lopes sound the way that we wish he had written. There were times when he seemed to lose track of his own sprawling sentences and where the translators should not just present an equally flawed English version. In those instances, we needed to make sure that Lopes really had gone wrong or 'nodded off'. Where there was an inconsistency or inaccuracy in the text, where doubt still remained about Lopes's meaning, where there was a suggestion of scribal or manuscript error, we have indicated this in a footnote. As a team, we felt confident when all of us agreed that there was a problem with the original. We had the great advantage of having every word of our English version scrutinised multiple times by colleagues who were highly competent and deeply committed to the project.

Lopes, in accordance with 15th-century practice, spelled all personal and place names in Portuguese. Our translation assigns persons in their national language and indexes them accordingly under their full name. The exceptions are those who are more widely known under another language, such as Latin, or persons who have become fully identified with a given place and society, such as Inês de Castro, as a rule associated with a Portuguese universe. Portuguese names are indexed under the last surname; Spanish (and Galician) names are indexed under the composite surname. Lopes habitually refers to persons by only two Christian names; to aid clarity, we have supplied the missing family name in square brackets where there is doubt about someone's identity. We have also dispensed with variant spellings of names and places. Where there was doubt about a Spanish name, we have followed the *Diccionário Biográfico Español*. Place names are spelled according to the country, except for universally accepted anglicised spellings, such as Florence, Venice, Seville or Rome.

Titles of rank are used prolifically by Lopes. We have rendered them into English, except where an important national distinction should be signalled: for example, 'Dom' and 'Dona' for a Portuguese nobleman or noblewoman, and the Castilian equivalent, 'Don' and 'Doña'. Where Lopes refers to ecclesiastical prelates, masters of military orders, and the nobility, it is principally by title not name. Given the many decades covered by the chronicles, there were numerous holders of such positions and rank. We identify these in footnotes to the translation at timely moments, but they are also identified by their full name in the Index.

Capitalisation: given the ubiquitousness of capital letters in the Portuguese text, used as a title but without a name, we have kept capital letters for a few, specific cases: 'Master' is reserved for João, Master of the Order of Avis; 'King' where the name or nation is mentioned (the 'King of Portugal', 'the King of Aragon', 'King Pedro'), 'Constable' or 'Count' for Nuno Álvares Pereira; and popes.

As regards specific lexical areas, a significant difficulty has been to translate offices and positions where there is no direct contemporary English equivalent or where an office has become obsolete. Frequently, offices of state had a Castilian equivalent which has guided our translation and definition. A typical example is *fronteiro* (Sp. *frontero*), the military official or commander responsible for guarding and defending a given frontier region of a country. Modern approximations such as 'frontier guard' or 'border guard' give a somewhat misleading or narrow idea of 'the frontier', so we have taken the concept of Marches to reflect the nature of that borderland and opted for 'Officer of the Marches' or 'Lord of the Marches'.

Readers will note that we have not provided a glossary, since our task was to render everything possible into English, providing footnotes for necessary explanation. Occasionally, a specific Portuguese term needs to be translated by a variety of English terms. Such is the case with *privado*, the role of whom was that of a confidential advisor and implied trust and close friendship of the *privado* with the monarch. Our translation renders it as 'confidential advisor', 'confidant', or 'privy counsellor', according to context.

The exceptions to translating into English are specific archaic items such as weights, measures, and coinage, and land reform terms. These have been left in the original Portuguese. Likewise, there is a very limited number of nouns that have no satisfactory English equivalent, as follows.

Criado: this term derives from the practice of *criação* (Latin *creatio*), the upbringing of a child or youngster placed under the authority of a person unrelated to him or her by blood. This originated a special bond of pseudo-kinship which could not be easily undone and marked the life of the *criado* by obligations similar to family ties. In Lopes's chronicles, the word is often used in this way, especially in the case of the nobility, and carries this sense of mutual obligation and ties, which cannot be conveyed by current English terms such as 'retainer' or 'servant'.

Nao: this was the sail-powered round ship (as opposed to the long ship, the galley, powered by oars), that was used for both trading purposes and warfare, as circumstances dictated. This type of vessel is clearly of the cog type, which goes under a variety of names, such as *nave, nef, nao,* and *nau.* Given that 'cog' is more associated with northern Europe, and *cocha* with the Mediterranean, especially Genoese fleets, given the lack of contemporary documents about Portuguese ship design and construction in the 14th century, and given the considerable presence of Castilian or Genoese vessels in the Portuguese fleet, we have deemed it best to retain the spelling *nao* (modern Portuguese *nau*) to denote this type of ship. Identifying such vessels is particularly relevant where naval exchanges are concerned, and the weather is a decisive factor.

Alcaçar: Lopes is very consistent in the use of this word whenever referring to fortresses or castles with Moorish architectural features and origins. In this, he follows the usage of his near-contemporary and main source for Castilian matters, Pero López de Ayala. As the word 'alcazar' exists in English, though only introduced in the 17th century, the reader will find it in the translation reflecting Lopes's own words and concept of fortress.

A note on dates: Lopes habitually used the Era of Caesar for year-dates. In medieval times in the Iberian Peninsula, such dates were regularly used and refer back to 38 BC, the year in which Caesar Octavianus Augustus took over the government of 'Hispania', the Iberian Peninsula. In Portugal, the Era of Caesar was used for year-dates until AD 1422, when King João I ordered the change to Anno Domini dating. Like other fellow chroniclers, although writing after the change, Lopes preferred to repeat the dates as he found them in his sources. For the reader's convenience the Era of Caesar has normally been converted to AD dates throughout this translation.

Finally, a word about the index. It has been our aim to mention all persons and places in the chronicles and this is the first time that this has been attempted. Despite the resulting length and detail of the index, our hope is that readers will be able to navigate the translation with confidence.

During a long-term project such as this translation, we have built up a debt of gratitude to many academic specialists in medieval studies. Their names appear in the Acknowledgements. Special mention should be made of Alan Deyermond, an early and enthusiastic supporter of the project, and of Nicholas Round. The latter gave unstintingly of his time and expertise to read the first full drafts. Without his keen eye, his skill as a translator, and unrivalled background in medieval Hispanic studies, our translation would be much the poorer.

Lopes's varied and complex chronicles have tested to the limit our abilities as translators and researchers. Inevitably, errors and inconsistencies have escaped our attention, but we trust that they are slight. We sincerely hope that readers will enjoy what we consider to be a truly important narrative of the medieval world.

Juliet Perkins
Philip Krummrich

ABBREVIATIONS

The royal families of Portugal, Castile and Aragon

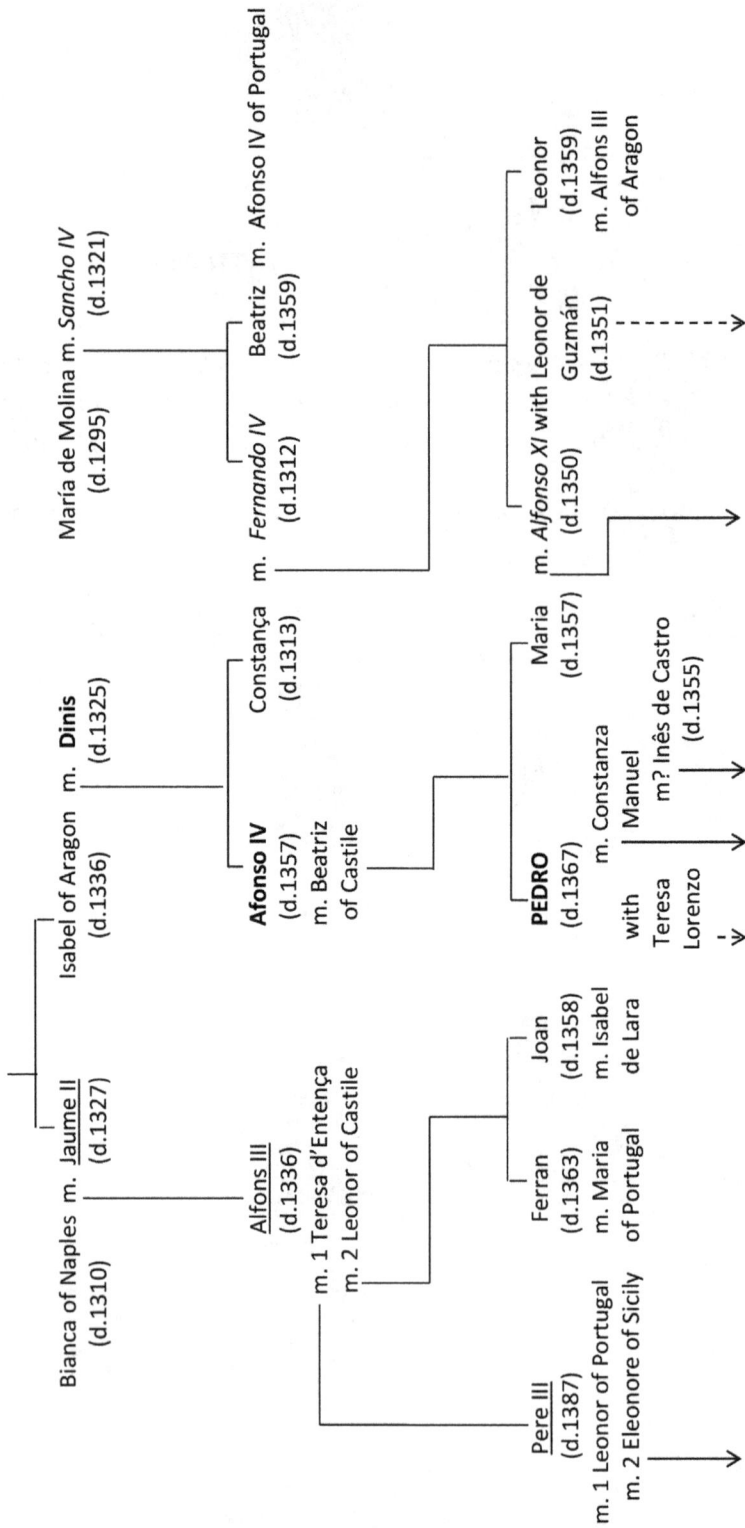

Bianca of Naples m. Jaume II
(d.1310)   (d.1327)

María de Molina m. *Sancho IV*
(d.1295)   (d.1321)

Isabel of Aragon m. **Dinis**
(d.1336)   (d.1325)

Alfons III
(d.1336)
m. 1 Teresa d'Entença
m. 2 Leonor of Castile

Afonso IV   Constança
(d.1357)   (d.1313)
m. Beatriz
of Castile

Fernando IV   Beatriz   m.   Afonso IV of Portugal
(d.1312)   (d.1359)

m.   Leonor
                         (d.1359)
                         m. Alfons III
                         of Aragon

m. **Alfonso XI** with Leonor de
(d.1350)   Guzmán
                   (d.1351)

Pere III
(d.1387)
m. 1 Leonor of Portugal
m. 2 Eleonore of Sicily

Ferran   Joan
(d.1363)   (d.1358)
m. Maria   m. Isabel
of Portugal   de Lara

PEDRO   Maria
(d.1367)   (d.1357)
m. Constanza
Manuel

with   m? Inês de Castro
Teresa   (d.1355)
Lorenzo

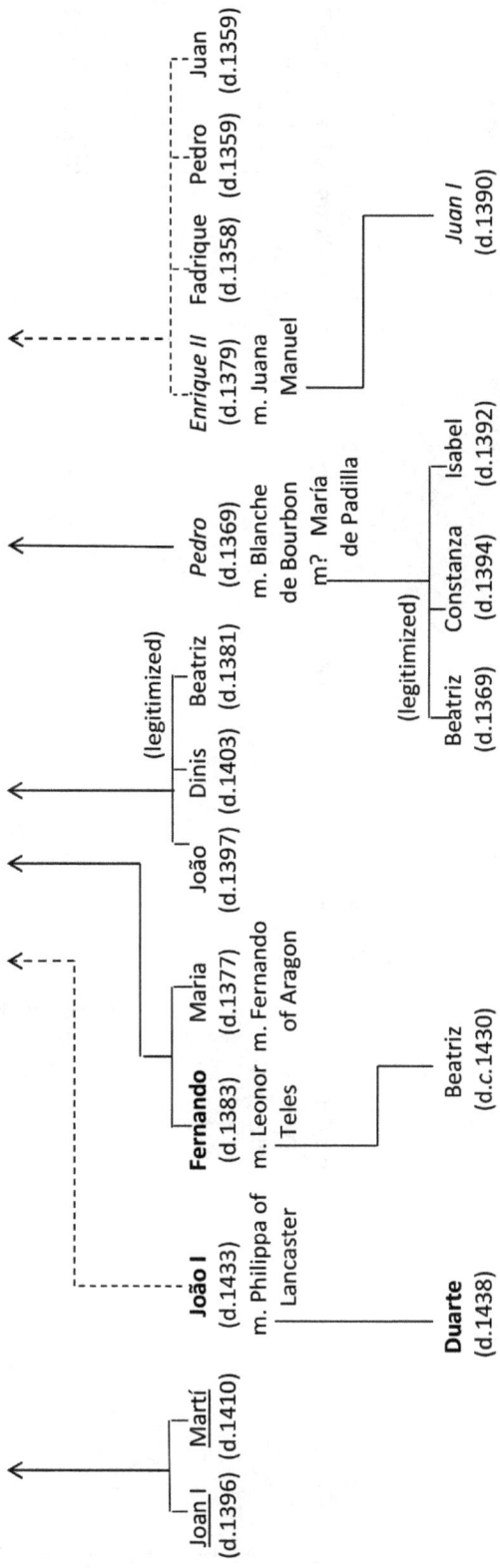

Joan I (d.1396) — Martí (d.1410)

João I (d.1433) m. Philippa of Lancaster — Fernando (d.1383) m. Leonor Teles — Maria (d.1377) m. Fernando of Aragon — João (d.1397) — Dinis (d.1403) — Beatriz (d.1381) (legitimized) — Pedro (d.1369) m. Blanche de Bourbon m? Maria de Padilla — Enrique II (d.1379) m. Juana Manuel — Fadrique (d.1358) — Pedro (d.1359) — Juan (d.1359)

Duarte (d.1438)

Beatriz (d.c.1430)

(legitimized) Beatriz (d.1369) — Constanza (d.1394) — Isabel (d.1392)

Juan I (d.1390)

Key

Name in **bold** = king of Portugal

Name in *italics* = king of Castile

Name <u>underlined</u> = king of Aragon

Illegitimacy = - - - - - - -

The Castilian connections of the Castro family

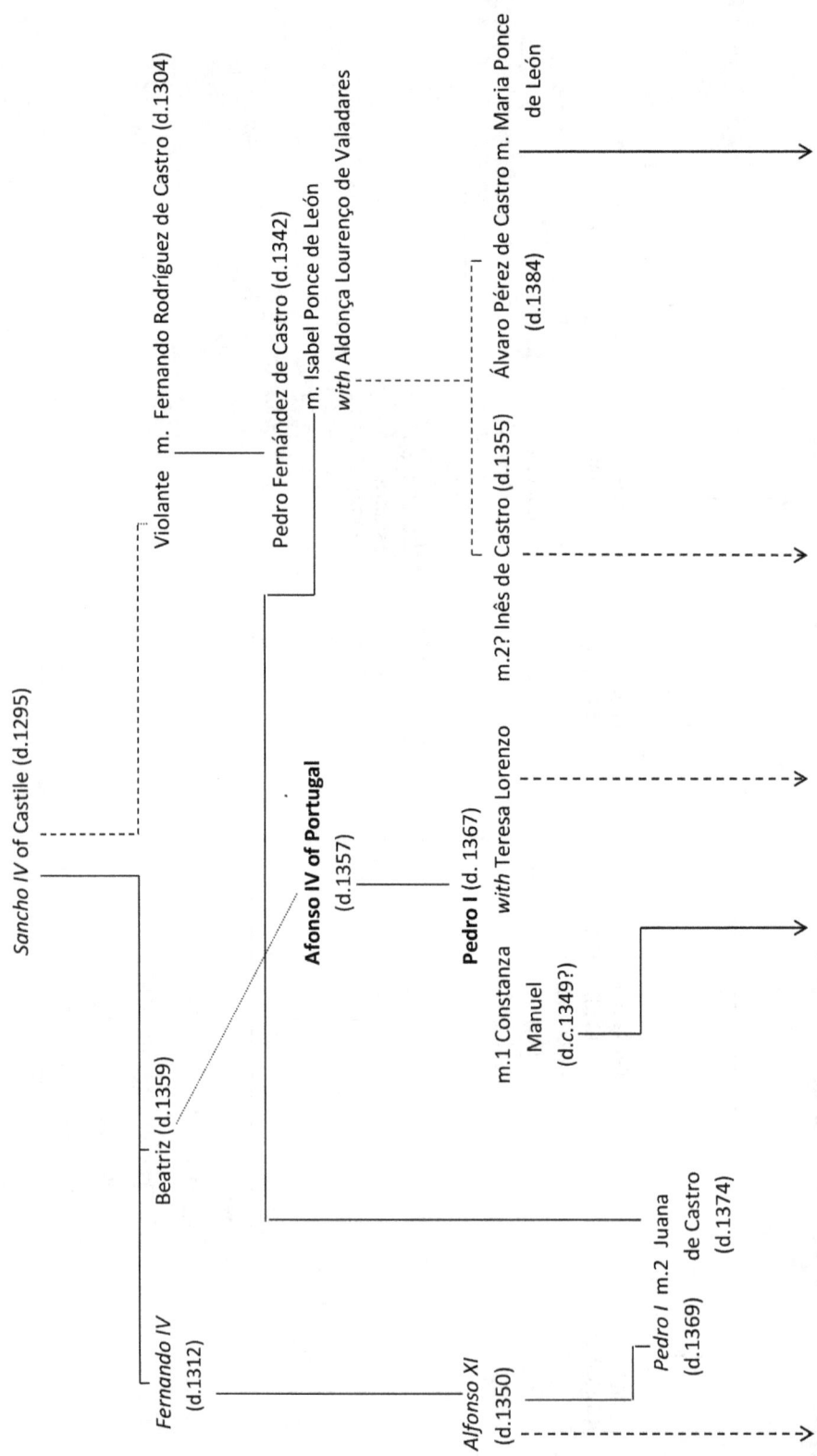

Sancho IV of Castile (d.1295)

Violante m. Fernando Rodríguez de Castro (d.1304)

Pedro Fernández de Castro (d.1342)
m. Isabel Ponce de León
with Aldonça Lourenço de Valadares

Álvaro Pérez de Castro m. María Ponce de León (d.1384)

m.2? Inês de Castro (d.1355)

Fernando IV (d.1312)

Beatriz (d.1359)

Afonso IV of Portugal (d.1357)

Pedro I (d. 1367) *with* Teresa Lorenzo

m.1 Constanza Manuel (d.c.1349?)

Alfonso XI (d.1350)

Pedro I (d.1369) m.2 Juana de Castro (d.1374)

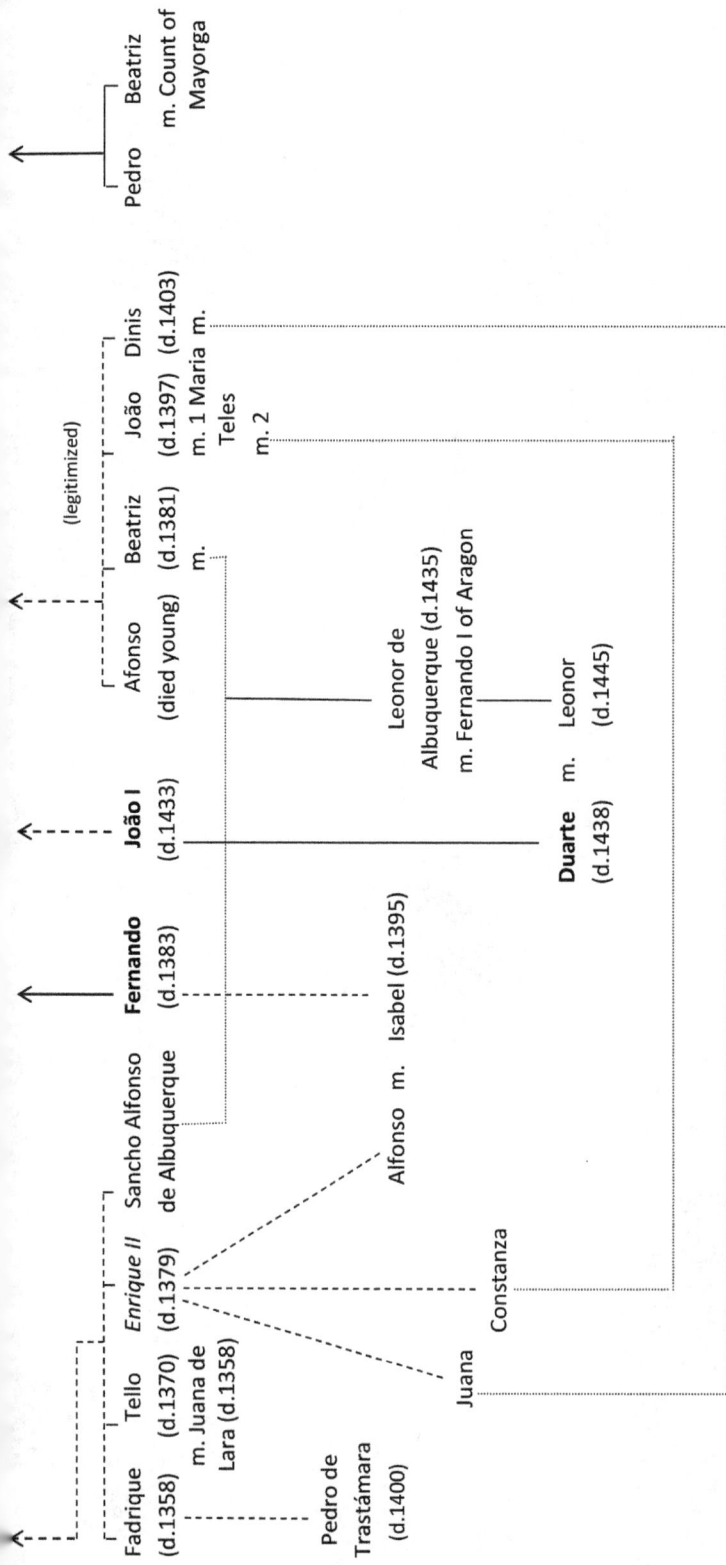

Pedro — Beatriz
m. Count of Mayorga

(legitimized)

Fadrique (d.1358)   Tello (d.1370)   *Enrique II* (d.1379)   Sancho   Alfonso de Albuquerque   **Fernando** (d.1383)   **João I** (d.1433)   Afonso (died young)   Beatriz (d.1381)   João (d.1397)   Dinis (d.1403)

m. Juana de Lara (d.1358)

Pedro de Trastámara (d.1400)

Alfonso m. Isabel (d.1395)

Juana

Constanza

m.

m. 1 Maria Teles

m. 2

Leonor de Albuquerque (d.1435)
m. Fernando I of Aragon

Duarte (d.1438)   m.   Leonor (d.1445)

Key
Name in **bold** = king of Portugal
Name in *italics* = king of Castile
Marriage = ————
Illegitimacy = – – – – –

INTRODUCTION

1

Fernão Lopes: the Father of
Portuguese Historiography

CHRIS GIVEN-WILSON

It would be hard to name a European chronicler whose work has a more pressing claim to dissemination to a wider audience than Fernão Lopes. The surviving chronicles, which were unquestionably authored by this 'father of Portuguese historiography' (or even, it has been said, of Portuguese prose), cover more than half a century (1357–1411) and amount to over half a million words, although it is unlikely that they represent his total output.[1] A self-proclaimed pioneer in the use of archival documents to present historical truth, he also thought deeply about the construction and purposes of history.

Although little of his early life can be verified, Lopes must have been born around 1380, probably in Lisbon, of relatively humble stock. Trained as a notary, he rose high in the service of the new Portuguese royal dynasty of

---

[1] Apart from the translated chronicles in this edition, which amount to over 570,000 words in English, the main sources used in writing this introduction are: P. E. Russell, *Portugal, Spain and the African Atlantic, 1343–1490* (Aldershot: Variorum, 1995), especially chapters 2 ('On the Sources of Fernão Lopes'), 3 ('Fernão Lopes and the Text of the Treaty of Santarém'), and 9 ('Archivists as Historians: the case of the Portuguese fifteenth-century royal chronicles'); Fernão Lopes, *The English in Portugal 1367–1387*, ed. and trans. D. W. Lomax and R. J. Oakley (Warminster: Aris & Phillips, 1988); S. Parkinson, C. Pazos Alonso, and T. Earle (eds), *A Companion to Portuguese Literature* (Woodbridge: Tamesis, 2009), especially the articles by H. Macedo ('Eight Centuries of Portuguese Literature') and S. Parkinson ('Fernão Lopes and Portuguese Prose Writing in the Middle Ages'); H. V. Livermore, *A New History of Portugal* (Cambridge: Cambridge University Press, 1966); T. Amado, 'Fiction as Rhetoric: A Study of Fernão Lopes's *Cronica de D. João I*', *The Medieval Chronicle*, 5 (2008), 35–46; T. Amado, 'Time and Memory in Three Portuguese Chronicles', *The Medieval Chronicle*, 6 (2009), 91–104. Other secondary sources used are referenced below, as are direct quotations from the chronicles or secondary sources.

Avis, acting as librarian to the heir to the throne, Prince Duarte, before being appointed in 1418 by King João I (1385–1433) as keeper of the royal archives in the Torre do Tombo (Archive Tower) in the keep of Lisbon castle. It was here, 40 years earlier, that King Fernando I (1367–1383) had established a repository for the mass of documentary material that underpinned Portuguese royal government. The next two decades saw the responsibilities entrusted to Lopes steadily expand. Continuing to act as the king's 'notary general', he was also private secretary to one of João's sons, Prince Fernando, with whom he established a close personal relationship.[2] When João died in August 1433, Lopes became secretary to King Duarte I (1433–1438), who on 19 March 1434 commissioned him to 'set down in a chronicle the histories of the kings who had previously reigned in Portugal, up to and including the great and noble deeds of my most able and virtuous father [João]'; in return, he was granted an annual salary of 14,000 *reais*.[3] This great task would occupy him for the rest of his working life, until 1454, when, 'being so old and feeble that he is no longer equal to the task', he was replaced by Gomes Eanes de Zurara. Lopes was still alive in 1459 but probably died in the following year.

It may well have been Lopes himself who suggested this undertaking to King Duarte in 1434; intimately acquainted by now with the wealth of archival material in the Torre do Tombo, he must have been well aware of the possibilities it offered for a comprehensive and securely-based history of the first 300 years of the independent kingdom of Portugal. Yet his appointment also reflected a tradition of officially-sponsored historiography in the western European kingdoms. The best-known example of this comes from France, where successive monks of Saint-Denis, near Paris, had been writing French history from a consciously royalist perspective since the 12th century, but the practice was also widespread in the Iberian kingdoms. Alfonso the Wise of Castile (1252–1284) and Jaume the Conqueror of Aragon (1213–1276) both commissioned histories of their realms. The *Chronicle of San Juan de la Peña*, commissioned by Pere the Ceremonious of Aragon (1336–1387), was an overtly nationalistic and teleologically-structured celebration of the dynasties of counts and kings who had created, defended, and expanded the Aragonese kingdom. Closer to Lopes's own time, and covering much the same period as his own, were the chronicles of the great Castilian poet and historian Pero López de Ayala. A soldier, statesman, and political defector to

---

[2]   He gave Fernando a book entitled *Ermo Espiritual* ('The Spiritual Hermitage') and was bequeathed 50,000 *reais* in the Prince's will; his son Martinho became Fernando's physician.

[3]   Lomax and Oakley, *The English in Portugal*, p. vi; Russell, 'On the Sources of Fernão Lopes', pp. 2–4.

the cause of Enrique de Trastámara (1369–1379), who ruled Castile following the overthrow and murder of his half-brother Pedro the Cruel, Ayala had an unfaltering commitment to the fate of the Trastámaran dynasty, despite his veneer of objectivity.

The fact that Ayala also served as a royal councillor and chancellor of Castile was symptomatic of a growing preference for institutionally-based royal historiography during the later Middle Ages. The monks of Saint-Denis may have been writing semi-official history for 300 years, but it was not until 1437 that one of their number, Jean Chartier, was formally appointed as *chroniqueur du roi* by Charles VII of France and granted a position at court. When Philip the Good, Duke of Burgundy, appointed George Chastellain as his official chronicler in 1455, he granted him lodgings in the ducal household and a salary equivalent to that of his councillors. Even in England, where the idea of 'official' history was never as well developed as in France or Spain, the 15th century witnessed a decisive shift from monastic-based to court-based historiography, in which chancery clerks and other royal servants played a prominent role. The fact that Lopes wrote in Portuguese was also character-istic of late medieval historiography; more and more chroniclers were turning away from Latin to the European vernacular languages, reflective of a growing sense of national identity as well as the attempt to reach a wider audience.[4]

Fernão Lopes's training and deep knowledge of the Portuguese royal archives thus made him an ideal candidate for the role of historiographer-royal, and no other European chronicler of the 15th century undertook the task as conscientiously as he did. His declared purpose, indeed his obsession, was to present historical truth.

> Just imagine how much care and diligence we have devoted to perusing vast numbers of tomes in diverse tongues and from sundry countries, not to mention public documents from many archives and other places, through which, after long vigils and hard study, we could not be more certain than we are about the contents of this work.[5]

It was from archives, therefore – especially the registers of the Portuguese chancery, which recorded the proclamations, diplomas, treaties, and other deeds of its kings, nobles, and churchmen – that the true facts of the nation's history were to be gleaned. Needless to say, chroniclers before Lopes had used

---

[4] C. Given-Wilson, *Chronicles: The Writing of History in Medieval England* (London: Hambledon Continuum, 2004), pp. 153–55; and 'Official and Semi-Official History in the Later Middle Ages', *The Medieval Chronicle*, 5 (2008), 1–16.

[5] *The Chronicle of King João I of Portugal*, Part 1 (present edition hereafter referred to as *CKJI*), prologue.

archival material, but none with such consistency or with such unshakeable belief that thereby lay the only route to authenticity.

At times this belief manifested itself as arrogance: of the great Portuguese victory at Aljubarrota in 1385, Lopes declared, 'we condemn, reject and regard as valueless all chronicles, books and treatises that fail to agree with the present volume'.[6] To make such an assertion about a battle seems strange, because the 'true events' of battles were not susceptible to documentary verification to the same extent as, say, diplomatic negotiations were. Lopes was aware of this problem and pointed out that he had painstakingly sifted through a variety of narrative sources as well as eyewitness accounts in order to arrive at his 'definitive' account of Aljubarrota. Yet ultimately, as he admitted on more than one occasion, he had to rely on his own judgment, guided by 'reason' and 'probability'; fortunately for him, he seems to have had implicit confidence in his own judgment (though less in that of his predecessors). There were, however, occasions when even he admitted that the bewildering contradictions of earlier writers made it impossible for him to be sure of his facts and that he must leave it to the reader to decide between them.

As this indicates, Lopes could not construct his history from documentary sources alone. In addition to Ayala's chronicles, he also made extensive use of annals, genealogies, and a number of Portuguese narrative sources, the most important of which were a passionately anti-Castilian life of João written by 'Doctor Christophorous', an anonymous cleric and canon lawyer, and the *Chronicle of the Constable*, an account of the deeds of the Portuguese general and faithful ally of the king, Nuno Álvares Pereira.[7] Nevertheless, when archival material – 'authentic truth', as Lopes called it – was available to him, he almost always preferred it to narrative or allegedly eyewitness evidence. The idea that documentary sources might present their own version of untruth seems not to have crossed his mind – or, if it did, he allowed it to pass. One thing at any rate of which he cannot be accused is falsifying the record: the originals of many of the documents he preserves have been lost, but where his versions can be compared to surviving copies, they reveal a high degree of accuracy.

Underpinning Lopes's approach to writing history was his knowledge of and respect for classical and early medieval authors. The Portuguese royal court under João, his English queen, Philippa of Lancaster, and their son Duarte I and grandson Afonso V (1438–1477) provided a welcoming environment for

---

[6]   *The Chronicle of King João I of Portugal*, Part 2 (present edition hereafter referred to as *CKJ2*), Chapter 37.

[7]   It has been suggested that Lopes himself may have written the *Chronicle of the Constable*, but this is unlikely (Russell, 'On the Sources of Fernão Lopes', pp. 6–11).

scholars. These early monarchs of the Avis dynasty not only wrote treatises and discourses but collected and commissioned both new works and translations and founded libraries. Among the authors who Lopes read and admired were Livy, Cicero, Eusebius, Bede, St Augustine, and above all Aristotle, 'that shining light of philosophy'.[8] What especially attracted him to Aristotle was the latter's insistence on setting down events in a clear and logical order in order to establish the process of causation. The failure to elucidate causation was, to Lopes's way of thinking, the besetting sin of medieval chroniclers; by using authentic documents, placing them in the correct chronological order, demonstrating the relationship between them, and thereby creating a sequential and rational progression of events, he believed (usually correctly) that he could not fail to improve on the work of his predecessors.

Although his theory of historical causation owed something to Renaissance humanism, Lopes also, like his medieval predecessors, had a strong sense of the role of providence and destiny in determining human fate. The over-arching theme of his chronicles – 'the transformation of a medieval kingdom into a new nation forged by the collective will of its people' – was for him the fulfilment of Portugal's destiny in the teeth of Castilian opposition, prefigured by the scene in which, in 1365, when the future João I was just seven, his father King Pedro dreamed that his son had single-handedly put out a fire that threatened to engulf the realm.[9] Lopes was certainly not as objective as he claimed to be. Portuguese through and through, he rarely missed an opportunity to point out instances of Castilian aggression or duplicity. Although he used Ayala's work extensively, he frequently criticised the Castilian chronicler for getting his facts wrong and refused even to refer to him by name, customarily citing him as 'a certain historian' or just 'an author'.[10]

Nevertheless, Lopes's Portuguese kings were far from being one-dimensional heroes. The great achievement of the 'stammerer' Pedro was to make the Crown solvent and assert the supremacy of royal justice over private and local jurisdictions, thereby bringing order to the kingdom and suppressing crime. But the king's passionate and obsessive character also revealed itself in a darkly sadistic streak, most memorably and horrifically described in the revenge he took on the murderers of his beloved mistress, Inês de Castro.[11] His successor Fernando was an even more equivocal figure, a spendthrift who dissipated the riches accumulated by his father and a slippery character with a

[8] See Chapter 29 below.
[9] See Chapter 43 below; quote from Macedo, 'Eight Centuries of Portuguese Literature', p. 3.
[10] See for example *CKJ2*, Chapter 118.
[11] See Chapter 31 below.

passion for hunting and women. The most striking example of the disastrous consequences of Fernando's inability to control his passions was his infatuation with Leonor Teles, which provided Lopes with the opportunity to develop at some length one of his recurrent themes, the instability caused by ill-advised royal matches and scandalous liaisons.[12] Yet if this meant that he often portrayed women as a disruptive political influence, his favourable treatment of the half-sisters Philippa and Catalina of Lancaster, the wives of João I of Portugal and Enrique III of Castile respectively, who did much to preserve peace between Portugal and Castile following the truce of 1389, went some way towards redressing the balance.[13] Lopes did not always view the English so favourably. Although the Anglo-Portuguese alliance naturally inclined him towards acceptance of England's interventions in Iberian affairs between 1366 and 1389, the Earl of Cambridge's chaotic expedition of 1381–1382 made him and many others question the value of having such an ally. It was only after John of Gaunt, Duke of Lancaster, agreed to give his daughter Philippa – the woman destined to become the mother of Portugal's 'illustrious generation' – in marriage to João that relations were repaired and the oldest alliance in European history cemented.

By this time, Lopes's focus had narrowed somewhat. The two parts of the *Chronicle of King João I* are more concerned with internal Portuguese affairs than the narrative of the years 1357–1383, in which Portugal's role is as one, albeit the leading, actor in a series of pan-Iberian wars and diplomatic machinations. Nevertheless, the reigns of Pedro and Fernando provided the essential backdrop to the momentous events of 1383–1385, the pivot of Lopes's narrative, for it was Fernando's diplomatic naivety and military failures against Castile that threatened to reduce Portugal to the level of a client state of its more populous neighbour. This was the predicament from which the royal bastard João, Master of the knightly Order of Avis, emerged as the anti-Castilian champion. His story reads in many ways like a study in royal charisma, most notably in the quasi-messianic quality of his leadership at Aljubarrota, but João is undeniably human and fallible. Initially hesitant and fearful of putting himself forward in 1384–1385, his first thought was to flee to England, and to some extent he was propelled by forces beyond his control, for the great tumult of 1383–1385 also threw up another hero, the citizenry of Lisbon. It was they who took the initiative immediately after Fernando's death, who came out decisively against the Castilian threat, and, despite enduring a brutal four-month siege, did not waver in their determination to maintain

---

[12] *The Chronicle of King Fernando of Portugal* (present edition hereafter referred to as *CKF*), Chapters 57–65.

[13] *CKJ2*, Chapter 98.

their independence. Lopes's graphic descriptions of the power and presence of the *Lisboetas* reveal his origins as a man of the people, as well as his understanding of the forces that went into the emergence of Portugal as a European power. The third hero of Lopes's story was Nuno Álvares Pereira, João's chief military commander, a less flawed and more chivalric figure than the king, aptly described as 'Galahad to his Arthur'.[14]

The events of October 1383 to April 1385 – Part I of the *Chronicle of King João I* – take up around a third of Lopes's entire narrative, more than the combined reigns of Pedro and Fernando and scarcely less than his subsequent account of the next 25 years of João's reign. The fact that Part II of the *Chronicle of King João I* begins with the build-up to Aljubarrota, and that the last event recorded by Lopes was the 1411 treaty with Castile, which appeared finally to guarantee Portuguese independence, gives an impression of calculated consummation to Lopes's narrative, but it may simply be coincidental, a consequence of the fact that he was too frail to continue writing. He may also have felt equivocal about the direction taken by Portuguese history. Beginning with the capture of Ceuta in 1415, the real 'story' of Portugal in the 15th century, or at least that on which his successors chose to focus, was of imperial expansion. Given that Lopes's son Martinho was captured, along with Prince Fernando, on the disastrous Tangier expedition of 1437, and died in a Moroccan prison, he can be forgiven for feeling less enthusiastic than many of his countrymen about their nation's African adventures.

Already marked out by his surviving *oeuvre* as one of the most prodigious historians of the Middle Ages, Lopes probably also wrote (much shorter) lives of the first seven kings of Portugal, from Afonso I (1139–1185) to Afonso IV (1325–1357). This was, after all, what he had been commissioned to do in 1434. Half a century after his death, these would be used as the basis for Rui de Pina's lives of the early Portuguese kings – indeed it has been claimed that the reason why Lopes's chronicles of the first seven kings were lost was because Pina, chronicler-royal from 1497 to 1521, destroyed them in an effort to disguise his dependence on them. Yet although his successors as chroniclers-royal admired and may even have cannibalised Lopes's work, they rejected his archivally-based approach to the writing of history; his immediate successor, Zurara, remarked that too much reliance on official documents produced dull history.

In fact, Lopes's chronicles are far from dull. His descriptive powers, his eye for detail and ear for dialogue (displayed both in the lengthy and carefully reasoned speeches and in the occasionally barbed retorts which he put into the

---

[14] Quote from Parkinson, 'Fernão Lopes and Portuguese Prose Writing of the Middle Ages', p. 51.

mouths of his characters), his sense of humour and irony, his psychological insight and desire to peer behind the curtain of human behaviour to elucidate character and motive reveal him to have been, despite his training, much more than an archivist. It was the seriousness of his mission – the legitimisation of the Avis dynasty and the destiny of Portugal as an autonomous kingdom – which determined the seriousness of his approach to the evaluation of evidence, but his rhetorical art and his grounding in romantic and chivalric literature were equally influential in shaping his writing. His legacy to both his successors and his people was to create the historical memory of a nation.

2

Fernão Lopes and the Writing of a Late Medieval Portuguese History[1]

NICHOLAS G. ROUND

Modern history begins when more and more people emerge into social and political consciousness, become aware of their respective groups as historical entities having a past and a future, and enter into history.[2]

I

Medieval historical writing is too diverse to admit of much valid generalisation. But those who produced it, virtually without exception, shared the belief that the ultimate object of their study was the working-out of God's purposes in human affairs. Not all medieval chroniclers would have defined their own immediate task in the terms applied to it by R. G. Collingwood: 'to narrate the *gesta Dei*'.[3] In English aristocratic chronicles, for example, reference to God has been characterised as 'comparatively rare and casual ... rhetorical rather than explanatory'. Yet few would have resisted the general

[1] This introduction in its opening sections (I–VII) greatly amplifies, and in its later sections (VIII–XI) largely reproduces, an article of mine ('The Revolution of 1383–84 in the Portuguese Provinces: Causality and Style in Fernão Lopes') that first appeared in *Dispositio*, 10:27 (1985), 65–84. I am grateful to the Department of Romance Languages, University of Michigan, for permission to reprint material from it here.
[2] E. H. Carr, *What is History?* (Harmondsworth: Penguin, 1964), p. 149.
[3] R. G. Collingwood, *The Idea of History* (Oxford: Clarendon Press, 1946), p. 53; further discussion in William J. Brandt, *The Shape of Medieval History: Studies in Modes of Perception* (New Haven, CT: Yale University Press, 1966), p. 82; Beryl Smalley, *Historians in the Middle Ages* (London: Thames and Hudson, 1974), pp. 28, 63.

presumption that human history was, in Beryl Smalley's phrase, 'the history of man's salvation in time'. Revealed religion seemed to imply as much, and also to predict the major crises of that history: the Second Coming and the end of the world. Before that cataclysmic outcome, the rest of history seemed all of a piece; to quote Smalley again, 'A medieval writer could distinguish stages in the history of salvation, but they were religious stages.' Whatever more immediate crises might occupy his attention, the writer of history in the Middle Ages was aware that the really significant upheaval was yet to come. This awareness found one expression in the influential tradition of the world's six ages. The sixth and latest of these was seen as dating from the Incarnation; the Seventh Age would follow, after the end of history, as the Kingdom of Heaven upon earth.[4]

Unusually among medieval historians, the 15th-century Portuguese chronicler Fernão Lopes was strongly conscious of living in a post-crisis era. Portugal under the early monarchs of the Avis dynasty was no Kingdom of Heaven; the disputes that brought the Infante Pedro to power as Regent in the late 1430s were a reminder of intractable social conflicts.[5] Yet Fernão Lopes, writing in 1443, remained profoundly impressed by the transformation in Portuguese affairs that had accompanied the installation of the ruling dynasty 60 years earlier.

The nature of those changes is, to this day, a matter of controversy.[6] Those historians who are agreed that the crisis of the early 1380s was socially revolutionary in its character tend to differ as to the kind of social revolution which it

[4] On the Ages of the World see Smalley, *Historians in the Middle Ages*, pp. 29–30; also, Luís de Sousa Rebelo, *A concepção do poder em Fernão Lopes* (Lisbon: Horizonte, 1983), pp. 61–71; Alan Deyermond, 'Historia universal e ideología nacional en Pablo de Santa María', in *Homenaje a Álvaro Galmés de Fuentes*, vol. 2 (Oviedo: University; Madrid: Gredos, 1985), pp. 313–24, at pp. 316–18.

[5] José Hermano Saraiva, introduction to his edition of *História de uma revolução: Primeira parte da 'Crónica de El-Rei D. João I de Boa Memória'* (Lisbon: Europa-América, 1977), p. 13; also, Luís de Sousa Rebelo, 'The Idea of Kingship in the Chronicles of Fernão Lopes', in F. W. Hodcroft et al. (eds), *Mediaeval and Renaissance Studies on Spain and Portugal in Honour of P. E. Russell* (Oxford: Society for the Study of Medieval Languages and Literature, 1981), pp. 167–79, at p. 167.

[6] Antonio Sérgio, introduction to Fernão Lopes, *Crónica de D. João I segundo o Códice no. 352 do Arquivo Nacional da Torre do Tombo*, *I* (Oporto: Civilização, 1945), esp. p. xxi; António Borges Coelho, *A Revolução de 1383: tentativa de caracterização*, 3rd ed. (Lisbon: Seara Nova, 1977), esp. pp. 105–06; Joel Serrão, *O carácter social da Revolução de 1383*, 3rd ed. (Lisbon: Horizonte, 1976), esp. p. 43; ibid, pp. 56–61 (on Jaime Cortesão); Joaquim Veríssimo Serrão, *História de Portugal*, *I. Estado, pátria e nação (1080–1415)* (Lisbon: Verbo, 1978), pp. 298–304.

was. António Sérgio sees the wealthy merchants of Lisbon and Oporto acting as the national leadership of a proletarian revolt against the nobility and their local middle-class clients. For António Borges Coelho the affair was a bourgeois revolution, both nationally and locally, at every stage. Divisions within the middle classes were not significant, and popular insurrection never managed to make its own 'revolution in the revolution'. According to Joel Serrão this was achieved for a time in the popular protests of 1383, but the movement's middle-class supporters gained control in the constitutional settlement of 1385. By contrast with all these, Jaime Cortesão's view that the upheaval was not socially but patriotically motivated still has its adherents. Joaquim Veríssimo Serrão, in particular, stresses the continuity of Portuguese social structures, and states flatly that 'Em 1383 não houve uma luta de classes.'[7] Dynastic right and national independence were the issues that, in this interpretation, led Portuguese of every class to support the Master of Avis, Dom João, against his Castilian rival for the Crown.

These competing views are, to a large extent, alternative readings of Fernão Lopes; there is matter in his *Crónica de D. João I* which can be cited in support of each one. On balance, though, his evidence tends to reinforce rather than to weaken the claim that the movement that brought João of Avis to power did have a measure of social-revolutionary content. The caveats advanced by Veríssimo Serrão, however, are important: Fernão Lopes does state that families were often divided against themselves; Chancery documents do make it clear that there were supporters of the Castilian cause who did manage to retain their lands and status; much other documentation has yet to be examined. The 14th-century *povo* was less restrictively defined than some modern interpretations of that term will allow. Yet Fernão Lopes, who after all had looked at a good many documents himself, and who was capable of much precision in his designation of particular social groups, leaves no room for doubt as to his overall assessment. For him the early 1380s were a period of profound change – change that went well beyond the dynastic shift. It involved, certainly, a great national victory over Castile. But it also witnessed much autonomous action on the part of the unprivileged classes of Portuguese society. Without these initiatives it was most unlikely that João of Avis would have become king at all. A further aspect of the process was a redistribution of lands and offices, in which some (not all) of the older nobility and gentry lost their fortunes, and some (not all) of João's low-born supporters made theirs. The social transformation may well have gone somewhat further; it appears

---

[7] 'In 1383, there was not a class struggle', editor's translation; Joaquim Veríssimo Serrão, *História de Portugal*, vol. 1, *Estado, Pátria e Nação (1080–1415)*, 2nd ed. (Lisbon: Verbo, 1978), pp. 298–304.

from other sources that even the economic grievances of landless peasants met with some relief in terms of wage rates.[8] All in all, it is not hard to see why it should have seemed to Fernão Lopes that nothing after these years was to be the same again.

II

The phrase in which this is most obviously registered is *outro mumdo novo* [another new world]. It is disconcerting, then, to find that Fernão Lopes had used these same words before, in the opening chapter of his *Crónica de D. Fernando*.[9] There he had meant little more than that the new king's reign was not much like that of his father. In Chapter 7 of the First Part of the *Crónica de D. João I* he uses the phrase again in the restricted sense of a time of inter-regnal change and the many uncertainties linked with it. But the new dispensation referred to in Chapter 163 of that chronicle (pp. 335–36) is far more elaborately presented, being linked quite explicitly with the Six Ages of traditional historiography. The Avis period is represented here as a seventh historical age, which will last 'until the end of time or as long as it pleases God' (p. 336). It is an emphatic enough assertion of the chronicler's post-crisis awareness, and goes far to explain the flavour of modernity that marks his historical writing.

Even so, it requires to be taken in context. What is distinctive about the new order, as Fernão Lopes presents it here, is that it is a 'new generation of people', in which persons of 'such low status as is unsuitable to relate' (p. 336) are raised to the highest rank. But, as we have already noted, this, while it happened, did not happen as universally as is here implied. It was even, to a degree, reversed before very long; already by the time of the *Cortes* of Coimbra in 1385, there were moves afoot to reinstate many displaced gentry

---

8   Sérgio, introduction, p. xviii; on the changes wrought by the new regime see Borges Coelho, *A Revolução de 1383*, pp. 119–46.

9   Sérgio, introduction, p. xi; Fernão Lopes, *Crónica de D. Fernando*, ed. Giuliano Macchi, 2nd edn (Lisbon: Imprensa Nacional-Casa da Moeda, 2004) Prólogo, p. 4; the parallels in *Crónica de D. João I*, Chapters 7 and 163, can be found in the present edition, volume 3, *The Chronicle of King João I of Portugal, Part 1*, henceforth *CKJI*, at pp. 23 and 336. Quotations from Fernão Lopes in sections I–VII of this introduction are from the English texts provided in the present edition; in sections VIII–XI, where the focus is on the chronicler's linguistic and stylistic choices, citations are in Portuguese and are taken from the following: Fernão Lopes, *Crónica de D. Fernando*, ed. Giuliano Macchi; Fernão Lopes, *Crónica del Rei Dom Joham I, Parte Primeira*, ed. Anselmo Braamcamp Freire (Lisbon: Imprensa Nacional-Casa da Moeda, 1977).

of allegedly pro-Castilian leanings.[10] Possibly Fernão Lopes's picture may be truer to the moment of history to which this portion of his chronicle refers – just after the lifting of the Castilian siege of Lisbon in 1384 – than to the eventual settlement of João I's established reign. The point of real interest, indeed, is that he applies the Seventh Age motif precisely where he does. It follows immediately after a section of his work (Chapters 159–62) in which lists of persons and communities contributing to the Castilian defeat are carefully drawn up.

Fernão Lopes announces his intention of arraying these lists in a traditional social hierarchy (Chapter 159): first the noblemen who took João's side, then the governors of castles who stood by him, and finally the citizens and residents of Lisbon itself. But the actual presentation does not quite conform to this. Its final chapters are spoken by an allegorical figure of the loyal city of Lisbon, celebrating those who shared her commitment to the *evamgelho portugues,* and culminating in a list of the other towns that followed her in this (Chapter 162). The effect is certainly not to detract from the importance of support at this level. The last paragraph in this chapter (p. 335) does indeed look forward briefly to the installation of João of Avis as king, seen as the long-desired marriage of the city with its *senhor e esposo.* There is a sense, then, that the new age does begin with the new reign. But the actual placing of the Seventh Age chapter tells against this. The reign does not actually begin until the events that occupy the final section of Part I of the chronicle (Chapters 182–92): recognition of João's claims by the *Cortes* of Coimbra, and acclamation of him as sovereign in the towns and cities. If the Seventh Age motif were intended to flatter the new dynasty it would have made a neat conclusion here. Placed earlier it points away from the question of kingship and towards the event that Fernão Lopes regarded as truly epoch-making: the deliverance of Lisbon.

This had been a crowning mercy of Providence; it had owed much, too, to João of Avis. Fernão Lopes acknowledges both these debts. But the city's successful resistance was, before all else, the culmination of what the Portuguese had, against every expectation, done for themselves. That is the emphasis which Fernão Lopes's disposition of his material at this point affirms; it is, precisely, the extraordinary event that precipitates the new age. The characterisation of that age as a 'new generation' is of a piece with this. However selective it may be as an account of Portuguese society at large, the sense of disrupted hierarchy that it expresses was clearly, in Fernão

---

[10] Saraiva, *História de Uma Revolução,* p. 504, quotes (from Marcelo Caetano, 'As Cortes de 1385', *Revista Portuguesa de História,* 5:2 (1951), 5–86, especially pp. 82–83) a petition submitted with this in mind.

Lopes's estimate, an appropriate response to the events of the early 1380s. Other chapters of his work will furnish details that might amplify or modify that response. But the New World and the Seventh Age are not attempts to summarise that detail in a sociological way. They are rhetorical expressions of how Fernão Lopes felt these events to be important.

Indeed, that is what he says they are: these concepts are introduced 'with daring words, as if in jest, by way of comparison' (p. 336). The three phrases are not quite identical in meaning; each in its way is apt. In an age when millenarian preaching was a potentially subversive force – and one that had certainly made itself felt in the movement that brought the Avis to power – there was indeed a measure of daring attached to such notions.[11] Fernão Lopes is at pains to distance himself from too radical an application of them. He disclaims any intention of predicting an early, or even a precise, date for the actual end of the world, and he is cautious here – more so than elsewhere – in using references to Jesus Christ to describe the role played by João of Avis. Only towards the end of the chapter does he allow himself the sly observation that João's patronage has enabled many of his supporters, by acquiring vassals, to become like the apostles, fishers of men. The rhetorical background of such uses of typology is familiar; this particular instance clearly belongs to the idiom implied by 'as if in jest'.[12] But this formula of pure play will not adequately cover Fernão Lopes' central purpose; it is the third term, 'by way of comparison', which best expresses that. On the one hand, something wholly intentional is being conveyed: the measure of the difference made by the events of 1384. On the other, Fernão Lopes does not seek to displace or deny the pre-existing term of his comparison. The scheme of traditional historical thinking, derived from Eusebius and Bede, is reaffirmed as valid.[13] Belief in

[11] On the millenarian tradition see Norman Cohn, *The Pursuit of the Millennium: Revolutionary Messianism in Medieval and Reformation Europe and its Bearing on Modern Totalitarian Movements*, 2nd edn (London: Mercury Books, 1962); on this element in the background to the Avis revolution see Rebelo, 'The Idea of Kingship', pp. 177–78, and *A concepção do poder*, pp. 57–61. One reason for Fernão Lopes's caution may well be that the whole topic had become less safe to approach openly, following the Hussite and Taborite controversies in Bohemia in the early 15th century.

[12] Mário Martins, *Estudos de cultura medieval*, vol. 3 (Lisbon: Brotéria, 1983), p. 215, considers that this qualifying phrase preserves the passage from being 'parodia do sagrado'. For a similar use of New Testament material compare Álvaro de Luna's reply to the admonition that 'se devia de tenplar en el ganar', citing the verse 'lo que viniere a mí non lo lançaré fuera' (Fernán Pérez de Guzmán, *Generaciones y semblanzas*, ed. R. B. Tate (London: Tamesis, 1965), p. 46.

[13] For the relevant passage from Bede, *De temporibus*, see Rebelo, *A concepção do poder*, pp. 137–38.

the conclusive outcome of history promised by Christian eschatology is not abolished by Fernão Lopes's sense of inhabiting a post-crisis epoch. Instead, the two attitudes coexist – the one more clearly sanctioned by authority, the other more directly rooted in experience.

III

This coexistence of the traditional with the new is a constant throughout his work. The *Crónica de D. Pedro*, his earliest surviving chronicle, may not have diverged very much from the pattern of its now lost predecessors. It is relatively short, covering a ten-year reign in a mere 44 chapters. Its principal subject, announced in the *Prologue*, is the traditional – even folkloric – theme of King Pedro's exemplary reputation as a *rei justiceiro* [justicer king]. Several other elements bear something of the same folkloric character: the king's addiction to dancing by night through the streets of Lisbon (Chapter 14); the prophecies of future greatness for his natural sons, João of Avis and João the son of Inês de Castro (Chapter 43); and, indeed, the whole Inês de Castro episode itself. Yet transcribed royal letters and similar documents appear from the outset (Chapters 2–3), as do well-documented details of monetary and fiscal policies (Chapters 11–13). A long central section on foreign affairs draws extensively on the Castilian chronicler Pero López de Ayala, whose tendentious portrayal of Pedro the Cruel is, at this stage, largely endorsed (Chapter 16). More remarkably, Fernão Lopes's own account of Pedro of Portugal as the model of an ideally just ruler has features – arbitrary, absolutist, capricious, and even sadistic (Chapters 5–9) – that can only undermine the King's credibility in any such role. The blend of selective memory (plainly troubling to Lopes's notions of integrity as a historian) and coercive revenge attaching to the Inês de Castro story (Chapters 27–31) is similarly unsettling. The popular verdict, cited in the final chapter, that Portugal had never experienced a decade like Dom Pedro's reign, hints at future turbulence, if only because King Pedro's sons could have inherited – as all of them, João of Avis not excepted, did – something of his deeply unstable temperament.

The agenda that all this implied for chroniclers – to provide examples, ethically assessed, of how great personages bore themselves under the pressure of great events – was in no sense a radical one. On one level, that kind of agenda continued to preoccupy Fernão Lopes for the whole of his writing life. The focus on the deeds of great lords, on their character and lineage, and the incentive to provide lessons for princes, are all affirmed at various points in the Second Part of the *Crónica de D. João I* (e.g. Chapters 88, 199). In Chapter 164 of the foregoing chronicle, following on immediately after his bold revision of the *mumdo novo* topic, he refers to the instructive value of exemplary 'deeds of chivalry'.

These priorities are not greatly altered by the rather broader array of fitting topics that from time to time he finds worth including in his narrative: major external events where these are relevant to what was happening in Portugal (*Crónica de D. Fernando*, Chapter 107); enactments of the *Cortes* of Coimbra, selected to illustrate the procedures adopted there (*Crónica de D. João I*, Part II, Chapter 1); the precise mandate of a negotiating team sent to Castile (ibid, Chapter 178). Conversely, when presenting the crucial battle of Aljubarrota (ibid, Chapter 36) he sets a conscious limit to his concerns, seeking to know 'what ought to be known': how many men were there, how the battle was won, how long it lasted, which captains took part, and what were the casualties. As for his allocation of praise and blame (mainly for loyalty or its opposite in relation to King João), his measured approach, grounded in St Augustine, includes the caveat that none of it should bring permanent reproach to those lineages that were later reconciled with him (*Crónica de D. João I*, Part I, Chapter 175). None of this would take us far beyond essentially class-defined notions either of Fernão Lopes's own preoccupations, or of the audiences he had chiefly in mind.

Yet that is not the audience he appears to envisage when, in the Prologue to Part I of the *Crónica de D. João I*, he declares his intention to 'set down the unadulterated truth, leaving out all feigned praise as regards the good events, and simply revealing to the people in plain terms whatsoever adverse occurrences there were and the way in which they came about'. Whatever uncertainties might attend his notion of what *o poboo* was, it clearly meant something more than the Portuguese ruling class. And his promise of a plain, corroborated and truthful account, here as later in his approach to the description of Aljubarrota, affirms a measure of autonomy from their particularised concerns, or those of any other group. The form that that autonomy took is made clearer in a remarkable sequence of chapters, extending across the whole of Fernão Lopes's output, in which issues of epistemology of the most fundamental kind are brought to the fore.

The earliest of these, Chapter 29 of the *Crónica de D. Pedro*, draws on Aristotle, the 'shining light of philosophy', for an associative theory of memory that renders King Pedro's alleged recollection of his marriage to Inês de Castro, and its confirmation by various third parties, deeply suspect. Though declining to rule formally on the truth of the matter, the chronicler does observe that 'reason cannot accept' these accounts – showing plainly enough what his own views were. Also Aristotelian in its source is his insistence in *Crónica de D. Fernando*, Chapter 139 that we cannot know how things are without an understanding of their remote and primary causes. His starting-point for the discussion (*Crónica de D. João I*, Part I, Prologue) of the environmental and hereditary roots of local identification may have lain in a critique of prevailing notions of 'natural bonds'. Such ideas, after all, provided compelling motives for the great number of Portuguese who rallied to the Avis cause. But when it came to the local partiality into which motives of this sort could lead historians, Fernão Lopes was insistent that such was not his way. He dwells at some length on the time and effort spent in research to avoid bias of any kind. Chapter 23 of the same chronicle lays out, in what is perhaps the most elaborate of all these essays, the varieties of revelation, physical and spiritual, and the five different kinds of dream. Though Fernão Lopes declines to record his specific sources, the background here is plainly scholastic. Its effect is to validate in these terms the notion that the life-story of Friar João da Barroca, the holy man whom João of Avis consulted, was indeed shaped by divine visitations. Chapter 37 of *Crónica de D. João I*, Part II, insists once again that the chronicler needs to be certain – as eyewitness, or through clear (that is to say, well-documented) knowledge – about what he sets down. Chapter 38, more enigmatically, observes that 'nothing is so well-demonstrated by the representation of things as by the thing itself' – hinting, perhaps, at a diagram or visual illustration of the disposition of troops at Aljubarrota, or simply stressing once again in his approach to this episode, the virtues of a plain tale, plainly told.

In this regard, indeed, we need to take Fernão Lopes's assertion with some degree of scepticism, for he also possessed and cunningly used a generous array of rhetorical tropes and techniques. Yet the outline of a basic theory of historical knowledge and how to attain it remains impressive. Grounded in personal witness, reliable memory and whatever documentation is to be had, its analysis supported from the best of medieval intellectual practice, the tale of unfolding causal chains is to be brought together in as coherent and credible a narrative as may be achieved – useful, no doubt, to those at whom it is first and foremost directed, but not determined in advance by their uses of it. The ideas informing this vision had been around for a long time, and did not in themselves impugn medieval notions of the supernatural and its role in historical causation. But to invoke Aristotle, the dominant presence in medieval logical theory, in order to underwrite the basic norms of specifically historical discourse was to take a gigantic step towards modernity. We can see what it means in practice in Chapters 47–48 of the *Crónica de D. Fernando*, when Fernão Lopes confronts the digressive, far-fetched and, in his view, defamatory accounts provided by Martim Afonso de Melo and another of the failed negotiations over a proposed marriage alliance between King Fernando and an Aragonese princess. He subjects these narratives (which, he declares, would have been better left unwritten) to a barrage of essentially Aristotelian questioning: what was the sum of the proffered dowry? who did what with it? why? how? why were other crucial decisions taken? and how were they, in their turn, implemented? Analysis along these lines, he declares, has led to a research programme, involving much hard work, on which the true version of events, which he now proceeds to give, has been based.

IV

Such is the method to which Fernão Lopes remains committed throughout his mature work. It is most explicitly applied in those cases where sources contradict one another, or in those others where he treats the account in one particular source as unreliable. Leaving aside the *Crónica de D. Pedro*, where such issues tend to be less clear-cut, his three longer chronicles offer just over 20 instances of the former type. Fernão Lopes only rarely seeks to fuse these conflicting versions into a single coherent narrative. Chapter 23 of the *Crónica de D. Fernando*, describing the assassination of Pedro the Cruel, is one exception. His discussion of the wildly disparate estimates of the numbers on either side at Aljubarrota (*Crónica de D. João I*, Part II, Chapter 37) might count as another. Here he finds some excuse for differences that arise because numbers were assessed at different points in the rallying of forces, but none at all for discrepancies designed merely to inflate the reputation of one side or the other. Equally – although he will sometimes admit (e.g. ibid, Chapter 15) to leaving out 'well-known contradictory accounts' – it was not his custom to reject out of hand sources that differed among themselves.

Rather, he prefers to set down both opinions, often adding that 'the reader is free to choose between them', or some phrase to that effect. Only on rare occasions, though, does he leave the issue entirely open, admitting, for example, that 'nobody knew for certain' who it was that had captured the Castilian banner at Aljubarrota (*Crónica de D. João I*, Part II, Chapter 45). Much more commonly, he privileges one or the other account with a fuller explanation of his own, sometimes adding a brief word of commendation: 'not to be rejected' (*Crónica de D. Fernando*, Chapter 100); 'more satisfactory' (*Crónica de D. João I*, Part I, Chapter 8); even 'a lengthier account' (ibid, Chapter 79). His preferences can also be linked to various shifts of focus: from the lukewarm resistance by certain Portuguese towns against Castilian capture in 1369–1370 to King Fernando's notoriously ineffectual performance against the invaders (*Crónica de D. Fernando*, Chapter 36); from Diogo Lopes Pacheco's reasons for fleeing to Castile to the results of his bellicose advice to the king there (ibid, Chapter 81); from the date at which the marriage of João I to one of John of Gaunt's daughters was first mooted, to João's own decision that his bride should be Philippa, unencumbered by her sister Catalina's claim to Castile (*Crónica de D. João I*, Part II, Chapter 91).

For the rest, Fernão Lopes's preferred versions find their justification either in terms of what appears (or fails to appear) in written documents, or through a process of contextualising within his broader narrative. An example of the former type occurs when, after presenting four accounts of João de Avis's intentions prior to the *Cortes* of Coimbra, he opts for the last of them (*Crónica de D. João I*, Part I, Chapter 181) because it coincides with the instruction (which he quotes) given by the loyal city of Lisbon to its *Cortes* delegates. Typical of the latter approach is his discussion (ibid, Chapter 172) of Nuno Álvares's abortive raid on Vila Viçosa. Here he concludes that allegations of his being lured there by false messages of support from within the town are likely to be correct: otherwise, those summoning him would have been punished, and that did not happen. Consistency with written (or, as in *Crónica de D. João I*, Part I, Chapter 64, eyewitness) record; consistency with related aspects of the story: these are the principles on which Fernão Lopes bases his discrimination between conflicting sources. In one instance only (the background to João I's move against Tuy in 1389) does he let his choice be determined by authority alone – the greatly trusted 'Doctor Christophorus' (*D. João I*, Part II, Chapter 140) – and by this late stage in his chronicle, Fernão Lopes's energies may have been running low owing to his advancing age.

In rather more cases – somewhere between 30 and 40 – he takes issue with the account offered by whatever source he is following at the time. Only a very few such instances fall outside the two basic types – the documented and the contextual – referred to above. He treats a couple of defective accounts with relative leniency: the manifold errors of other historians regarding Princess Beatriz's betrothal (*Crónica de D. Fernando*, Chapter 104) are attributed not to malice but to mere ignorance; again, in the *Crónica de D. João I*, Part II, Chapter 114, he is content simply to observe that other writers 'do not speak at much length' about what most concerns him. He notes that the highly improbable story of the Castilians at Aljubarrota cutting the shafts of their own lances (ibid, Chapter 42) is actually true: they had realised that, contrary to expectations, the battle was going to be decided on foot, not on horseback. These few exceptions aside, Fernão Lopes's overt rejection of sources is always grounded either in documentary evidence or in contextualising argument. The *Crónica de D. Fernando* has rather more examples of the former kind, though both types do occur there. In the First Part of the *Crónica de D. João I*, all instances follow the contextualising pattern. The latter still predominates (in a ratio of rather more than four to one) in the Second Part, though other examples with a documented basis also occur there. This preponderance was in one sense natural: as Fernão Lopes's work advanced, it created more contexts through which the accounts furnished by others might be tested. But the national and patriotic themes that he was developing were, in themselves, contexts into which these other versions of events might be fitted either more or less easily. This does not lead him to abandon, or even consciously to suspend his principles of historical judgement. But his application of those principles can be very far from neutral in its willed effects.

Some contexts, of course, were wholly straightforward – those, for example, relating to chronology. When King Fernando sent ships to support Castilian and French naval activity against England, it was easy for some writers to interpret that as an outcome of the treaty he later arrived at with Castile. But they were wrong in making that link, and Fernão Lopes (*Crónica de D. Fernando*, Chapter 93) duly records the fact. The gifts and titles bestowed on Nuno Álvares's wife by João I probably do date, as the chronicler believes, from after Aljubarrota rather than from their earlier meeting in Oporto (*Crónica de D. João I*, Part II, Chapter 9). Reports of Castilian moves for a renewed invasion of Portugal shortly after that battle (ibid, Chapter 78) are discounted, very reasonably, because at that stage the military aid promised by the French had not yet arrived. Other varieties of contextual testing can be more complex, and yet remain uncontentious. The story that the Castilian fleet kept its station off Lisbon continuously from the end of the siege until Juan I's second invasion in 1385 (highly improbable in strategic terms) earns from Fernão Lopes the blunt comment that its author 'should be told that he was dreaming when he wrote that'. Inevitably, though, some turn out to be more problematic. Carefully researched as it was, his treatment of the battle of Aljubarrota cannot quite withstand Peter Russell's criticism: 'too patriotic to be entirely convincing'.[14] Lopes's estimate of Castilian numbers is rather too high to be credible, while that given for the Portuguese falls towards the lower end of any plausible range, and minimises the role of Gascon troops and English bowmen. These shortcomings do not invalidate Fernão Lopes's claims to be following a sound historical method; they do remind us, though, that such claims serve the ends of a rhetorical strategy, designed to advance a nationalistic reading of events. One obvious marker of this, here and elsewhere, is his overtly forceful criticism of other historians.

---

[14] P. E. Russell, *The English Intervention in Spain and Portugal in the Time of Edward III and Richard II* (Oxford: Clarendon, 1953), p. 384n. For Russell's detailed response to Fernão Lopes's estimated numbers, especially with reference to Gascon men-at-arms and English archers, see ibid, pp. 384–86.

V

This too can have a range of different motives. The attack on Martim Afonso de Melo in *Crónica de D. Fernando,* Chapters 47–48 does appear to turn on issues of professional competence: Fernão Lopes is against those who undertake the writing of history too lightly. By contrast, three stories that he rejects with particular force in the *Crónica de D. João I*, Part I, all cast doubt on the ideal solidarity pictured as obtaining between João of Avis and the besieged people of Lisbon: that he had been negotiating in secret with Juan of Castile (Chapter 130); that he was tardy in his response to a plot to betray the city (Chapter 138); that towards the end of the siege he proposed a compromise settlement with the Castilian king (Chapter 141). Fernão Lopes finds the first of these claims implausible in terms of King Juan's own behaviour, adding that it is 'a fabrication [...] very far from true'. The second he treats as a slur on João's character, offering his own alternative version based on other sources. The third he denounces outright, as a product of bias and 'a great disservice to the truth'. Here, where the new social compact forged between the future João I and his people is being brought into question, there is little doubt that the target of his reproach is the Castilian royal chronicler, Pero López de Ayala. Writing a generation earlier, often an eyewitness, and indeed a participant in much that he describes, Ayala too had worked to produce an official history in a national interest. He had done so, moreover, ably enough to demand direct refutation from Fernão Lopes who wrote, again officially, from the opposing viewpoint.

It is no surprise, then, that Ayala becomes yet more overtly a target in Part II of the *Crónica de D. João I.* He is not directly arraigned for questioning the loyalty of Nuno Álvares's forces to their leader (Chapter 24) – a suggestion, unlikely in itself, that attracts an angry response: 'such a wretched and erroneous opinion [...] should get down on his knees and plead for pardon from the truth'. Nor is he particularly associated with the statement – here denounced as a simple falsehood – that, in the run-up to Aljubarrota (Chapter 28), King João had been secretly disposed to reach a compromise with King Juan. But Ayala is very much the object of two further clusters of criticism, both of them affecting essential landmarks in the story Fernão Lopes has to tell.

One, dealing with Aljubarrota itself (Chapters 35–38), has been discussed in its other aspects already. Our concern with it now involves the series of adverse comments that are brought home to Ayala in person. Finding inconsistencies in his description of the battlefield, Fernão Lopes (though perhaps himself lacking in what Russell calls 'a soldier's understanding of ground'[15]),

---

[15] Russell, *The English Intervention*, p. 384, n. 1 from previous page.

follows these up damningly, deeming the other's work 'of little value, seeing that in certain passages he conveyed the opposite to the truth, so as to diminish the victory won by his enemies'. He observes again in Chapter 38 that if, as was alleged on their behalf, the Castilians' battle position was badly drawn up, that was the fault of 'all the honourable great lords present' (of whom Ayala, of course, had been one). Plainly he wanted readers to see Ayala as one of those denounced earlier in his discussion of numbers (Chapter 37) for seeking on behalf of one of the parties 'fraudulent reasons to justify their adverse fortune'. The more detailed and damaging case duly follows: 'others, in order to favour the Castilians, [...] gave the Portuguese a much higher total than they amounted to and supplied no figure at all for the Castilians'. This is repeated a few lines later in almost identical terms: 'these writers, while knowing for certain how many their own men amounted to, chose not to supply their numbers, whereas, though ignorant of the number of their opponents, they recorded specific figures'. They did this 'in order to diminish the battle-honours earned by the other side'. Fernão Lopes himself, as we have seen, was not above using a degree of spin in presenting such numbers as these. He may even have felt that Ayala was entitled to do the same – but not in outright violation of the principles on which history had to be written: 'one should not assert as true whatever lies in doubt, nor conceal whatever is quite certain'.

The second cluster of such reproaches relates to comments made on King João's alliance with John of Gaunt, and his marriage to Gaunt's daughter, Philippa. These were crucial matters for the acceptance of the new Portuguese order among European monarchies – an issue still far from resolved when Ayala was writing. His strategy, then, was to make the whole episode appear vaguely disreputable. João I was shown as pressing peremptory financial demands on John of Gaunt: a dowry for his marriage, together with the expenses of their joint campaign in Galicia. The effect is to suggest an under-current of ill-feeling between the two men during at least some part of the period between João I's marriage in February 1387 and his father-in law's departure for Bayonne and a settlement of his own with the Castilians in the autumn of 1387. There were, of course, plenty of reasons for tension, mostly over the rather unsuccessful invasion of León in which both were engaged. But the suggestion of a long-standing rancour is not one that Fernão Lopes is willing to countenance: he sees it as being offered 'more to be defamatory than to write history' (Chapter 118). After pointing out at length all the things that make such claims implausible in context, he cites a letter from John of Gaunt, written in early 1387, and addressing João I in the friendliest and most deferential of terms.

Yet even this, for Fernão Lopes, was scarcely the main matter. At the date of King João's marriage to Philippa, the required papal dispensation from the bridegroom's previous vow of celibacy as Master of Avis had been sought but not yet obtained. Its absence might be regarded as impugning the validity of the marriage itself. João's haste in receiving the sacrament with Philippa could be made to appear unseemly, or canonically dubious, or even a standing affront to his Lancastrian in-laws. Fernão Lopes will have none of this. It is, he declares, 'false [...] totally contrary to the truth [...] an outright lie', a product either of malice or of ignorance. The truth is 'quite the opposite of what the aforesaid author maliciously wrote' (Chapter 118). His more detailed rebuttal, explaining why the dispensation was so long in coming, and stressing its unconditional character when it did arrive, is given in Chapters 123 to 126; it culminates in transcriptions of two documents from the newly-elected Pope, Boniface IX. As a postscript to them, Fernão Lopes invites his audience to consider how 'that historian' (he clearly means Ayala)

> was so bold as to say such things to support his defamation, which, devoid of all substance as they are, deserve no credence whatsoever. For where the truth is certain and clear, anything that may be said to the contrary proceeds from a warped imagination or a perverse and malicious intent.

So much, we might well feel, for Ayala. Yet he was, for much of what Fernão Lopes wrote, especially about events in Castile, a largely trusted source and, of all his sources, the one who was literally doing the same job. Lopes can scarcely have been unaware of the extent to which his own figures for the forces at Aljubarrota were themselves being deployed to make a case. Some of the feeling behind his comments on Ayala may well reflect a sense of their referring not just to issues of necessary contention but to lapses from what ought to have been a shared practice. Chapters 51 and 62 of the *Crónica de D. João I*, Part II, dealing with Ayala's captivity and eventual ransom after Aljubarrota, may embody something of this mixed reaction. The story they have to tell of Ayala's concern to keep the cost of his ransom down is by no means creditable to him; this, one feels, is where Fernão Lopes might have denounced him once for all as a defaulting chronicler, perverting the record in the Castilian interest. In fact, all he allows himself to say at this point (Chapter 51) is that Ayala was 'an honourable knight and a highly respected Castilian nobleman'.

VI

One inherited aspect of their common calling was the medieval sense of providential shaping at the heart of the historical process. Like other medieval chroniclers Fernão Lopes remains conscious of the events he is recording as the outcome of God's will. Distinctively, though, he finds it at once more elusive and more urgent to grasp how that process of shaping operates. He maintained a prudent distance, for example, from the systematic, yet never entirely trusted, attempt to comprehend such processes offered by the study of astrology. Regarded as reliable enough in principle, that science also attracted to itself an anecdotal tradition showing the perils of over-detailed or over-confident attempts to probe God's designs. Much in line with stories that relate to Henry IV of England, to Álvaro de Luna and to the *Libro de Buen Amor*'s fictitious King Alcaraz,[16] Pedro the Cruel of Castile, acting on astrological advice, was said to have massively fortified the tower of La Estrella in Carmona, only to find that there was another tower, similarly named, at Montiel. This tale Fernão Lopes rather circumspectly accepts (*Crónica de D. Fernando*, Chapter 46). Yet in Chapter 110 of the same chronicle there is a brisk modernity about his explanation of why the eclipse that preceded the death of Enrique II of Castile could not be causally linked with it. Eclipses, he explains, occur at particular times as foreknowable 'works of nature'; the king had simply died at the time when the eclipse was due to occur. This key distinction between naturalistic forecast (astronomy) and astrological prediction is still rather less than securely established in Fernão Lopes. He is still disposed to believe in stories of the latter kind attending the birth of Nuno Álvares Pereira (*Crónica de D. João*, Part I, Chapter 33). Here he tells how Nuno's father identified him among his children as the one who, so astrologers foretold, would be invincible in battle, and took action accordingly by attaching him at an early age to the Portuguese court. Alvaro Gonçalves Pereira's conduct in this would seem to be marked out mainly by his scrupulous secrecy – a clear sign of his desire not so much to exploit the predictive power of astrology as to act conformably with the providential design it disclosed. More significantly for Fernão Lopes, the whole episode comes from the *Crónica do Condestabre*, a source that, like the Arthurian material on which it is so largely calqued, could accommodate a fair measure of the supernatural without forfeiting its claim to be written as history. Here and elsewhere, Fernão Lopes was disposed to go along with that.

He does much the same, again in a context defined by the *Crónica do Condestabre*, when another, far more widely-accepted mode of discerning the hand of God behind events comes into play. The young Nuno Álvares, he declares (*Crónica de D. Fernando*, Chapter 138) escaped from peril more

---

[16] See Nicholas G Round, *The Greatest Man Uncrowned: A Study of the Fall of Don Álvaro de Luna* (London: Tamesis, 1986), p. 214n (Luna, Henry IV, and other examples); also, Juan Ruiz, *Libro de Buen Amor*, ed. G. B. Gybbon-Monypenny (Madrid: Castalia, 1989), pp. 136–38, stzs. 129–39 (rather closer to the astrologers' point of view).

through what appeared to be a miracle than through any natural course of events, because God meant to preserve him for greater things. This was, of course, virtually a default reaction to improbable outcomes of a favourable kind. Applied more broadly, the same attitude made it easy to discern the active approval of Providence behind the unlikely sequence of events that brought João I to power. Some of these events, like the plague that finally broke the Castilian army's grip on Lisbon (*Crónica de D. João*, Part I, Chapter 149), could hardly be construed in any other terms. Fernão Lopes, being both an official historian and a committed one, was not at all disposed to resist this line of thinking; on the contrary, he builds it quite deliberately into the presentation of his work. Many of his typological references to Scripture are deployed to this end, with the Master of Avis as a Christ-figure, Nuno Álvares Pereira his St Peter, and their partisans the disciples and apostles of this 'Portuguese gospel' (ibid, Chapter 159). The providential theme is again underlined, by reference to Fernão Lopes's history of the conquest of Portugal from the Moors (ibid), with the defenders of the realm against Castile now being equated with its liberators then.

Much of this is of a piece with the treatment of these topics of divine favour in the sermons preached to the people of Lisbon, on the deliverance of the raised siege, and on the similar 'crowning mercy' of Aljubarrota. These, to judge from the Franciscan Friar Pedro, quoted extensively on the latter occasion (*Crónica de D. João*, Part II, Chapter 48), were scrupulous in avoiding the term 'miracle', which would have implied a supernatural reinforcement of some aspect of the Christian faith.[17] By contrast, they were happy to expound events in Portugal (including, as well, feats of arms, portents, prophecies, and reported breaches of the natural order) as 'marvels', analogous to Biblical instances of divine favour. Yet when Fernão Lopes's more direct account offers us events that go beyond the natural, the emphasis laid on corroboration is especially strong. The lights that inexplicably appeared on the tips of lances during the defence of Lisbon were witnessed, he records, by 'seven Christians and three Moors'; stories from Montemor-o-Velho of a rain of wax were formally witnessed in a notarised document, and a sample was brought to Lisbon (*Crónica de D. João*, Part I, Chapter 111). Reports of these things motivated a religious procession in Lisbon, headed by a Bishop: people clearly

---

[17] Cf. St Thomas Aquinas, *Summa Theologiae: A Concise Translation*, ed. Timothy McDermott (London: Eyre and Spottiswoode, 1989), p. 523, IIIa, 43.1: 'God empowers men to work miracles principally in order to confirm teaching which is beyond proof by human argument and must be proved by the argument of divine power, and secondarily that we may believe God is dwelling by the grace of his Holy Spirit in the men working the miracles.'

took them seriously. So did Fernão Lopes. But where the responsibility for including them was his, he felt the need to give reasons for believing that they had actually occurred. Marvels, great and small, then, were evidence of divine favour, but still in principle requiring to be properly documented. In a sense, his entire historical undertaking was to document the overall marvel that was Portugal's independent survival under the Avis line.

History in its wider scope was, by convention, a providential work, and had been so regarded since St Augustine. Yet not entirely so: for many, it was also what it had always been: a sequence of more or less arbitrary ups and downs. What was in theory providence was, for more immediate purposes, experienced as fortune. For that, there was a long-established allegorical and visual representation: the woman with the wheel. There was also a more diffuse and primary sense of impersonal forces (which might yet obey some personal attachment), going by such names as fate, chance, *wyrd* or luck. It was, broadly, the educated way to treat these last as superstitions, and to present the experiences that were allegorised as Fortune's doing as the humanly knowable enactments of an inscrutable Providence. The challenge to Fernão Lopes, as to other medieval historians, was to uphold this hierarchy and still allow an intelligible scope for human free will. Exercising one's free will, of course, could involve getting these governing historical principles wrong, as King Fernando did in reaching his decision to go to war with Juan I of Castile. Believing that Juan's father, Enrique II, had owed his victories against Portugal more to 'good luck and the stars' than to any personal qualities, Fernando now sought a war, being convinced that the luck was bound to change. His self-confident assertion to a sceptical adviser that 'God will counsel me' amounts to little more than a reiteration of that ill-considered hope (*Crónica de D. Fernando*, Chapter 114).

Fernão Lopes further refines his own view in several chapters that deal with João of Avis's killing of the Queen's lover, Juan Fernández Andeiro. He rejects the naïve explanation that Fortune put off the event until the moment that would bring Andeiro maximum dishonour. Instead, he offers a more contextualised account of Providence furthering its own design that João of Avis should become king (*Crónica de D. João I*, Part I, Chapter 1). When he wants to suggest (Chapter 7) that this design operated by way of a flaw in Andeiro's character, Lopes himself deploys the allegory of 'Dame Fortune' as a secondary agent in this dubious work. A little later (Chapter 8), João of Avis, finally resolved on the killing, is described with virtually no allegorical implications as 'open to whatever outcome fortune might bring'. Finally, in Chapter 36 of the *Crónica de D. João I*, Part II, Fernão Lopes defines his own attitude to this kind of language. After declaring that 'Dame Fortune [...] had already ordained that matters should take a different course' from the one assumed by the advisers who encouraged Juan I to offer battle to the much smaller Portuguese army, he warns his readers that all such references to her stand for the workings of a deeper, more inscrutable, divine judgement.

To tell what was essentially the story of God's providential mercies to the Portuguese, and yet to do so in terms that were humanly convincing and grounded in the evidence available to him, was, of its nature, an essentially plural task. It was Fernão Lopes's awareness of this that carried his historical writing beyond the customary limits of his time. One consequence was a certain ironic dimension, distinctive because it was liable to emerge at moments when the providential theme was also very clearly in play. Friar João da Barroca's credentials as a holy man and prophet who can advise João of Avis reliably on God's intentions for him (*Crónica de D. João I*, Part I, Chapter 23) are established beyond any doubt. Yet he also has some down-to-earth and technically specific advice to give on the kind of siege-tower Dom João will need in order to take possession of the castle of Lisbon. The incongruity is there because Fernão Lopes put it there – and he need not have done so. Again, in *Crónica de D. João I*, Part II, Chapter 41, his comment on the prayers for victory being offered on either side before Aljubarrota could be directed simply at Castilian over-confidence, but it is framed as something more widely-applicable and more troubling: 'Anyone pleading on behalf of large numbers would certainly believe that his or her prayers would be more swiftly heard by God and more easily answered.' On the battlefield itself (Chapter 42), an archbishop's sermon reminds the Portuguese that their enemies are schismatics, and they should go into battle with the text *verbum caro factum est* on their lips. 'What's he saying?' ask some of the more ignorant soldiery (surely a majority on this occasion). 'This is a very expensive business', their scarcely better-informed comrades tell them. And though Fernão Lopes rather primly reports others as insisting that God would, after all, make it a better bargain, one cannot escape the notion that this was an authentic snatch of worm's-eye-view dialogue, figuring here because he felt that this was where it belonged.

More broadly, it became, from a very early stage, a second nature to Fernão Lopes's writing of history to keep the operation of more than one kind of cause in view. In the Prologue to the *Crónica de D. Fernando,* he notes how differently things might have turned out for Portugal had the king been content to live in peace and not to squander the vast wealth he had inherited. But that, he reflects, was perhaps not ordained from above. Here the two orders of causality – providence and King Fernando's defective judgement – are arrayed side by side, with no detail as to their interaction, though plainly we are being invited to think that they do interact. A more complex and dynamic model occurs in the account given (*Crónica de D. João I*, Part I, Chapter

49) of João of Avis' financial policies. These, though Fernão Lopes avoids
mentioning the similarities, had features much in line with those of his prede-
cessor: overspending, backed by currency manipulation, to meet the costs
of war. 'By such changes and the minting of coins', Lopes concludes, 'and
with the help of Almighty God the Master defended the kingdom of Portugal
[…] though his people felt the harmful effect of certain shortages.' Victory
is achieved through divine favour, but also through well-tried secular guile,
and – importantly – through a degree of suffering, stoically endured, on the
part of the people. Even this, though, is by no means the full picture. That
would involve at least two further major factors: the new style of warfare,
making effective use of its new social basis, that Nuno Álvares, his aura of
chivalric glamour notwithstanding, was able to devise and exploit, and the
explosion of popular initiative that preceded it in 1383–1384. Of the latter,
Fernão Lopes declares (ibid, Chapter 43) that it was wonderful to see the
courage God instilled in the commoners and the cowardice with which He
afflicted their adversaries; yet he also notes (here and in Chapter 44) that a
ruthless use of hostages was decisive for the insurrection in Estremoz and
Évora. Again, the providential cause is being linked with the most extreme
and unexpected line of secular causality.

VII

This last attains its full significance only towards the end of the *Crónica de
D. Fernando*. As late as Chapter 115, Fernão Lopes can write of the growing
closeness between Queen Leonor and Juan Fernández Andeiro, insisting that
'everything that followed later […] first started here'. This certainly invokes
an autonomous line of secular cause and effect, but this is the line – associated
with great personages, their characters and desires – that medieval historians
at large would have identified as the human dimension of their story. Hints at
a wider social perspective begin much earlier in King Fernando's chronicle,
with the rhyming rebuke on his ineffectual campaigning, quoted in Chapter 36.
They acquire a clearer institutional context in Chapter 60, where townsfolk and
villagers formulate responses to the King's intended marriage to Leonor Teles,
meeting 'in groups, as is their custom'. They took the view that Fernando's
high-born counsellors had failed in their duty: they – the commoners – were
left to tell him that he was in the wrong.

The main work in this fell, naturally enough, on the people of Lisbon
where, so the narrative implies, a more developed set of customary institutions existed: an assembly capable of electing delegates, and an armed militia,
numbering several thousands, drawn from 'artisans of all the trades', with
more specialist soldiery attached. Perhaps because of this latter factor, their

spokesman, the tailor Fernão Vasques, was allowed to deliver his uncom-
promising message, to which the king offered only a mild and temporising
reply. Next day (Chapter 61), Fernão Vasques reiterated the point that the
magistrates and other dignitaries there present ought to be giving the advice
that he, on behalf the commoners, was delivering. But King Fernando was
not there to hear it: rather than renewing contact as promised, he had fled
the city in company with Dona Leonor. Such was her dominance over him,
even so, that she was later able to have Vasques and his associates arrested
and brutally punished.

Confrontation with the common people, however, though clearly exacerbated by Fernando's marriage, attains its full force only with a subsequent issue
– the succession, after his death, of his daughter Beatriz, now the child-bride
of Juan I of Castile. Here again, there is an institutional background. Part of
the ritual of recognising a legitimate heir was his or her acclamation by the
people, in which members of the governing class proclaimed the new heir,
and rode through the streets with banners flying amid cries of loyal attachment
from the populace. On this occasion, though, the populace declined to play
the role assigned to it. In Lisbon (Chapter 175) they found little to choose
between falling into Castilian hands and becoming captives of the Moors;
the kingdom, so dearly won, was, they declared, 'being sold for nothing'. A
markedly tentative and lukewarm effort at rallying support petered out in the
Cathedral square; those who had ventured further among the people brought
back reports discouraging to any renewal.

It was worse than that in Santarém (Chapter 176), where the appointed
cheerleader for the Castilian queen met first with silence, then with a wave of
support for Prince João of the Castro line (currently a prisoner in Castile) as
the only true heir, and finally with threats to his own life. In Elvas (Chapter
177), the leader of a rival demonstration, hailing a different flag with cries of
'Arreall, arreall por Portugall!', was briefly arrested, but escaped when, as he
had predicted, the *arraya meuda* returned from their work in the vineyards and
came to his rescue. He and they then took over town and castle and expelled
the governor. Similar events happened elsewhere. On the ominous contrast
between these disruptive outbreaks and the pledges of loyalty demanded by
Juan of Castile, and willingly granted by most of the 'counts, masters and
knights' in Portugal (Chapter 178), Fernão Lopes brings his chronicle to an end.

The insurrectionary mood among the people is now plainly in view; it
will remain a central strand of causality in Part I of the *Crónica de D. João
I*. It can become either more or less prominent as Fernão Lopes follows
out his chosen strategy of pursuing one narrative thread at a time (Chapter
29). But it is a crucial mover of what happens in various provincial towns
before Lisbon is besieged, and it is yet more essential to all that concerns

the city's epic resistance. The striking contrast drawn in Chapters 114 and 115 between Juan I's opulent and immensely powerful siege-camp and the austere battle-readiness of the defenders, the latter's extreme sufferings of hunger and loss (Chapter 148), all help to register the defence of Lisbon as a collective achievement. That achievement is triumphantly identified with the story of providential favour in the *mumdo novo* chapters (159–163), which also function as a listing of people and communities whose actions brought victory to the Avis cause, and permanent change to Portugal. The account of political issues and activities finally merges with the theme of providence through the long and structurally prominent treatment of João I's recognition as rightful king by the *Cortes* of Coimbra. The arguments of João das Regras, the principal legal spokesman for the Avis claim, are rehearsed in almost pedantic detail (Chapters 183–190). Coming where it does, at the climax of Part I of the *Crónica*, this elaborate vindication of João I's legal right – which includes as its final element (Chapter 192) the acclamation of his banner through the streets of Lisbon – also becomes the sign of that providential warrant that is being claimed, not only for his kingship, but also for the extraordinary process of events that has brought it about. Human jurisprudence, accessible to human reason, demonstrates that João's succession fulfils the ancient laws of Portugal. In the inscrutable design of Providence, we are led to think, the *mumdo novo* of the Portuguese revolution must after all be the fulfillment of a divinely-established order.

Disconcertingly, little of this applies in Part II. There are reasons for this, however. The later chapters of that chronicle exhibit a falling away in completeness, organization, and urgency, consistent with its being a late work of Fernão Lopes, and still in need of some final revision. After the second great Castilian reverse of Aljubarrota, the tale of protracted minor wars and negotiations, first to promote Lancastrian claims in Castile, and then to secure a settlement that would bring full recognition for the new Portuguese order, is distinctly less than compelling. If it has a focus, that is provided by the figure of Nuno Álvares, an exemplary leader in battle, and a pattern of chivalric virtues – moderation and justice – in which his more humanly fallible sovereign, João I, can sometimes fall short. The insurrectionary people are nowhere to be seen. They could, of course, have been rather more perceptible to readers at the time: Nuno Álvares owed much of his success (at Aljubarrota especially) to his practice of a new form of warfare, less predictably dominated by mounted knights. And the assumption of an achieved social change, not to be disrupted by the claims of returning exiles, is crucial to the long struggle for a settlement with Castile.

That said, there may have been other elements at work. A description quoted earlier from their opponents (*Crónica de D. João I*, Part I, Chapter

29) regarding the people of Lisbon, observes that 'they are people of very mixed origins and between them, give vent to a variety of opinions and cause many uprisings'. The first of these statements is clearly true, and underlies the distinction, scrupulously observed by Fernão Lopes, between *çidadãos* (the birthright citizens of Lisbon) and *moradores* (the members of other communities resident there). Support for João of Avis is represented as coming from them both (ibid, Chapter 160). There is evidence elsewhere in the chronicle of his maintaining good relations with local Jews and Muslims, as with Genoese and English merchants. Diversity itself could well have helped to foster the robust independence of mind of the inhabitants of Lisbon. Yet in the 11-month period between the lifting of the siege and the victory at Aljubarrota their mood seems to have been, with some reason, an acutely anxious one – so much so that the city held a formal consultation with learned theologians on how to ensure that God would heed their prayers (*Crónica de D. João I*, Part II, Chapter 41). The response, a wide-ranging condemnation of laxity in religious belief and practice, from sorcery and spells to seasonal commemorations and public mourning for the dead, was to enforce a degree of conformity not known until now. Proposed by Dominican friars and sponsored by city officials and high-ranking guild members, the programme was quickly put into practice. Such was the uncertainty of the times that the *lisboetas*, for all their diversity, accepted it. Of their earlier anarchic radicalism there survived only the strands that had the full sanction of the authorities: the fierce nationalistic attachment to the Avis cause and their Romanist allegiance in a divided Church. Their history in this regard would appear to have been that of a good many other revolutions. Or so this line of speculation would suggest.

As to how we ought to read the later chapters of Part II, the most important single factor is probably still the relative decline in Fernão Lopes's energies. His treatment in Chapter 168 of what motivated certain defectors to the Castilian cause is revealing: those who complain about the lack of an explanation, he admits, would be raising a serious question, which they might care to answer for themselves. One could hardly imagine the Fernão Lopes of Part I leaving it at that. The very different response represented by his ordering of Part I of the *Crónica*, however, arguably reflects him in the full exercise of his powers. It also falls broadly within the terms of Luís de Sousa Rebelo's account of the complexities involved in reading his work.[18]

Rebelo describes a progression from the literal meaning, via the moral meaning offered by the work's ethical and juridical dimensions, to an allegorical meaning, disclosed at the level of its providential concerns. This hierarchy of

[18] Rebelo, 'The Idea of Kingship', p. 177; *A concepção do poder*, pp. 26–30 and 58–59.

literal, moral, and spiritual senses would have been familiar to any medieval reader trained in the handling of Scripture. Fernão Lopes would certainly have expected his work to be read like this, and his strategies of exposition appear to take that into account. But his priorities as a writer of history were rather different. In particular, the literal record of events counted for more in Fernão Lopes than in many other medieval historians, whose preference was, in Collingwood's words, for 'looking away from man's actions in order to detect the plan of God'.[19] That outlook led naturally to a certain impatience with basic factual research; just how far removed Fernão Lopes was from this is made clear in his prologue to the *Crónica de D. João I*, Part I, and clearer still in the *Crónica* itself.

This is not only full of concrete incident: it insists on giving prominence to precisely those incidents that create most problems for the providentialist theme. The fanatical, often violent, support lent to João of Avis by the rebellious commoners of the Portuguese towns was hard to relate to the constitutional niceties of the *Cortes* lawyers, and harder still to connect with the detailed working-out of any divine purpose. The links could be established only in the most general and rhetorical of terms, on the lines sketched out above. Fernão Lopes's easiest course, if he wanted simply to reinforce these rhetorical connections, was to avoid going into too much detail, highlighting perhaps those episodes which demonstrated exemplary daring or fortitude, and passing rapidly over all the rest. Yet that, conspicuously, is what he does not do. The reason for this seems clear. The rugged indiscipline of these plebeian groups had been a crucial factor in winning control of both Lisbon and a number of provincial towns for the Avis faction at the start of the civil war. If Fernão Lopes was concerned to show the causes of events he had to show all this too.

It is evident that he was so concerned. Peter Russell has observed how often he criticises earlier chroniclers for neglecting questions of causality.[20] The reproach was likely to be well-founded. In many medieval chroniclers, as W. J. Brandt demonstrates, the very perception of causal relationships is inhibited in principle.[21] Aristocratic chroniclers are concerned 'to celebrate,

[19] Collingwood, *The Idea of History*, p. 55; contrast *Crónica de D. João I*, pp. 2–3.

[20] P. E. Russell, '*As fontes de Fernão Lopes*', *Revista Portuguesa da História*, Colecção Universitas (Coimbra: Coimbra Editora, 1941), p. 7; see also Borges Coelho, *A Revolução de 1383*, p. 25: 'Percorre a história todo um fio explicativo' [There is an explanatory thread running throughout the narrative].

[21] Brandt, *The Shape of Medieval History*, pp. 88, 171; also p. 62; Smalley, *Historians in the Middle Ages*, p. 189, and see pp. 129–30 (Gerald of Wales), 140–41 (William of Tyre) for instances of causal pluralism.

not to explain' the events they describe. Those of clerical background tend to envisage historical action as the disruption of an otherwise static norm, and to account for each such disturbance in terms of the inherent properties of things. More generally, belief in the providential movement of history discouraged further causal speculation; questions about historical explanation, as Beryl Smalley observes, 'were non-questions to a disciple of Orosius'. Certainly any notion of multiple causality is unusual; it tends to arise only when a chronicler's experience of adversity leads to dissatisfaction with a simple providentialist view. To all this Fernão Lopes stands as an exception. His world is precisely what Brandt declares the medieval chronicler's world could never be: 'interrelated causal processes'. His writing stands in contrast with Froissart or Ayala very largely because of its greater plenitude of explanation. His view of the causes of events is habitually plural; the workings of providence, the interplay of political initiatives, and the dynamic thrust of popular agitation all combine to bring about the events of his story. But his pluralism is not the fruit of an attempt to rationalise adversity; the events of the 1380s had gone the way Fernão Lopes wanted them to go. The case is, rather, that these events were so unusual in themselves, and so manifestly the determining crisis of Portuguese history that they called for a new intensity of explanatory effort. Here indeed we have a decisive step towards modernity in Fernão Lopes's historical method.

VIII

Much of the rest of this introduction will be concerned with the detail of how the revolutionary process is presented, and more particularly of how issues of causality are handled, in Fernão Lopes's account of the popular capture of a number of provincial centres in the closing months of 1383.[22] Two obvious reasons suggest themselves for concentrating our attention on these provincial developments. The first is that Fernão Lopes's Lisbon-centred chapters have already been the object of intensive study, by Maria Lúcia Perrone de Faro Passos and others. The second is that the social-revolutionary aspect of the pro-Avis movement, queried by Veríssimo Serrão, is so transparently present here that time need not be spent on arguments to establish its authenticity. The following analysis seeks primarily to assess the relative importance that Fernão Lopes assigns to providential favour, political activity, and social turbulence, as vehicles of historical causality, and to illustrate his concept of the relations

---

[22] *Crónica de D. João I*, Part I, pp. 72–82 (Chapters 42–46); on the revolution in Lisbon see Maria Lúcia Perrone de Faro Passos, *O herói na crónica de D. João I de Fernão Lopes* (Lisbon: Prelo, 1974), pp. 214–40.

obtaining between them. No attempt is made to deal with detailed questions of historicity, or with the wider historical implications of the events described. But by concentrating on the historian's artistic ordering of his material, and on how this relates to his concept of historical process, it should be possible to speak with a little more precision about Fernão Lopes's originality as historian and literary artist.

At first reading the tale of events in these five chapters seems oddly random and disjointed. *Crónica de D. João I*, Part I, Chapter 42 begins with the letters sent out by the Queen Regent in furtherance of the Castilian cause, and passes to an account of their reception in Estremoz; this then breaks off, and we learn of more dramatic events in Beja. Chapter 43, having mentioned that there were similar risings elsewhere, alludes briefly to one such, in Portalegre, and then returns to Estremoz. The next two chapters are set in Évora. Chapter 46, the last of the group, describes a letter sent by João of Avis to the kingdom at large, and its impact on the city of Oporto, ending with further comments on the general turbulence. It is this interplay between the overall picture and the local vignettes that provides the clue to Fernão Lopes's strategy of exposition. The number of towns that declared, then or later, for the Avis interest was large; the chronicle later names fifty-two.[23] By moving the focus of attention rapidly among five locations Fernão Lopes is able to offer a typifying sample of events. Unease at the Queen Regent's attitude (Estremoz and Beja) leads to a takeover by Avis partisans (Beja, Portalegre, and Estremoz again). The outbreak may go further, as respectable leaders are displaced by extremist commoners (Évora). But when the leadership of João of Avis is formally accepted, a new unity of purpose can be the result (Oporto). There are enough generalising formulae on the lines of 'Desta guisa que avees ouvido' (the opening phrase of Chapter 43)[24] to make the typifying function clear. At the same time, the shifts of focus provide an adequate though still concise image of the revolution's confused spontaneity.

A second feature of Fernão Lopes's general presentation is his deployment of documentary sources. At least four of these have a clearly stated authorship here. Queen Leonor sends out an instruction that her infant daughter, Beatriz, betrothed to the King of Castile, should be recognised as sovereign; she also writes to Juan of Castile, urging him to enter the country, and follows this up

---

[23] The list in Chapter 162 (pp. 306–07) includes all the towns mentioned here except, unaccountably, Beja; it is avowedly not quite exhaustive.

[24] 'In the very way you have heard about.' This and all future translations from chronicles were selected from the respective passage in the present edition of *The Chronicles of Fernão Lopes*. Whenever appropriate, we have also translated incidental brief notes by other authors.

with a letter to the city of Beja, detailing her further requirements (Chapter 42). João of Avis, for his part, responds to the news from his partisans in Évora that they have taken the town (Chapter 44); their original letter to him (not reproduced here) may or may not have supplied the foundation for Fernão Lopes's description of events there. Finally, the public letter from the Master of Avis urging resistance to the Castilians, under his leadership as *Regedor e Defemsor dos rregnos*, is paraphrased in Chapter 46. This local density of documentary support bears out the account in Fernão Lopes's prologue of how he has sought to base his 'clara certidom da verdade' on 'pubricas escprituras de muitos cartarios' (p. 2).[25] But it serves another purpose too; the documents are made to illustrate an important contrast in political styles. The Queen Regent, ordering the municipalities to recognise her daughter's rights, addresses the 'alcaides dos castellos' – the military aristocracy – and the 'homeẽs boõs das villas e çidades' (p. 72)[26] – the traditionally dominant social authorities. And even they are not treated as having much choice in the matter. The tone of Fernão Lopes's summary is curt and official: after complaining of recent events in Lisbon, Queen Leonor goes onto specify 'a maneira que *aviam de teer* [my italics], em tomar voz por sua filha' (ibid).[27] The summaries of letters written by João of Avis are very different.

João writes in response to a report from the original leaders of the revolt in Évora 'que eram huũs dos gramdes que hi avia' (p. 77, with names given there and at p. 78).[28] Later he writes to 'alguũas villas e çidades' – not necessarily to their magistrates, who had in many cases been set aside – as well as to certain individuals, presumably his partisans (p. 81). His tone on each occasion is sympathetic, even respectful, and he makes skilful use of currents of popular feeling already evident in the various provincial revolts. Writing to Évora he picks up the familiar rebel claim that their enemies are traitors to the country and appeals for the revolutionaries' continued support as 'verdadeiros naturaaes do rregno' [true natives of the realm] (p. 78). In his more widely circulated letter, he enlarges on the same appeal, playing on already awakened fears of Castilian rule: 'elRei de Castella viinha pera os tomar, e meter os poboos delles em sua sobjeiçom' (p. 81).[29] The key word here is *sobjeiçom*; we have encountered it before, in the sneer of Queen Leonor's aristocratic

---

[25] 'clear grasp of truth' on 'public documents from many archives'; *CKJ1*, Prologue.

[26] 'governors of the castles' and 'leading citizens in towns large and small'; *CKJ1*, Chapter 42.

[27] 'how to proceed in declaring their loyalty to her daughter'.

[28] 'who were among the men of rank who lived there'; *CKJ1*, Chapter 44.

[29] 'the King of Castile was on his way to seize them and subjugate the people'; *CKJ1*, Chapter 46.

supporters at the political naivety of the pro-Avis commoners: 'chamavõ-lhe poboo do Mexias de Lixboa, que cuidavom que os avia de rremiir da sogeiçõ delRei de Castella' (p. 75).[30] We shall meet it again later in Chapter 46, in the sermon of the Oporto friar: 'servir ho Meestre [...] pois que sse poinha a deffemder o rregno, pera o livrar da sobjeiçom delRei de Castella' (p. 82)[31]. A positive note, no less potent than this negative theme of subjection, is sounded by another phrase in the Master's letter: 'todos de boom coraçom' [all those with a noble heart] (p. 81). Again, this is made more explicit in the friar's sermon: 'todos deviam de seer dhũa voomtade e desejo' (p. 82).[32] The appeal in both cases is to the sense of solidarity inherent in the popular movement, and implicit in the term most commonly used for such movements: *huniom*. There were overtones of dangerous radicalism about *huniom* itself. Froissart uses closely-related language ('Mais vouloient être tout un') in an unmistakably hostile spirit, about the almost exactly contemporary Peasants' Revolt in England.[33] And the instigator of the Avis faction's resistance to authority in Beja, when challenged with the words 'Que huniom he essa [...]?' is quick to disclaim the term: 'Isto nom he huniom, mas queremos saber [...]' (p. 74).[34] Yet Fernão Lopes, who in other contexts finds a strongly positive value in concepts like *prol comunal, bem comunal,* or *prol de todos,* was almost bound to give his approval to the sense of collective belonging and purpose expressed in this language of unity. The wholly acceptable instance of such language used here by João of Avis is clearly meant to sound rhetorically appropriate. And this is indeed the effect of the overall contrast between the two letters. We know from studies by Russell and by Mário Martins that Fernão Lopes's style can reflect in a local way whatever source he is exploiting at this or that given moment.[35] It seems very likely that the formulae cited above were

[30] '[they] called them "the Lisbon Messiah's people" for believing that the Master was bound to save them from subjection to the King of Castile'; *CKJ1*, Chapter 43.

[31] 'serve the Master [...] since he was standing ready to defend the realm and to rid it of subjection to the King of Castile'; *CKJ1*, Chapter 46.

[32] 'that they should all be of one heart and mind'; *CKJ1*, Chapter 46.

[33] Jean Froissart, *Chronicles,* trans. Geoffrey Brereton (Harmondsworth: Penguin, 1968), p. 212; for Fernão Lopes' use of *prol comunal,* etc., see Rebelo, 'The Idea of Kingship', p. 174 (examples from *Crónica de D. Fernando*). Significantly enough, it is for the murderously-disposed crowd of Évora, that the chronicler reserves his own use of the term *huniom* in these chapters (*Crónica de D. João I,* Part I, p. 79); also in *CKJ1,* Chapter 45.

[34] 'What faction is that [...]? [...] This no faction! But we want to know [...]'; *CKJ1*, Chapter 42.

[35] Russell, *'As Fontes de Fernão Lopes',* p. 38; Mário Martins, *A Bíblia na literatura medieval portuguesa* (Lisbon: Instituto de Cultura Portuguesa, 1979), pp. 78–79.

taken directly from the documents used. But whether that is the case or not, the resulting contrast is deliberate and highly germane to his theme. João of Avis knew how to address himself to a situation in which a spontaneous mass movement existed; indeed, he knew how to address its leaders. Queen Leonor did not.

Other formulae used in the summaries of João's letters were almost certainly taken from the original texts. The Master describes his supporters' successful coup in Évora as an achievement carried through 'por serviço de Deos e homrra do rreino e de sua pessoa' (p. 78).[36] He declares that he will fulfill his task as *Regedor e Defemsor* 'com a graça de Deos' [with the grace of God] (Chapter 46, p. 81). This is not quite the royal 'by the grace of God', but such phrases were readily associated with kingship – as they were doubtless meant to be. Though he had not yet laid claim to the kingship, the João of Avis's newly assumed office embraced many of its functions. Moreover, it was clearly in his interest to claim that the political enterprise on which he was embarked was divinely inspired and favoured. This concern becomes quite explicit at another point in the Évora letter: 'e que esperava em Deos, que fora começo de taaes feitos, que seeria boõ meo e fim delles' (p. 78).[37] João's plebeian supporters would have responded still more readily to such language if, as seems to be the case, their movement had a messianic and millenarian aspect. But it was in any event true that the Master of Avis finally became king; he and his successors did claim to rule by God's grace. As their subject and their client, Fernão Lopes was bound to believe – and on some of the evidence already examined, he clearly did believe it – that the movement which brought them to power was in some sense an implementation of God's will.

And yet between the letters of Chapters 44 and 46, with their claims to divine approval, the chronicler sets the sacrilegious murder of an abbess by Avis partisans in Évora. The revolt in Beja is followed (Chapter 42) by the treacherous killing of the Admiral, a prisoner in rebel hands; in Estremoz (Chapter 43) even the women engage in murderous vendettas; the citizens of Oporto and of other towns that declare for the Avis cause 'nom guardavom divido nẽ amizade a nehuũ que sua teemçom nõ tevesse.' (p. 82).[38] There is more in question here than Fernão Lopes's faithful adherence to the programme outlined in his prologue: 'nuamente mostrar ao poboo quaaes quer comtrairas

[36] 'in the service of God, for the greater honour of the realm and in his own honour'; *CKJI*, Chapter 44.

[37] 'he trusted that God, Who had been the beginning of their great deeds, would also be their righteous middle and end'; *CKJI*, Chapter 44.

[38] 'family ties and friendship were of no avail to anybody who failed to share their intent'; *CKJI*, Chapter 46.

cousas, da guisa que aveherõ' (p. 2).[39] We are faced with a series of contrasts that are created for the reader precisely by the way in which the chronicler has chosen to order his material. The issue, inescapable for Fernão Lopes as a loyal believer in the divine justification of the pro-Avis movement, is made inescapable for us too: what sense can be made of these contrasts?

Some kinds of sense Fernão Lopes does not even try to make of them. He nowhere states his approval of the atrocities, or attempts to explain why it should have been right for any one of them to happen. What he does try to make clear is their place in the process of events that leads to the Avis triumph. He was too much a child of his time to find no role in that process for the providential will of God. With entire orthodoxy he sees that will as acting inscrutably, and as leaving freedom of action to the human will.[40] The practical effect of this is to allow him to show, in a strikingly modern way, the range of purely human causes that bring about historical events. By contrast with the normal run of aristocratic chronicles of his day, he does not see the springs of this autonomous human action as lying solely within the policymaking activity of the great. The process of causality can also arise, and does arise, from collective and plebeian social movements. In effect, the interplay of these two factors stands as a sufficient explanation of events, side by side with the providential model.

The chapters dealing with the provincial revolution record an important shift in the causal balance between national high politics and local popular unrest. As Chapter 42 begins, the former element seems to prevail decisively over the latter. The Queen Regent's letters are 'grave cousa douvir' [were very hard to swallow] (p. 72) to the commoners, but they can do little about it. The plebeians of Estremoz are restricted to a mute but visible 'torvaçom e mall comtemte' [troubled mind and discontent] (p. 73), and the reaction of the controlling elite even to this is brutally assured: 'logo disserom que mester avia na praça çepo e çaator pera deçepar os que comtradissessem o que elles faziam'.[41] The appointment of João of Avis as *Regedor e Defemsor*, it next appears, brought comfort to his supporters – here, as elsewhere, identified primarily as the 'poboos meudos' [common people]. It also proved a source of annoyance to the Queen's party, notwithstanding their conviction that 'todo era

---

[39] 'simply revealing to the people in plain terms whatsoever adverse occurrences there were and the way in which they came about'; *CKJI*, Prologue.

[40] See his comment on the murder of the Abbess in Évora (*Crónica de D. João I*, Part I, p. 80), discussed below.

[41] 'they immediately declared it essential to install an executioner's block and axe in the main square for beheading those who opposed what they were doing'; *CKJI*, Chapter 42.

vaidade' [it all was vainglory] (p. 73). This is still no more than a change of mood. Yet by Chapter 43 the power situation too has changed. The 'gramdes' [grandees] dare not so much as answer the charge that they are betraying their country by their support of Queen Leonor. To anyone who attempted to do so, Fernão Lopes declares, 'morte maa tiinha logo prestes' [a grim death would swiftly follow] (p. 75). What, then, has brought about this change?

For readers of the *Crónica de João I* the answer has to be sought in the intervening episode: the confrontation of the two parties in Beja. There, a second letter from the Queen Regent, demanding collaboration with the King of Castile, is received but not immediately promulgated; suspicion among the commoners leads to a movement to discover what the new orders are. The issue is succinctly put by the town notary: 'Se querees teer amte com a Rainha, ou com ho Meestre' (p. 74),[42] and the response of the citizenry is decisively for the latter. The 'boõ escudeiro' [worthy squire] Gonçalo Nunes makes a dash for the castle and, with support from the crowd, who set fire to the gates, manages to take it over before the garrison can secure it for the Castilian cause. The rebels then hear that the Admiral, Micer Lançarote, will pass close to the town on his way to join the Castilians. They take him prisoner, and he is held in a tower of the castle, from which he is lynched by the enraged townsfolk. 'Desta guisa que avees ouvido', Fernão Lopes continues in Chapter 43, 'se levantarom os poboos em outros logares, seemdo gramde çisma e divisom amtre os gramdes e os pequenos.'[43] He adds that the term used for the militant 'ajumtamento' of the latter was 'arraya meuda' (p. 75). That, indeed, has been the significantly new element throughout the episode. The immediate occasion of the revolt was a political choice between allegiances: Queen or Master? But that choice was posed in a context that was being actively reshaped by the commoners' own demand that they too should be made party to it: 'Pervemtuira esta villa ha sse de manteer e deffemder per quatro ou çimquo que vos aqui sooes? Çertamente nom, mas per nos outros que aqui moramos' (p. 74).[44] Their spokesman in this, the esquire Gonçalo Nunes, is a relatively moderate figure ("Isto nom he huniom […]"). But he is able to secure the castle only with the aid of the angry crowd, and the deputy whom he leaves in charge there is unable to protect their prisoner, the Admiral, against the

[42] 'Whether you wish to stand with the queen or with the Master?'; *CKJI*, Chapter 42.

[43] 'In the very way you have heard about, the people rose up in other towns, and there was a great rift between people of rank and ordinary folk.'

[44] 'Is this town, by any chance, going to be maintained and defended just by the four or five of you gathered in this spot? Of course not! It'll be by us, who live here'; *CKJI*, Chapter 42.

violence of the *arraya-meuda*. It is this insurrectionary force whose actions, repeated across the country, transform the national situation.

In the chapters that follow, Fernão Lopes continues to present these actions in a general relationship to the issues of nationwide politics. The accusations levelled by the pro-Avis commoners against their opponents are of this order: 'chamavomlhe treedores çismaticos, que tiinham de parte dos Castellaãos, por darem o rregno a cujo nom era' (p. 75).[45] Ecclesiastical, chauvinist, dynastic – none of this motivation is specifically or exclusively of concern to the lower orders. In terms of the attention that he devotes to it, however, Fernão Lopes quite clearly attaches a far greater importance to the dynamic, self-sustaining momentum of their revolt. He also allows Providence a role, and this, in Chapter 43 at least, is rather more than merely permissive. It is remarkable, he observes, that castles that had proved their strength against armies should now have fallen to the ill-equipped and leaderless commoners, 'tamto esforço dava Deos nelles, e tamta covardiçe nos outros' (p.75).[46] Thus Portalegre 'com a ajuda de Deos' [with God's help] falls in a single morning (p. 76). But Fernão Lopes's second example, that of Estremoz, is differently explained. The townsfolk set the families of the castle garrison on a cart before the walls and let the implied threat to these hostages do its work. The defenders sue for peace. When the same stratagem is repeated at Évora (Chapter 44), we learn that 'era huũ jogo que os poboos meudos ... muito costumavom emtom de fazer' (p. 77).[47] It goes far to account for the sudden vulnerability of so many castles. Thus, a totally naturalistic causality stands alongside the notion of providential agency. No overt choice is made between them. But the Estremoz incident is dealt with at much greater length than the affair at Portalegre, and offers the reader a much clearer sense of a process at work.

IX

The passage dealing with Estremoz (Chapter 43, p. 76) is a brief one, of fewer than 300 words, but it is an instructive example of Fernão Lopes's treatment of such processes. His alertness to each stage of its working is registered in a sequence of explanatory phrases. 'Semelhavellmente' [similarly], the first term in the series, links the naturalistically-explained events in Estremoz with

---

[45] '[the ordinary folk] called grandees "schismatic traitors" for siding with the Castilians in order to hand over the kingdom to someone to whom it did not belong.'

[46] 'how much courage God instilled in the common people and how much cowardice in the others'.

[47] '[this] was a ploy, in such circumstances, which the common folk customarily resorted to in those days.'

the 'providential' taking of Portalegre – a linkage that can work both ways. In the succession of such phrases that follows, the use of verbal participles expresses with particular clarity Fernão Lopes's instinctive sense that events develop out of one another: 'postos em gramde allvoroço' [mightily aroused], 'Veemdo elles sua rreposta' [On receiving his answer], 'Quamdo esto virom' [On seeing this], 'Veemdosse elle em tall apertada' [Realising the predicament that he was in], 'mas suas fallas nom prestamdo nada' [But, as his arguments availed him nothing], and finally – explanatory because everything else has been explained –'porque nom pode mais fazer' [because he was in no position to do anything else]. But the passage is also shaped by a further sequence of phrases, involving verbs of saying: 'cometerom' [proposed], 'disse' [said], 'disserom' [they said], 'mamdou dizer' [sent word], 'propos muitas rrazões' [advanced many arguments], 'Outorgou' [Conceded]. Within his political narrative, besides his reflective commentary on God's will, Fernão Lopes provides a virtual dramatisation of crucial events such as this.

He dramatises the parallel episode at Beja in a more literal sense. The progress of the *arraya-meuda* from sullen suspicion of the Queen's message and the intentions of local notables to self-confident insurrection is marked by no fewer than seven passages of direct speech, amounting to almost half the 300 or so words of text devoted to the matter (pp. 73–74). A further four verbs in the same narrative refer to other speech-acts. Five of the interlocutors are named – two of the gentry and three spokesmen for the people; the others are the town notary and the citizens at large, clamouring their support for João of Avis 'todos a huũa voz' [with one voice]. Direct and indirect speech are more evenly balanced in the chapters dealing with events in Évora and Oporto, but a similar dramatic structure is present in parts of both.

This use of speech to carry the substance of the action is not, of course, unique to those chapters of Fernão Lopes's work that deal with popular revolutionary outbreaks. It is as much a part of his habitual way of seeing historical reality as his reliance on documents.[48] Chapters 9 and 10, for example (pp.

---

[48] It is impossible to tell how far the two features are really one. Fernão Lopes describes his use of sources in terms which can be understood as covering both written documentation and oral tradition: 'Nem emtemdaaes que certeficamos cousa, salvo de muitos aprovada, e per escprituras vestidas de fe' [Do not conclude that we assert anything unless it has been confirmed by many people and ascertained by reliable documentation] (*Crónica de D. João I*, Part I, Prologue, p. 2). At a distance of some 60 years, oral material that was 'de muitos aprovada' [confirmed by many] could have come from actual witnesses, and was likely to be derived from them at no more than one remove. Memories of what people had said (or were thought to have said) would naturally have been prominent in such material.

16–21), present the killing of the Queen's lover, the Count of Ourem, by João of Avis – an episode whose immediate setting is the royal court at Lisbon. Yet here too the narrative is carried forward through a series of conversations, involving the Master of Avis successively with the Queen, the Count of Barcelos, Andeiro, and so on. The difference is that these speakers are great personages, whose exchanges advance the story of high politics as if it were essentially a tale of personal aspirations and rivalries. That is how the Master justifies his action: 'Comde, eu me maravilho muito de vos seerdes homem a que eu bem queria, e trabalhardesvos de minha desomrra e morte' (p. 19).[49] Other chapters make it clear, of course, that wider issues are involved, but the history dramatised in such episodes as this is still close to that of earlier aristocratic chronicles.

The speakers in Fernão Lopes's accounts of revolutionary activity, on the other hand, are important because of their part in an essentially social and collective process. Some are given their names, because Fernão Lopes was scrupulous in his concern that names should not be forgotten.[50] But it is of more moment that we should be able to identify one of them as 'huũ boo escudeiro', another as the lieutenant of a castle, another as a goatherd, and so forth. What matters in these passages is not individual rivalry, but the interaction between quite well-defined social factions. The most significant voice of all, indeed, is that of the anonymous *arraya-meuda* itself, with its rumours, its slogans, and its newly-awoken sense of power and purpose. Fernão Lopes's use of direct and indirect speech responds to a well-founded sense that the sequence of historical events is a sequence of interactions, that one action responds to another. But the method achieves its fullest effect only when it is placed at the service of new priorities of historical interest – a non-aristocratic, collective history. When that happens, Fernão Lopes is enabled to make historical change intelligible as dramatic development. He is able to present the dialogue of the indignant commoners with their rulers, and to show how the action develops out of this dialogue in a series of effectual gestures. Much of the remarkable success achieved by João of Avis derived from his acceptance of this dialogue, his willingness to admit the claims of previously passive social groups to a fuller historical role. Fernão Lopes, for his part, gives these same groups and their claims an artist's and a historian's recognition.

---

[49] 'Count, I'm astonished that you're a man whom I held in high esteem, yet you strive to bring about my dishonour and death'; *CKJ1*, Chapter 9.

[50] See the introductory remarks to his list of Avis supporters in Chapter 159 (*Crónica de D. João I*, Part I, pp. 298–99); see also *CKJ1*, Chapter 159.

X

He withholds from them, as the mature artist or historian must, the wholesale approval of the too-absolute moralist. He does not evade or excuse the violent excesses of the revolutionary movement. But his account of them is discriminating and specific; there is none of the blanket imputation of atrocity that marks Froissart's treatment of the *Jacquerie*. Sensational tales of rape and sadism are absent here; the violence described is arbitrary and sometimes appalling, but still in its essence political. This tension between what Fernão Lopes plainly regarded as a praiseworthy political stance and the disreputable practice of some Avis partisans was a natural incentive to irony. A detached observer of a more conventional turn of mind might have emphasised the dangerous naivety of these interventions in high matters by people who should have known their place. But Fernão Lopes's detachment is not of that kind. He simultaneously approves of the political action and deplores the form that it sometimes takes. As a result, the irony in his description of these atrocities is largely a dramatic irony.

The Admiral is killed by the mob to whom he surrenders: 'cuidando de achar em elles piedade e compaixom, matarom no de maa e desomrrada morte, e assi acabou seus pustumeiros dias' (p. 75).[51] The effect of this is nicely balanced between the perfidy of the crowd and the Admiral's own ill-fortune. The women of Estremoz are as violent as any of the men, denouncing and murdering Maria Esteveěz's son because 'dissera mall do Meestre, e que era Castellaão'; but Fernão Lopes leaves it open whether this was more than the upshot of a personal feud. The chilling strangeness of their conduct is left to speak for itself: 'e ellas per ssi o matarom e forom no lamçar do muro afumdo' (p. 76).[52] At its most explicit his irony is still enigmatic. Of the zeal with which fugitives to the Castilian zone were pursued – a zeal that might well secure their properties for the pursuers – he observes 'buscavom nos e premdiam nos tam de voomtade, que pareçia que lidavom polla Fe' (p. 82).[53] But this whole passage, as José Hermano Saraiva has shown, is a considerable toning-down of a petition from the *Cortes* of Coimbra seeking to reinstate some of those

---

[51] 'hoping that they would show him pity and compassion, yet they inflicted on him a grim and dishonourable death, and so he ended his last days'; *CKJI*, Chapter 42.

[52] Translation of this and the previous quotation: 'had slandered the Master and that he was a supporter of the Castilians [...] they took it upon themselves to kill him and hurled him down from the ramparts.'

[53] '[they] went in pursuit of them, and so willingly hunted and captured them that it was as though they were fighting for the Holy Faith itself'; *CKJI*, Chapter 46.

who had been dispossessed.[54] Moreover, it appears very probable that many of the rebels did believe themselves to be fighting for true religion, and that Fernão Lopes, though he sometimes felt that they had an odd way of going about it, might well in other contexts have agreed with them.

Essentially his way of seeing these episodes is morally informed but not moralistic; that is to say, his moral vision is made present, but it does not itself shape his account. That remains the function of his historical sense, his awareness of how a mass movement acquires its form and direction. Events in Évora provide a case in point. Fernão Lopes is sharply critical of the second phase of the revolt there, in which the well-to-do leaders of the Avis faction were purged by their plebeian followers: 'Tomado o castello [...] ficou o poboo da çidade cheo de gramde alvoroço, fora de todo boo costume; começarom de sse mover per brava sanha, multiplicamdo novos queixumes, comtra quem lhe nom avia feito erro' (p. 79).[55] The only phrase here to carry any hint of reproof for insubordination of a specifically social kind is 'fora de todo boo costume', and even that is no more than ambiguous. Otherwise, the terms of the criticism are wholly moralistic; its basic concern is with a kind of natural justice and reciprocity in human dealings, irrespective of social status. With 'contra quem lhe nom avia feito erro' here we might compare 'nom guardavom divido nẽ amizade' (Chapter 46, p. 82), in the general description of the revolution at the end of the Oporto chapter. But the criticism is also an explanation; each phrase marks a stage in the process whereby the shifting mood of the *poboo meudo* assumes this dangerous form. The starting point is the prevailing excitement; this leads to a sense that normal rules of conduct no longer apply; hence the surrender to anger, and to arbitrary hostility. In this state, we are told, the people 'husavom de seu livre poder, desdenhamdo quem aa primeira tomavõ por capitaães'.[56] Their new leaders proceed to act 'como lhes dava a voomtade' [as they pleased] (p. 79).

The direction in which their untrammelled wills now take them is pointed by a series of snatches of direct speech. First comes the rallying cry 'Abite! abite! Aqui dos dabite!' (p. 79). This may have had millenarian or even antinomian overtones;[57] it may simply reflect an uneducated public's deformation of the

---

[54] Saraiva, *História de uma revolução*, p. 504.

[55] 'Once the castle had been captured [...] the townspeople became passionately aroused, far beyond what good practice normally allows; they began to be driven by a wild rage, inventing all manner of new grudges against people who had done them no wrong'; *CKJI*, Chapter 45.

[56] 'Unrestrained in their power, they showed contempt for those whom they had at the outset regarded as leaders.'

[57] See the note by Saraiva, *História de uma revolução*, p. 503; it seems unlikely,

title of João, Master of Avis, or it may have been as unintelligible to Fernão Lopes as it is to 21st-century readers. Its importance is that it is, precisely, a rallying cry, an 'apellido'; we are now in the presence of a movement of that kind. The cry will be echoed again when the crowd, hunting down the Abbess, break into the cathedral. There follows something much more specific: 'Vaamos a foaõ, matallo, e rroubemollo!' that will be taken up by the goatherd Gonçalo Eanes: 'Vaamos matar a alleivosa da Abadessa, que he paremta da Rainha e sua criada.'[58] As happens characteristically in Fernão Lopes, the general observation leads on to the particular instance. The factors of crowd psychology are again stressed at this point: 'amdamdo o poboo em este alvoroço, sem outra ocupaçom em que despemdessem tempo'.[59] And so, from causes that have been made amply clear, 'naçeo huũa voz' [a sudden voice cried out] against the Abbess.

But here Fernão Lopes encounters a conflict of sources. Some accounts – the use of the verb 'rrecomtam' [retell] suggests that we are dealing with alternative oral traditions – trace the origin of the voz and the prompting of the murder to Gonçalo Eanes. Other versions attribute to the Abbess an imprudently public criticism of the rebels in the haughty tone that seems characteristic of the Queen's supporters. 'Ex os bevados! amdam com sa bevedice […]' (p. 79)[60] may, indeed, be closer to 'poboo do Mexias de Lixboa' (p. 75) than the literal sense implies, if we take it that the latter carries overtones of millenarian religious enthusiasm. At all events, Fernão Lopes prefers this latter story, on the grounds that 'pareçe mais rrazom' [it appears more reasonable], meaning not that it is a slightly better excuse for what was done, but that it provides a clearer line of causality. On evidential grounds, however, there is nothing to choose between the two explanations, so he leaves the issue open. Effectively, then, we have two alternative lines of causality from the very start of the episode.

A third is offered at the point where the rebels, ignoring the pleas of the priests, tear the Communion chalice from the Abbess's hands, and drag her out of the sanctuary 'sem nehuũa rreveremça do Senhor que nas maãos tiinha, que os por emtom leixou husar de seu livre poder, per juizo a nos nõ conheçido' (p.

---

though, that even the most antinomian of rebels would have identified themselves, as Saraiva thinks, with sinners rejected by Christ.

[58] 'Let's go and kill so-and-so, let's go and rob him!' […] 'Let's kill that treacherous abbess: she's a relative of the queen and a former member of her household.'

[59] 'With the common people so aroused and with nothing else with which to occupy themselves'.

[60] 'Just look at those drunks! See how drunk they are!'

80).[61] The 'livre poder' [unrestrained power], whose exercise was previously accounted for in terms of a recognisable process of crowd psychology, is now seen as the result of a permissive disposition of Providence. But if there is any providential warrant for this particular incident, Fernão Lopes disclaims all attempt to discover what it might be. He merely notes the result: that the rebels were left to act according to their free will. In effect, this invocation of providential causality merely leaves him free to explore other kinds of causality that have already engaged his interest. In no sense does it attenuate his presentation of that undisciplined, dynamic impulse towards extreme violence that was so central a feature of the revolutionary movement.

It is this impulse and its workings that Fernão Lopes is at pains to dramatise here. First (pp. 79–80) he conveys the growth of the rebels' frustrated rage by counterpointing their search for the Abbess with a series of obstacles: her absence at the Cathedral, the attempt of a servant to warn her, her reliance on the consecrated cup for protection, the intervention of the priests. None succeeds: the rebels drag her out and, with a chilling symmetry, Fernão Lopes marks each stage of her unwilling journey by registering a new outrage. Before they reach the staircase they tear off her headdress; before the Cathedral door is passed they cut off her skirts; in the main square one of them kills her with a blow to the head, 'e desi os outros começarom de acuitellar per ella, cada huũ como lhe prazia' (p. 80).[62] The precise linking of place and action makes the account at once outrageous and inexorable; the exercise of 'livre poder' is carried to such extremes as these by a momentum of its own. Before the chapter ends, Fernão Lopes the moralist allows himself a characteristically controlled yet damning irony. The rioters, leaving the Abbess's body to lie in the square, 'forom comer, e buscar outros desemfadamentos' [went off to eat and look for other amusements] (p. 80); they are, horribly, still normal men with normal needs. But by the end of the chapter Fernão Lopes the historian has reasserted himself. The sympathisers who rescue the body from the cattle-yard where it was dumped that evening bury it secretly because 'doutra guisa nom eram ousados de o fazer de praça' [they did not dare to do so openly] (p. 80). It is to the precise nature of the revolutionary situation that our attention is finally returned. Fernão Lopes, shocked and puzzled by the form the revolution sometimes took, sought to impress those reactions on his readers. But he shaped his narrative to convey something else: the historian's understanding of how these things came to be.

---

[61] '... without any reverence for Our Lord, Whom she held in her hands (that very Lord whose reasoning was unbeknown to us...)'.

[62] 'whereupon the others began to slash at her, each one as he saw fit'.

Matters did not invariably reach the same pass as in Évora. In some places the more moderate and middle-ranking leadership was able to impose its will on the turbulent commoners. This happened at a later stage, for example, in Vila Viçosa (Chapters 98–99), whose commander, Vasco Porcalho, suspected of dealings with Castile, was saved from a lynching. He then appealed to João of Avis in Lisbon, and was reinstated by his orders 'e pero lhes muito pesasse e aos da vilha' (Chapter 99, p. 167).[63] This was decorum itself compared with Évora, but the outcome was unfortunate: Porcalho did change sides, causing much trouble in that frontier area. Fernão Lopes and his readers may very well have felt that the crowd that had bayed 'Moira o treedor com quamtos tem!' [Death to the traitor and all his men!] (Chapter 98, p. 165) had not been so very wide of the mark. Yet another possible line of development could be observed in Oporto, the kingdom's second city, where the declaration of support for João of Avis was prompted by his letter to the municipalities, assuming the title of *Regedor e Defemsor* (Chapter 46, pp. 81–82). This order of events lent a certain legitimacy to the revolution in Oporto; it could be seen as an expression of loyalty rather than of insubordination. Moreover, this pattern was, Fernão Lopes tells us, frequently paralleled elsewhere. There were good rhetorical grounds, then, for making the Oporto outbreak a wholly exemplary episode. Instead, his analytic temper and keen eye for the actual process of events dominate this account as they do others.

The Oporto chapter is constructed around three items of formal record, all of them contributing to the dignity and authority of João of Avis. His letter, with its appeal to all 'verdadeiros Portugueeses' [true Portuguese], is at once kingly in its assumption of authority and communicative in its appeal for the recipients to act, 'todos de boom coraçom' [all those with a noble heart] (Chapter 46, p. 81). His proclamation through the city as *Regedor e Defemsor* anticipates the ceremony of acclamation by which he will eventually become king.[64] The sermon preached in the Cathedral by a rebel friar urges the audience to 'servir ho Meestre leallmente e de boom coraçom, come verdadeiros Portugueeses' (p. 82).[65] Several of these phrases come from João's own letter, but the claim to loyal service in a context of religious exhortation adds one more element to the quasi-royal status with which he is invested. This emphasis, as Fernão Lopes nears the end of his provincial survey, is part of the rhetoric through which the revolution is made to appear more legitimate.

---

[63] 'though both they and the townsfolk were greatly disturbed at this'.

[64] Here (p. 82) 'Arreall! Arreall! por o Meestre dAvis, Regedor e Deffemssor dos rregnos de Portugall'; there (Chapter 192, p. 372) 'Arreall! por elRei dom Joham!' Cf. the note by Saraiva, *História de uma revolução*, p. 504.

[65] 'serve the Master faithfully and with all their will, as true Portuguese'.

But it is not an invention; it also reflects the actual political strategy of João of Avis at this point – acting like a king, but not yet claiming to be one.

Throughout the chapter the popular response to these initiatives is conveyed in the familiar language of unity. The theme is introduced by João of Avis's own phrase 'todos de boom coraçom' (later taken up by the friar), and further developed through a sequence of expressions that trace the process whereby such a unity is forged. There are mass meetings (p.81) to consider João's letter ('logo sse jumtarom todos, espeçiallmente o poboo meudo')[66] and to arrange and witness the ceremony of his proclamation ('jumtaromsse todos ho outro [dia] seguimte' [they all assembled the following day]). This picture is reinforced by a reference to the 'praça da çidade, homde ja todos eram jumtos' [main square, where everybody had gathered] (pp. 81–82), and amplified as the banner-bearer parades the city 'acompanhado de muita gemte, assi clerigos come leigos, braadamdo todos a huũa voz' (p. 82).[67] This demonstration is followed by the friar's appeal for a yet closer unity: 'que todos deviam de seer dhũa voomtade e desejo, e nom amdar entrelles desvairo nẽ huũ' (p. 82).[68] The response is all that he could have desired: 'Muito foram todos comtemtes [...] todos dhuũ tallamte se desposerom a teer e seguir a teemçom do Meestre'.[69]

Thus far the emphasis in the Oporto chapter is triumphalist rather than conflictive. But Fernão Lopes does not lose sight of the conflictive dimension of events there. Once the Master's letter was received, he declares 'logo se jumtarom todos, espeçiallmente o poboo meudo, ca alguũs outros dessa comunall gemte duvidamdo rreçeavõ de poer em tall feito maão' (p. 81).[70] The doubters are commoners but not, by this account, members of the *poboo meudo*; by implication, then, they come from the ranks of the relatively well-to-do. The initiative, however, lies very clearly with the lower orders: it is the *arraya-meuda* that makes the decisions, selecting the standard-bearer for João's proclamation. Their first nominee refuses the task 'mostrãdo que o nom devia de fazer' [arguing that he ought not to do so]; these scruples, whatever their substance, are enough to have him branded a traitor and hacked to death

---

[66] 'all gathered together at once, with great determination and at the ready, especially the humbler folk'.

[67] 'followed by a huge crowd, clergy as well as laymen, and with everybody shouting out with one voice'.

[68] 'that they should all be of one heart and mind and that there should be no discord among them'.

[69] 'They were all very pleased [...] their common aim was to uphold and further the Master's intentions.'

[70] 'the people all gathered together at once, with great determination and at the ready, especially the humbler folk, for a number of others among the common people hesitated and were afraid to set about such a task'.

on the spot. Their second choice, Afonso Eanes Pateiro, forewarned by friends, volunteers before being asked, and carries out the task with much enthusiasm. How far this was the fruit of his advance warning, and how far of personal conviction, Fernão Lopes does not speculate; here as elsewhere we are left with a choice of motivation. But there is no doubt at all of the formidable character of the *arraya-meuda*'s resolve; when they begin, systematically, to infringe the interdict placed on the Cathedral, 'nehuũa pessoa ousava esto comtradizer' [nobody dared to speak out against this] (p. 82).

Generalising from the events in Oporto to those in other towns, Fernão Lopes continues to highlight the radical impulse behind the revolution, and to trace its workings (p. 82). The characteristic events, he suggests, were the taking of castles by the *poboos meudos*, and the acclamation of the Master of Avis by patriotic crowds. But he also stresses the dissolution of existing bonds of family, friendship, or obligation, and the arbitrary purges of supposed Castilian supporters. The mere arousal of suspicion – 'E Foaão delles he' [So-and-so is one of them] – was fatal, especially to the well-to-do and the gentry, many of whom fled. The commoners' enthusiastic pursuit of them was like a holy war. All these elements are recognisable from the foregoing chapters, and they keep firmly before us the complex and troubling reality of the Avis revolution. Such items as the gratuitous killing of the Admiral, the murderous women of Estremoz, and the horrors of Évora are as much a part of that reality as the personal daring of Gonçalo Nunes in Beja or the patriotic exuberance of Oporto. 'Husavom de seu livre poder' implies both the fact of freedom and the abuse of it; 'todos […] dhuma voomtade e desejo' and 'nehuũa pessoa ousava esto comtradizer' are two aspects of the same situation. Fernão Lopes clarifies both the relationship between them and the origins of each one.

XI

He is able to do so because he maintains a pluralistic view of causality, allowing Providence a role, but one that will not usurp the place of actual historical judgment. He recognises that the political activity of the great is carried on in a relationship with deeper social movements, and often depends on them. In such movements he is aware of the interaction between individual and collective initiatives, and of the complexities of motive that can underlie either. Yet the centre of his interest in these chapters is firmly maintained; it lies with that dynamic social unrest that, ultimately, made the Avis victory possible. That element is made central by a feat of essentially literary technique: the creation of a dramatic style that can match it in both momentum and complexity. Part of that complexity lies in the candour with which even the less creditable aspects of the movement are recorded. The very certainty of touch with which Fernão Lopes places these aspects historically adds credibility to his overriding belief that the victory of the Avis faction was an event to be welcomed.

That, at all events, is what happens for many modern readers,[71] for reasons so closely bound up with Fernão Lopes's precise deployment of language that the effect can hardly be accidental. This way of reading the *Crónica* might be seen as reversing the approach outlined by Rebelo, for whom the providentialist meaning governs and justifies the work's more literal senses. That approach too has good textual warrant; it would certainly have commended itself to a great many readers of Fernão Lopes's own day. It is not at all surprising, however, that he should have produced a work capable of being read coherently on widely differing assumptions. That is what great writers often do; there is no reason why the great historian should be an exception. The control that he exercises over his audience is, of course, built into this at every level. In a single line (*Crónica de D. Fernando*, Chapter 113), he can shift from a hard-headed focus on the international diplomacy of the Great Schism, by way of a language of orthodox pronouncement, to a slippery and grotesque run of images – 'com duas cabeças, assi como corpo monstruu, que era fea cousa de veer'[72] – that draws his hearers into a directly visceral identification with anti-Avignonese feeling in Portugal. On a rather larger scale (though again in a context of aural delivery), the surrender of Portel by the humorous and foul-mouthed Fernão Gonçalves works to a different effect. Placed as it is in *Crónica de D. João I*, Part I, Chapter 158, between Juan I's sombre withdrawal from Lisbon (Chapter 156) and the definitive celebration of Portuguese victory (Chapters 159–63), it punctuates these solemnities with a moment of broad comic relief. At this level of control, a whole narrative section, like the story of Prince João of the Castro line (*Crónica de D. Fernando*, Chapters 98–106), can have a self-sufficient poignancy about it. His many attractive qualities as a youth, his secret attachment and marriage to the Queen's more thoughtful sister, the temptations dangled before him to believe the worst of her to his own future advantage, his murder of her and his flight to Castile – all these elements are interwoven in a fully convincing story of personal motives, as tragic as his mother's better-known story and in human terns more circumstantial. Yet it is there for a very immediately persuasive

---

[71] Manuel Rodrigues Lapa, *Lições de literatura portuguesa: época medieval*, 6th edn (Coimbra: Coimbra Editora, 1966), p. 385, offers a similar reaction: 'O escritor parece compreender, embora os não aprove, estos excessos habituais das multidões' [The writer seems to understand these habitual excesses of crowds, albeit not approving of them].

[72] 'two-headed, just like the body of a monster, which was an ugly thing to behold'.

purpose: this man, rather than João of Avis, was for many Portuguese the primary focus of their dynastic hopes in opposition to Princess Beatriz and her Castilian husband. Their outlook still commanded support in the *Cortes* of Coimbra. Fernão Lopes's telling of his story at this earlier stage serves to convince readers later on that the man was simply not capable of that role. It has to be admitted that the tale of the younger Castro brother, Prince Dinis (*Crónica de D. João I*, Part II, Chapter 130) provides less convincing proof of its similar dynastic priorities, containing as it does several uncharacteristically crude factual distortions.[73] Prince Dinis's story, however, is a rare, late, and very marginal lapse from Fernão Lopes's usual standards.

His historiography has more than once been described – not always with approval – as closely akin to the novelist's art.[74] The present analysis certainly points to a number of qualities common to them both: the wholeness of vision; the artistic ordering of that vision to point up significant relationships; the power of conveying an illusion of lived reality. But Fernão Lopes has other attributes that are more professionally specific. His evidential grounding, his awareness of social phenomena as realities, and his acknowledgement of a plurality of potential causes for historical events – these are the things that make him still, and primarily, one of the first great modern historians.

[73] Derek W. Lomax and R. J. Oakley, *The English in Portugal*, p. 328 describe this chapter as 'inaccurate and designed to discredit Prince Dinis'. For a different and fuller account of his mission to England and its outcome, see Russell, *The English Intervention*, pp. 516–18. Some of the inaccuracies are just that – an unusual thing in Fernão Lopes; why, for example, have the prince captured by Breton rather than Frisian pirates? Possibly Chapter 130 was one of a number of later chapters in the *Crónica de D. João I*, Part II, that have come down to us in a drafted but unrevised state.

[74] The view that 'a Crónica é mais um romance histórico' [the Chronicle is more like a historical novel] is advanced as a negative criticism by Oliveira Marques (see Borges Coelho, *A Revolução de 1383*, p. 12); the comment made by Martín de Riquer, *Resumen de literatura portuguesa* (Barcelona: Seix Barral, 1947), p. 31 that 'Fernão Lopes es un historiador con temple de novelista' [Fernão Lopes is an historian with a novelist's temperament] forms part of a strongly positive evaluation.

3

The Chronicle of King Pedro of
Portugal: Historical Context

DAVID GREEN

For Fernão Lopes the reign of Pedro I of Portugal and the Algarve (r. 1357–1367) was remarkable: 'there had never been ten years in Portugal like the ones in which King Pedro ... ruled'.[1] Born in 1320, Pedro was the third but only surviving son of Afonso IV (r. 1325–1357) and his wife, Beatriz of Castile (1293–1359). As with many royal children, little is known about Pedro's upbringing and education. He was married in 1336 to Constanza Manuel of Castile who, not long before her death in 1345, bore him one son, the future Fernando I (r. 1367–1383). Pedro's early years, however, would be dominated by another woman and by his affair with one of Constanza's ladies-in-waiting, Inês de Castro. The remarkable story of their relationship, her murder perpetrated on King Afonso's orders, and the astounding brutality with which Pedro took his revenge on her killers, had major personal and political implications that would shape the king's reputation for the rest of his life and for posterity.

That reputation was and remains conflicted. The assiduousness with which the king sought out crimes, real or imagined, committed against himself or his nation was such that he became known to some as 'the Just' and to others as 'the Cruel'. The latter appellation sometimes leads to confusion with his nephew, Pedro 'the Cruel' of Castile (r. 1350–1369), not least because the careers of the two men were closely entwined.[2] This was, in part, because of

---

[1] See Chapter 44 below.

[2] Peter Russell has described Pedro of Portugal as 'unpleasantly eccentric' and suggested 'he was ... guilty of ... acts of refined brutality, often of a clearly sadistic character': *The English Intervention in Spain and Portugal in the Time of Edward III and Richard II* (Oxford: Clarendon Press, 1955), pp. 17, 54. On the suitability of the title 'the Cruel' for Pedro of Castile see Clara Estow, 'Royal Madness in the Crónica de Rey Don Pedro', *Mediterranean Studies*, 6 (1996), 13–28, at p. 20. Unlike

the series of somewhat Byzantine dynastic crises and civil wars that bedevilled the Iberian Peninsula in the middle years of the 14th century. These struggles and the entangling alliances they involved encouraged the intervention of foreign powers, and it was during Pedro's reign that Spain and Portugal became deeply embroiled in the Hundred Years War (1337–1453), providing alternative theatres in which the Anglo-French conflict could be fought. Fernão Lopes recognised the wider European implications of these clashes, especially those that developed from the Castilian civil war fought between King Pedro and his half-brother, Enrique of Trastámara (King Enrique II, 1369–1379) and, because of this, he dedicated a considerable proportion of his chronicle to these events. Nineteen of the chronicle's 44 chapters concern Pedro of Castile.[3]

Lopes was, in general, a firm advocate of Pedro of Portugal. He described him as a fine ruler, one whose zealous search for justice was, for the most part, 'driven by noble intent'; a king who possessed many fine qualities and who spent his time wisely, honing those skills valued in a monarch.[4] Like his contemporary Gaston Phébus, Count of Foix-Béarn (1331–1391), Pedro had a passion for hunting and hawking, and he was often to be found in the company of huntsmen, hounds, and birds of prey. Such masculine activities were considered worthy and suitable for a king, since they taught courage in the field and control of men and resources. According to Gaston's *Livre de chasse* (1387), hunting brought spiritual benefits also: 'it makes one avoid all of the seven deadly sins; secondly it makes one a better and faster rider, more intelligent and more skilled, more at ease and more daring and more familiar with all kinds of lands and situations'.[5] Pedro was also said to manage his relationships with the nobility effectively; he recognised the importance of *largesse* and the appropriate distribution of patronage. Furthermore, the king established a suitable environment in which to govern; his court was a civilised and cultured space, a haven of feasting, dancing, and music – Lopes remarked on his particular fondness for long trumpets.[6] A number of these qualities were

---

the generally positive description of Pedro of Portugal offered by Fernão Lopes, the Castilian chronicler, Pero López de Ayala (1332–1407), describes 'a ruler whose cumulative acts of cruelty and terror gradually and inevitably alienate ever larger segments of Castilian society': *ibid*, 14.

[3]   Angus MacKay, *Spain in the Middle Ages: From Frontier to Empire, 1000–1500* (London: Macmillan, 1977), p. 121.

[4]   See the Prologue below.

[5]   Richard Vernier, *Lord of the Pyrenees: Gaston Fébus, Count of Foix, 1331–1391* (Woodbridge: Boydell Press, 2008), pp. 130–38, quotation at p. 132.

[6]   See Chapters 1, 4 and 14 below; see also Rita Costa Gomes, *The Making of a Court Society: Kings and Nobles in Late Medieval Portugal*, trans. Alison Aiken (Cambridge: Cambridge University Press, 2003), pp. 204–90.

central to the effective exercise of royal power during a period of political
unrest, religious disturbance, and socio-economic dislocation, which affected
Portugal and her neighbours in the later Middle Ages.

The Iberian Peninsula in the 14th century consisted of several distinct states,
of which the three largest were Castile, Aragon, and Portugal. In addition, to
the north, lay the kingdom of Navarre in the western Pyrenees. This gravitated,
politically, towards France as much as Iberia, not least because its ruler,
Charles 'the Bad' (r. 1349–1387), inherited the county of Evreux and other
estates in Normandy, as well as a claim to the French throne. Meanwhile,
Granada in the south remained under Muslim control, although it was nothing
more than a remnant of the great territory of al-Andalus which had dominated
the region until the early 13th century and left such a deep cultural imprint.[7]
Indeed, the geo-political dynamic of all Hispania was in a constant state of
flux because of the ongoing *Reconquista*, although the recapture of Muslim
territory was not a major priority for much of the 14th century. Progress
had, in any case, been uneven after the Christian victory at Las Navas de
Tolosa (1212), but new opportunities continued to emerge and all three major
kingdoms sought to extend their territorial authority within the Peninsula. This
often led to conflict between the Christian powers, a situation often exacerbated, somewhat perversely, by the many marriages that had been contracted
in order to establish peace. These usually served only to generate further
friction and increased the likelihood that familial disputes would escalate into
international incidents.

In addition to territorial expansion within the Peninsula, the Iberian nations
sought to extend their commercial influence overseas in this period, and
considerable efforts were expended in trade and maritime affairs. Fernão Lopes
regularly emphasised the importance of naval forces in his chronicle.[8] In 1248,
Castile captured the great river port of Seville, which became its key naval
base. Cadiz, with its unique position on the south-western coast, was taken
in 1262. It would become the departure points for many expeditions into the

---

[7] The Granadan monarch, Muhammad V (1354–1359, 1362–1391) succeeded his
father Yūsuf I (1333–1354). His reign was interrupted in 1359 when he was overthrown
by his half-brother, Ismail, Yūsuf's favourite younger son by a second wife. He ruled
briefly as Ismail II (1359–1360) and was in turn deposed by a cousin, Abū Saad. In
1362 Pedro of Castile provided military support to help Muhammad regain his throne:
Clara Estow, 'War and Peace in Medieval Iberia: Castilian-Granadan Relations in
the Mid-Fourteenth Century', in *The Hundred Years War: A Wider Focus*, ed. L. J.
Andrew Villalon and Donald Kagay (Leiden: Brill, 2005), pp. 151–75, at pp. 152–53.
Lopes discusses Granadan-Castilian relations in Chapters 32–33 and 41 below.

[8] See, for example, Chapters 18, 19 and 24 below.

Atlantic. For Aragon, the Balearic Islands (captured in 1229–1235), Valencia (1238), and Sicily (1282) provided important bases, alongside Barcelona, from which trade developed with North Africa and in the eastern and central Mediterranean. Portugal, which had gained independence from Castile in the 12th century, was bounded by the Atlantic Ocean to the west and Castile to the east. As a consequence it, too, sought to expand overseas. The opening of the straits of Gibraltar in the middle of the 13th century was an important step in developing Mediterranean and Atlantic trade links. And it seems likely that a series of expeditions directed or financed by the Portuguese reached the Azores, Canaries, Madeira, and other Atlantic islands as early as the 1330s and 1340s. Such concerns with expansion would, however, soon come to an abrupt halt.[9]

The decade prior to Pedro's accession to the Portuguese throne was deeply disturbed both politically and socio-economically. For the population as a whole the greatest tragedy came in the form of the Black Death, which struck Portugal in 1348. Spread by shipping along the coast and inland via the river system, plague raged through the Peninsula. It may have been further encouraged by the huge numbers of pilgrimages to Santiago de Compostela undertaken to try and assuage this most virulent manifestation of God's wrath with a sinful world. Estimates of mortality from plague are as high as two-thirds, even 90% in some areas, although such figures are difficult to substantiate. There is no doubt, however, that casualty rates were appalling, and, by the end of 1348, about a third of the Peninsula had been subjected to plague and much of the remainder would have to face the disease in the following year.[10]

For Pedro, tragedy in this period took a more personal form. Inês de Castro arrived in Portugal in 1340 to join the entourage of the prince's wife, Constanza. Pedro soon made Inês his mistress and, when Constanza died in 1345, their relationship became public and common knowledge. By 1351 Inês had given birth to three sons and a daughter. Given the political turbulence

[9]   J. R. S. Phillips, *The Medieval Expansion of Europe*, 2nd edn (Oxford: Clarendon Press, 1998), pp. 137, 149–50; Fátima Regina Fernandes, 'Nobles and the Crown on the Eve of Portugal's Atlantic Discoveries', *Mediterranean Studies*, 9 (2000), 35–41, at p. 35.

[10]   Ole J. Benedictow, *The Black Death, 1346–1353: The Complete History* (Woodbridge: Boydell Press, 2004), pp. 83–85, 89, 277, 282–83; Teofilo F. Ruiz, *Spain's Centuries of Crisis: 1300–1474* (Chichester: Blackwell Publishing, 2011), p. 33; Peter Linehan, 'Castile, Navarre and Portugal', in *New Cambridge Medieval History VI, c.1300–c.1415*, ed. Michael Jones (Cambridge: Cambridge University Press, 2000), pp. 619–50, at p. 637.

throughout the Peninsula and the potential threat of internecine war, Afonso IV began to fear that Inês and her children could pose a threat to the established royal dynasty. These fears reached such a pitch by January 1355 that Afonso ordered Inês to be killed.

Pedro, grief-stricken and enraged, led a revolt against his father. However, not all the ramifications of the relationship were yet apparent. It was only in June 1360 that Pedro chose to make a sensational declaration and claimed, swearing an oath on the Gospels, that he and Inês had, in fact, been married secretly. This act essentially legitimised their children, the princes João and Dinis. Statements were offered by two witnesses, Dom Gil, the bishop of Guarda, and Estevão Lobato, a *criado*[11] of the king, confirming that Pedro and Inês had, indeed, been married, but Fernão Lopes noted their evidence was far from convincing and many doubted its validity. More still wondered why he had taken so long to reveal the 'true' nature of the relationship. Given the king's growing reputation, however, it is not surprising that those with qualms voiced their doubts quietly.[12]

Towards the end of his reign, Pedro would have Inês reburied in suitable style. Her body was exhumed from its resting place in Coimbra and taken with great solemnity to Alcobaça, where it was interred in the royal monastery in what Lopes believed to be 'the most honourable transfer that had ever been seen in Portugal'. There, Pedro had two tombs constructed, one for each of them. The monuments show Pedro and Inês facing each other, inscribed with the words 'Até o fim do mundo' [Until the end of the world].[13]

By this time Pedro had meted out 'cruel justice' to Inês's murderers. Although these men had been pardoned by King Afonso, they had prudently sought and been offered sanctuary across the border when Pedro came to the throne. Unable, at that point, to punish them personally, Pedro instead confiscated their property; he sub-divided it and granted the smaller parcels of land to a number of his courtiers. He did this so that the estates could never be re-established. Some time later, however, he reached an accommodation with the King of Castile, offering to exchange the exiles for three Castilians who had, in a similar fashion, fled to Portugal to escape 'justice'. It was this breach of faith, by both kings, rather than the barbaric punishment which followed that so appalled Fernão Lopes:

---

[11] For a definition of '*criado*' see Chapter 6, note 12 below, as well as the 'Translators'note' above, p. xxvii.

[12] See Chapters 27–29 below.

[13] See Chapter 44 below.

The king lost much of his good repute as a result of this exchange [of prisoners], which was seen as a great infamy, both in Portugal and Castile. All the noblemen who heard of it declared that both kings had made a very grave mistake in going against their word, given that these nobles had been granted sanctuary in their respective kingdoms.[14]

The accused, Alvaro Gonçalves and Pero Coelho, were swiftly found guilty of Inês's murder, and Pedro devised a suitable punishment for those who had, by their actions, broken his heart. He ordered that their hearts were to be removed from their living bodies, one torn through his back, the other dragged through his chest. He then commanded their bodies to be burned. The king watched and enjoyed a meal while the sentence was carried out. A third man implicated in the assassination, Diogo Lopes Pacheco, escaped extradition through enormous good fortune, and was later found to be innocent. The executions of the assassins appear to provide the most compelling evidence for Pedro's alleged cruelty. However, although this specific incident is particularly striking, Pedro was far from alone in employing such extreme punishments. In later medieval France and England revolt and treason became subject to brutal retribution in the late 13th and early 14th centuries – this period saw the introduction of hanging, drawing, and quartering, a means of dispatch designed not only to degrade and destroy the individual in the present but also to prevent him from gaining salvation in the afterlife.[15]

The king's search for 'justice' was for Fernão Lopes the most distinctive aspect of his reign. The chronicle opens with a discussion of justice, which he described as 'the very basis of royal power, in that it punishes evildoers and allows good people to live in peace'.[16] Pedro is said to have loved justice with a particular passion, and he appears to have taken enormous, possibly sadistic, pleasure in punishing evildoers personally. The early part of the chronicle provides a litany of crimes and punishments: two of Pedro's favourites are decapitated for robbing and killing a Jewish spice merchant; a squire is castrated for having an affair with a married woman; and a married woman is burned at the stake for taking a lover. The king was only restrained with great

---

[14] See Chapter 31 below.

[15] J. G. Bellamy, *The Law of Treason in the Late Middle Ages* (Cambridge: Cambridge University Press, 1970), pp. 1–58; J. S. Bothwell, *Falling from Grace: Reversal of Fortune and the English Nobility, 1075–1455* (Manchester: Manchester University Press, 2008), pp. 36–46; S. H. Cuttler, *The Law of Treason and Treason Trials in Later Medieval France* (Cambridge: Cambridge University Press, 1981), pp. 145–46; Jacques Krynen, *L'empire du roi: Idées et croyances politiques en France XIIIe–XVe siècle* (Paris: Gallimard-Jeunesse, 1993), pp. 384–414.

[16] See the Prologue below.

difficulty from torturing the bishop of Oporto, who was found to be having an affair; and his order to behead Admiral Lançarote Pessanha,[17] who was accused of various sexual misdemeanours, was only rescinded following pleas from Gabriele Adorno, Fifth Doge of Genoa (1363–1370). Many of Lopes's anecdotes seek to show Pedro's obsession with becoming 'o rei justiceiro'; whether his wish to do so meant he crossed the line into tyranny remains a matter of debate.[18]

Pedro was also concerned with the wider reform of the machinery of justice in Portugal; he wished to use it to augment royal power and extend secular authority over the Church. By a series of measures promulgated at the *Cortes* of Elvas (May 1361) the respective jurisdictions of secular and ecclesiastical tribunals were defined and the practice of submitting papal letters to royal veto was confirmed. Pedro insisted on the 'beneplácito régio', that is, the royal approbation of all papal orders before they were published in his kingdom.[19]

Pedro gained the opportunity to extend secular authority over the Church in Portugal, in part, because of the relocation of the papal curia from Rome to Avignon that had taken place in the early years of the century. The Avignon papacy deeply compromised the spiritual standing of the Church, a state of affairs exaggerated by anti-clerical attitudes generated in the course of the Black Death. There had been good reasons for the papacy's move, not least Rome's disruptive political climate and uncomfortable summer weather. Indeed, because of such considerations it had not been uncommon for the papal curia to reside outside the Eternal City for extended periods, although it tended to remain in the Papal States. Pope Clement V (1305–1314), however, never even managed to get to Rome after his election. Poor health, a fondness for his home in southern France, and the political chaos of northern Italy were

---

[17] Son of the Genoese Manuel Pessanha, originally Emanuele Pessagno, was appointed admiral by King Dinis I (1279–1325) in *c.* 1320. Thereafter the title of High Admiral ['almirante-mor'] of Portugal became hereditary in the Pessanha family: Gomes, *Making of a Court Society*, p. 257.

[18] See Chapters 6–9 below; Stanley L. Rose, 'Anecdotal Narrative in Fernão Lopes's *Crónica de D. Pedro I*', *Luso-Brazilian Review*, 8:1 (1971), 78–87, at p. 81. On the appropriate balance between the legitimate exercise of royal authority and the rights of subjects see Antony Black, *Political Thought in Europe* (Cambridge: Cambridge University Press, 1992), pp. 148–52.

[19] See Chapter 7 below. The situation in Portugal is comparable to that in England where Edward III issued the Statutes of Provisors (1351, 1365) and Praemunire (1353, 1365): W. Mark Ormrod, *Edward III* (New Haven, CT and London: Yale University Press, 2011), pp. 367–68, 434–35.

among the reasons that led to the papal curia taking on a somewhat peripatetic existence until 1309, when it became fixed, more or less, in Avignon.[20]

Located in the Comtat Venaissin, Avignon was a possession of the Church on the borders of but not, technically, within the Capetian kingdom. However, outside France and certainly in those countries not allied to France, this soon became seen as a 'Babylonish captivity', and for much of the 14th century the Avignon Papacy was seen by many as little better than a tool of the French monarchy. Because of this the Church enjoyed few successes in its traditional role as an arbiter in European affairs. For example, under orders from Pope Innocent VI (1352–1362), Cardinal Guy de Boulogne and the Cardinal-Legate, Guillaume de la Jugie, made several attempts to resolve the Castilian-Aragonese war – an ongoing series of campaigns with which Lopes was much concerned.[21]

The divisions in Western Christendom highlighted by the Avignon Papacy were reflected in and to some extent caused by the Hundred Years War. The outbreak of hostilities between England and France in 1337 was the product of a number of disputes that had been simmering for many years. The central argument, however, focused on the question of sovereignty in the 'English' duchy of Gascony, the last remnant of the Angevin empire, which had extended southwards as far as the Pyrenees in the early 13th century. This was exacerbated by a contest for the French throne that followed the death of Charles IV, the last Capetian monarch, in 1328. Edward III (r. 1327–1377) of England's claim was rejected in favour of that of Philip, Count of Valois, who took the crown as Philip VI (r. 1328–1350).[22]

The war did not have major implications for Portugal immediately, but it would shape political events throughout the Iberian Peninsula from the 1360s. In the early phase of the struggle Portugal offered token support for England, although this was rarely more than a gesture of friendly neutrality. In general, Anglo-Portuguese relations had been amicable up to this point, if not always close. Commercial ties had developed in the 13th century, and trade increased

[20] Yves Renouard, *The Avignon Papacy, 1305–1403*, trans. D. Bethell (Hamden, CT: Archon Books, 1970).

[21] See Chapters 22–23, 26 and 32 below; T. N. Bisson, *The Medieval Crown of Aragon: A Short History* (Oxford: Clarendon Press, 1991), p. 112; Karsten Plöger, *England and the Avignon Popes: The Practice of Diplomacy in Late Medieval Europe* (London: Legenda, 2005), p. 23.

[22] Malcolm Vale, *The Origins of the Hundred Years War: The Angevin Legacy, 1250–1340* (Oxford: Clarendon Press, 1996); David Green, *The Hundred Years War: A People's History* (New Haven, CT and London: Yale University Press, 2014), pp. 4–11.

somewhat in the 1340s with a significant agreement made in 1352. It was, however, only in 1369, with the breakdown of Anglo-Castilian relations, that trade with Portugal truly flourished.[23] By that stage the Hundred Years War had made a great impact in Iberia. As with situations elsewhere, in Brittany and Flanders, for example, succession crises and competing political claims across the Iberian kingdoms saw them drawn into the orbit of the Anglo-French war. Castile was at the centre of these disputes.

The proximity of the duchy of Gascony had ensured that Anglo-Castilian commercial and political links had been close for some time before the outbreak of the Hundred Years War. This was most evident in the marriage of Eleanor of Castile (1241–1290) and King Edward I (r. 1272–1307). With the outbreak of the Hundred Years War, France and England courted Castile because of its growing naval strength, and Alfonso XI (1313–1350) conducted negotiations with both sides before agreeing an alliance with Edward III, founded on the marriage of the Castilian king's son, Pedro, to the English king's daughter, Joan of the Tower. Joan, however, contracted plague in 1348 and she died at Bordeaux, *en route* to Castile. Policy shifted early in Pedro's reign when, under considerable pressure from his mother and a number of the ministers of state, he agreed to a marriage with Blanche of Bourbon, Philip VI's niece. This proved to be an unmitigated disaster, in part because Pedro had by this time fallen in love with María de Padilla, who became his mistress. The king fulfilled the most minimal conditions of the marriage contract and then, two days after the wedding, effectively imprisoned Blanche in the alcazar of Toledo, never to see her again. She died in 1361 in mysterious circumstances.[24]

Pedro's behaviour scandalised the French and the Papacy and had major implications for domestic Castilian politics, which were already unstable. Pedro had only been 15 years old at his accession in 1350. Troubled by sickness and forced to fight off the competing claims of eight illegitimate half-brothers, conditions were far from ideal. The major contender for the throne was his elder half-bother, Enrique, 'the Bastard' of Trastámara. The son of King Alfonso XI and his mistress, Leonor de Guzmán, Enrique had received a wide range of valuable and prestigious estates and titles. Indeed, Alfonso had shown a clear preference for his illegitimate children, and this, essentially, created a power bloc to rival King Pedro – it was a state of affairs

---

[23] Wendy R. Childs, 'Anglo-Portuguese Relations in the Fourteenth Century', in *The Age of Richard II*, ed. James L. Gillespie (New York/Stroud: St Martin's Press/ Sutton Publishing, 1997), pp. 27–49, at pp. 27–28, 32–33.

[24] See Chapter 16 below; Clara Estow, *Pedro the Cruel of Castile, 1350–1369* (Leiden: Brill, 1995), pp. 11, 136–50; Joseph F. O'Callaghan, *A History of Medieval Spain* (Ithaca, NY: Cornell University Press, 1975), pp. 419–20.

that brought 'untold grief to the realm'.[25] Pedro was able to defeat a major Trastámaran rebellion in 1354–1356, but a series of wars with Pere III, 'the Ceremonious', of Aragon (1336–1387) soon weakened his position, and drew the Aragonese, Trastámaras, French, and the Papacy into an alliance against him.[26] Pedro sought to shore up his own position by concluding alliances with Portugal and England (June 1362), but these were not sufficient to save him. In 1365, Enrique invaded Castile supported by mercenary forces despatched by King Charles V (r. 1364–1380), recruited and led by Bertrand du Guesclin, the future Constable of France. They succeeded in deposing Pedro, who turned to his allies for help.[27]

Pedro of Portugal's policy towards Castile was highly pragmatic and shifted throughout his career according to changing conditions. In 1354, prior to his own accession but amidst the disturbance of the Castilian succession dispute, he had advanced his own claim to the Castilian throne. When this proved unsuccessful, he made an alliance with Castile and betrothed his son Fernando to Beatriz, his nephew's daughter. Thereafter he often provided support in Pedro's war against Aragon.[28] However, in 1366, when Pedro of Castile was driven from his kingdom and sought shelter in Portugal, his uncle quickly discovered good reasons to adopt a more neutral stance. He clearly had obligations to his Castilian ally, but to harbour the exiled king was to invite an attack from Enrique, du Guesclin, and the Free Companies. Consequently, Pedro offered no more than the bare minimum of assistance. The exiled king and his daughters were refused sanctuary but granted safe conduct through Portugal. Pedro further emphasised his change of position by cancelling the

---

[25] Ruiz, *Spain's Centuries of Crisis*, 78.

[26] Donald Kagay, 'The Defense of the Crown of Aragon during the War of the Two Pedros (1356–1366)', in *The Hundred Years War (Part II): Different Vistas*, ed. L. J. Andrew Villalon and Donald Kagay (Leiden: Brill, 2008), pp. 185–210; Donald Kagay, 'Battle-Seeking Commanders in the Later Middle Ages: Phases of Generalship in the War of the Two Pedros', *The Hundred Years War (Part III): Further Considerations* (Leiden: Brill, 2013), pp. 63–84; Bisson, *Medieval Crown of Aragon*, pp. 111–14. Lopes discusses the Castilian-Aragonese war in Chapters 15, 18–19, 22–24, 26 and 34–35 below.

[27] See Chapters 36–41 below; R. Delachenal, *Charles V*, 5 vols (Paris: Picard, 1916), vol. 3, pp. 303–64; Kenneth Fowler, *Medieval Mercenaries: The Great Companies* (Oxford: Blackwell, 2001), pp. 155–90; Ormrod, *Edward III*, pp. 437–42; Jonathan Sumption, *The Hundred Years War, II: Trial by Fire* (Philadelphia: University of Pennsylvania Press, 1999), pp. 480–82, 525–39.; Richard Vernier, *The Flower of Chivalry: Bertrand du Guesclin and the Hundred Years War* (Woodbridge: Boydell Press, 2003), pp. 81–102.

[28] See Chapter 15 below.

betrothal between Fernando and Beatriz. Greatly angered, Pedro of Castile travelled first to Galicia, from where he opened negotiations with the English and the Navarrese, and then he made his way to Bordeaux in Gascony – to the court of Edward III's eldest son, Edward the Black Prince (1330–1376).[29]

Pedro of Castile found the Anglo-Gascons more amenable to his pleas for help. In temporary alliance with Charles 'the Bad' of Navarre, the Black Prince gathered an army of mercenaries, Gascon lords, and troops from England led by his younger brother, John of Gaunt (1340–1399). By the terms of the treaty of Libourne (23 September 1366), the prince agreed to finance the campaign until January 1367, after which Pedro would, in theory, repay and reward those who had supported him with land and money.[30] The alliance between Pedro and the Anglo-Gascons had major implications for Portugal. It was clear that Pedro of Castile would soon return to Iberia with his new allies and, if he were to reclaim his throne, attention might then turn to Portugal. Pedro and his daughters had clearly been slighted when their requests for sanctuary had been refused, and the Castilian was not a forgiving man. The English, too, interpreted Portuguese actions as hostile and had, in response, begun to detain trade ships in their ports. Pedro of Portugal, therefore, sent envoys to Bordeaux to explain his actions and defend any accusations that might be made against him. These explanations, although far from convincing, were accepted in return for guarantees of his friendly neutrality in the forthcoming campaign.[31]

That campaign proved successful and resulted in victory at the battle of Nájera (3 April 1367), where du Guesclin was captured but Enrique escaped. Relations, however, soon soured between the allies and Pedro, who was quite incapable of repaying his vast debts. All attempts to secure payment failed, and the army was forced to return over the Pyrenees due to illness in the camp, which also affected the Black Prince.[32] Pedro, however, did not enjoy the

---

[29] Russell, *English Intervention in Spain and Portugal*, pp. 55–56; David Green, *Edward the Black Prince: Power in Medieval Europe* (Harlow: Pearson Education, 2007), pp. 107–08, 129–30.

[30] Treaty of Libourne (1366): Thomas Rymer, *Foedera, conventiones, litterae etc*, ed. A. Clarke, F. Holbrooke, and J. Coley, rev. edn, 4 vols in 7 parts (London: Record Commission, 1816–1869), vol. 3, pp. ii, 799–807; Richard Barber, *Edward Prince of Wales and Aquitaine: A Biography of the Black Prince* (Woodbridge: Boydell Press, 1978), pp. 189–91; Carlos Andrés González Paz, 'The Role of Mercenary Troops in Spain in the Fourteenth Century: The Civil War', *Mercenaries and Paid Men: The Mercenary Identity in the Middle Ages*, ed. John France, rev. edn (Leiden: Brill, 2008), pp. 331–43.

[31] See Chapter, 42 below; Russell, *English Intervention in Spain and Portugal*, p. 75.

[32] On the Nájera campaign and its consequences see Sumption, *Hundred Years*

Castilian throne for long. Enrique returned once more and his half-brother's deposition was, this time, permanent: Pedro was murdered at Montiel in 1369. In the immediate aftermath, English political efforts in Iberia centred on a diplomatic strategy to encircle Castile, now firmly allied to France, by making links to Portugal, Navarre, and Aragon.[33]

Pedro of Portugal did not live to see this next phase of the war, he died in January 1367. Whatever his personal reputation and despite the upheaval caused by plague and war in the Peninsula, there is no doubt that the country and the crown had prospered during his reign. Trade had flourished, especially in Lisbon and Oporto, and by the time of his death he enjoyed an annual income of 240,000 *dobras* (about £45,000). According to the chronicler, he bequeathed a greater fortune than any previous king had ever possessed – 800,000 pieces of gold and 400,000 marks of silver.[34] He was succeeded first by Fernando I and then João, his son with Teresa Lorenzo. João I (1385–1433) had been the Master of the military Order of Avis, and he would become the founder of the Avis dynasty.[35]

War II, pp. 540–85; L. J. Andrew Villalon, 'Spanish Involvement in the Hundred Years War and the Battle of Nájera', in *The Hundred Years War: A Wider Focus*, ed. L. J. Andrew Villalon and Donald Kagay (Leiden: Brill, 2005), pp. 3–74. For an eyewitness account of the campaign see Chandos Herald, *La vie du Prince Noir*, ed. Diana B. Tyson (Tübingen: Max Niemeyer, 1975), vol. 2, pp. 1669–3772.

[33] MacKay, *Spain in the Middle Ages*, p. 122.

[34] Jonathan Sumption, *The Hundred Years War III: Divided Houses* (London: Faber and Faber, 2009), p. 118.

[35] See Chapter 20 below; Linehan, 'Castile, Navarre and Portugal', p. 641. The Order of Évora, a crusading military fraternity, was founded in 1175/6 to defend Portugal's southern frontier and to defend the town of the same name, which had been captured from the Muslims in 1165. It assumed the name Order of Avis when granted that fortress in 1211. In Chapter 43 below, Lopes describes how João became Master of the Order aged only seven.

THE CHRONICLE OF
KING PEDRO OF PORTUGAL

Prologue

Leaving aside the various forms and definitions of justice, about which many authors have written in their sundry ways, it is our intention in this prologue to limit ourselves to considering that particular justice which is the very basis of royal power, in that it punishes evildoers and allows good people to live in peace. In doing this we shall not pretend to create or devise new theories of our own; rather, we shall assemble from certain authors a handful of those views that have appealed to us. Our first aim is to guide our audience[1] into understanding what our narrative is about; our second aim is to follow precisely the order set out in our first prologue.[2]

King Pedro, whose reign we shall now describe, meted out justice, and, as the saints have written, to dispense justice is more pleasing to God than any other worthy action that a monarch can perform. Moreover, since some people wish to know what that virtue consists of and to what extent such virtue, which must be found in a king, is also appropriate in his people, you will now be able to read about it in the straightforward style that corresponds to our understanding of it.

Justice is a virtue which is recognized as embracing all virtues, in the sense that any person who is just is entirely virtuous, because justice, being God's law, forbids fornication and gluttony, and in its observance we uphold the virtues of chastity and temperance. The same applies also to the other vices and virtues.

This virtue is essential to a king and, indeed, to his subjects, because if the king possesses the virtue of justice he will enact laws so that all should live lawfully and in peace, and his subjects, themselves also just, will observe

---

[1] Frequently, in all the chronicles, Lopes uses words implying 'to hear' or 'listeners' when referring to how the public will react to his accounts. Apart from the occasional public reading that is known to have still been performed at Court in the 15th century, this is generally thought to be a literary device to place the chronicles in the old and noble tradition of historiography which, in medieval terms, was intended for oral communication.

[2] Lopes wrote the chronicles of all seven Portuguese kings who preceded King Pedro, going back to the conquests of Count Henry of Burgundy (d. 1112), father of the first King of Portugal, Afonso Henriques. No reliable version of that part of his work has reached us. Here, he is probably mentioning the prologue he placed at its beginning. Sixteenth-century copies of older chronicles of the same kings appear to be partially connected with those earlier chronicles, but they are the result of subsequent interpolations and no longer represent Lopes's texts. There is still considerable scholarly debate about this.

the laws that he enacts and in their observance will commit no wrong against anyone. Such justice as this can be acquired by anyone of sound judgement. In some instances people are born with a natural sense of justice and enthusiastically put it into practice, even if they are prone to certain vices.

The reason why this virtue is necessary to the prince's subjects is that it causes them to observe his laws, which should always be framed for the public good. Anyone observing such laws will always act with decorum, because the laws set the rules that subjects must follow. They are the 'inanimate prince' [princeps inanimatus], whereas the king is an 'animate prince' [princeps animatus], and his laws express with silent voices that which the king declares from his own mouth.[3] This is why justice is most essential, both to his people and to the king, for without it no town or realm can live in harmony. Accordingly, a realm wherein the whole populace are beset with evil cannot survive for long, since, just as the soul sustains the body, and on leaving it the body perishes, in the same way justice sustains kingdoms, and when it abandons them they too perish.

If, therefore, the virtue of justice is essential to the people, it is all the more essential to the king, because, if law governs how a person should behave, then all the more just must be the monarch who enacts it and the judge who administers it. Law is a prince without a soul, as we said earlier, and the prince endows justice and the rule of law with a soul. Just as anything with a soul has the advantage over anything soulless, so the king must occupy a position of excellence over the law, because he must have all the necessary justice and integrity to enforce its execution. Otherwise, his kingdom would present the wretched spectacle of having good laws yet evil practices. Indeed, to harbour doubts on the monarch's need to value justice is nothing less than to doubt whether rulers need to be straight, for if the ruler lacks rectitude, then nothing right will come of it.

Another reason why justice is most essential in a king is that justice brings beauty to the monarch, endowing him not only with bodily virtue but also with spiritual strength: just as spiritual beauty prevails over that of the body, so justice in a king reigns above the other forms of beauty.

---

[3]   The Latin references here are derived from Book I, Part II, Chapter XII of the *De regimine principum* ('On kingship') of the theologian Giles of Rome (*c.* 1247–1316). See the translation of Ernst H. Kantorowicz in *The King's Two Bodies: A Study in Mediaeval Theology* (Princeton, NJ: Princeton University Press, 1981, reprint 1997), p. 134: 'the king or prince is a kind of Law, and the law is a kind of king or prince. For the Law is a kind of inanimate prince; the prince, however, is a kind of animate Law. And in so far as the animate exceeds the inanimate the king or prince must exceed the Law.'

The third reason rests on the perfection of goodness: we say that something is perfect when it is capable of reproducing itself. Accordingly, a thing is described as good from the degree to which its goodness extends to other people, at least in the example it sets, with the result that, when given the power to govern, it is by a man's deeds that one judges how good he is. It is, therefore, incumbent on kings to act justly, so as to serve the best interests of all their subjects and to cause them no harm, and to strive to ensure that justice is meted out not only to those living in their realm but also to those living beyond its borders. To deny justice to any person is a grave offence both to the sovereign and to his entire realm.

This virtue of justice, which finds few people willing to entertain it, is, as Tully says,[4] the queen and supreme lady of the other virtues. It was King Pedro's constant practice. Those who wish to ascertain this fact can do so simply by reading his story, and, since he was driven both by noble intent and natural inclination to curb evil deeds, he ruled his country well, despite shortcomings for which he could have been duly penitent. It may thus be assumed that he received the reward of justice, the leaves and fruits of which comprise an honoured repute in this world and eternal rest in the next.

Chapter 1

Concerning the reign of King Pedro, the eighth king of Portugal, and about the qualities that he possessed

After the death[5] of King Afonso [IV], about which you have heard, he was succeeded by his son Prince Pedro, who was then thirty-seven years, one month and eighteen days old. As we have recorded[6] at length the children that he sired, by whom and under which circumstances, there is no need to return to such matters here. At a later stage we shall very briefly describe their talents, qualities and status at appropriate points where we report on what they did with their lives.

King Pedro was plagued with stammering. A great hunter, he had always pursued game large and small, both as a prince and later as king; he kept a large household of huntsmen for small game and foot-huntsmen, and kept

---

4   That is to say, Marcus Tullius Cicero (106–43 BC), the Roman statesman, orator, and writer.

5   On 28 May 1357.

6   See note 2 of the Prologue.

all kinds of birds of prey and hounds as were suited to such pastimes. He took pleasure in his food, though he ate no more than the average man, and everywhere he went he had the reputation of keeping an open house where food was available in great abundance.

He did much to foster hereditary nobles in his Royal Court, because at that time custom demanded that no man could become a vassal unless he were already the son, grandson or great-grandson of a hereditary noble. At that time it was customary to pay the allowance nowadays known as *maravedís*[7] to the noble's son from the moment of his birth, in the cradle, and to no other. King Pedro greatly enhanced the allowance given to his nobles after the death of his father, King Afonso. Indeed, although the latter drew acclaim for his courage and honourable deeds, he was criticized for being a miser and lacking in largesse. King Pedro, by contrast, happily gave money away to the point where he often said that he wished to loosen his belt (and belts then were not worn very tight) in order to ease his movements and thus increase his generosity. He declared that the day the king failed to distribute money he did not merit the title of king. Moreover, he took a benevolent approach to those who sought his gifts and favours: the motto of his household was that, after putting a request to him, no one would be kept waiting for long.

King Pedro was fond of dispensing justice in accordance with the law. He passed through his kingdom as if conducting an inspection and, having visited one particular area, he never failed to visit another, so that he seldom spent an entire month in the same place. He zealously upheld the law and keenly insisted that verdicts be fully carried out, ever striving to ensure that people should not suffer ruin through court actions and prolonged litigation. Moreover, when Scripture proclaims that storms and tribulations befall a people when the king fails to dispense justice, such words cannot apply to King Pedro, for throughout his reign we find not a single case in which he pardoned anyone for killing another person, even if the latter deserved it in some way. Nor did he commute the penalty so that the murderer might keep his life. He rewarded everyone who gave service to him and those who had

---

[7] *Maravedís* were originally gold coins, issued by the Almoravid rulers of north Africa and Muslim Spain. The name passed first to gold and then to silver coinages minted by 12th- and 13th-century Christian rulers (including those of Castile and Portugal). By 1300 all these had passed out of actual circulation, though the term had a long history after that as the name of a Castilian unit of account. In Portugal too it was so used, though more rarely; the specialised sense in which Fernão Lopes deploys it here may derive from this. See Peter Spufford, *et al.*, *Handbook of Medieval Exchange* (London: Royal Historical Society, 1986), pp. xxiii, 155–62.

served his father. He never withdrew a favour previously granted by King Afonso; on the contrary, he maintained and added to it.

King Pedro refused to marry again after the death of Dona Inês [de Castro]. Both as a prince and later as a king he showed no wish to take a wife, though he took mistresses with whom he slept. By none did he sire children, save in the case of a lady named Teresa [Lorenzo], a native of Galicia. She gave birth to a son, Dom João, who was to become Master of the Order of Avis in Portugal and later the nation's king, about whom you will hear in due course. Dom João was born in Lisbon on the eleventh day of April at three o'clock in the afternoon during the first year of King Pedro's reign. The king ordered that in early childhood Dom João be reared by Lourenço Martins da Praça, an upright citizen of that city who lived close to the cathedral in the Praça dos Escanos [the Square of the Benches]. Later, he entrusted his upbringing to Dom Nuno Freire de Andrade, Master of Chivalry of the Order of Christ.

Chapter 2

How the King of Castile sent for the body of Queen Maria, his mother, and concerning the letter he sent to the King of Portugal, his uncle

As mentioned elsewhere in this book,[8] at the beginning of King Pedro's reign, the King of Castile gave orders in which he sent for the body of Queen Maria, his mother. She had passed away in Portugal whilst King Afonso [IV], her father, was still alive. He let it be known through a letter to King Pedro, his uncle, that it was his wish to transfer her body and lay it to rest in Seville, in the Royal Chapel, alongside King Alfonso [XI], his father. Accordingly, he ordered the Archbishop of Seville and other prelates from his kingdom to accompany the body of the queen. In addition, he commanded that Gómez Pérez, his Purveyor of the Royal Household, to whom the body was to be entrusted, should travel ahead to make all appropriate preparations for the body to be transferred in an honourable manner and to organize everything necessary for the transfer, so that when the prelates arrived they could find everything ready and leave immediately.

---

[8] 'In this book' concerns what Lopes seems to consider to be the first volume of his writings, including the chronicles of the first seven Portuguese kings (see note 2 of the Prologue).

This greatly pleased King Pedro, who wrote asking the King of Castile to send for the body whenever he saw fit. The King of Castile immediately sent his purveyor, who was entrusted with the body in the town of Évora, where it lay, so that he could organize the preparations in accordance with the orders he had been given. When the archbishop and the other prelates and people came for the queen's body, a letter was brought to King Pedro from his nephew, the King of Castile, which read as follows:

Dear king and uncle, we the King of Castile and León, send you our salutations as to one whom we greatly admire and for whom we would desire a long life and health with honour, just as we would wish the same for ourself. We wish to inform Your Grace that we have seen a letter of credence that you sent to us through your vassals Martim Vasques and Gonçalo Eanes de Beja, who have presented on your behalf the credentials with which you invested them. Furthermore, dear king and uncle, our wish is to love you, to maintain at all times the good relations afforded by our kinship, and to act in your honour as we do in our own.

Moreover, since for our service and yours it was important to make certain declarations regarding the positions we must establish between ourselves, namely the marriages of your sons with our daughters, we have spoken to Martim Vasques and Gonçalo Eanes about all our plans, and on this matter we have sent over Juan Fernández de Melgarejo, the Chancellor of our Privy Seal. We beg you to believe what he tells you on our behalf. Likewise, we are sending the archbishop of this city and other prelates of our kingdoms to bring the body of the queen, our mother, to be buried here in Seville. We do beg you to arrange that those jewels which she left behind be handed to Juan Fernández. For that, we shall be deeply grateful. Dated, etc.'

King Pedro allowed the body of Queen Maria, his sister, to be vouchsafed to the King of Castile's ambassador. Indeed, great honour was done to her, both by King Pedro and by the prelates who had come for her. She was most honourably escorted to the border and from there as far as the city of Seville, where her son, the king, came out to receive her, accompanied by many clerics, grandees and noblemen. The obsequies having been carried out with full honours, her body was placed in the Royal Chapel, where she now rests alongside King Alfonso, her husband. As for the marriages of the sons of King Pedro with the daughters of the King of Castile, for which purpose Juan Fernández had been sent, many matters were discussed with the King of Portugal. However, since at that time they could not agree on certain aspects, it was at a later stage that they reached agreement on all these questions, as you will hear in due course.

Chapter 3

Concerning the letters that the Pope and the King of Aragon sent to the King of Portugal upon the death of the king his father

King Pedro had written to the Pope and to the King of Aragon when King Afonso died to inform them of his father's death and of his own accession as King of Portugal. Each having taken the trouble to reply to him, their replies arrived at this time. The Pope's letter read as follows:

> Innocent,[9] bishop and servant of the servants of God, to my dearly beloved son in Christ Dom Pedro, most noble King of Portugal, greetings and our apostolic blessing. When, well-beloved son, through your letters and by public rumour we received confirmation that the most illustrious sovereign of noble memory, King Afonso, your father, had left this world, his death was and still is for us a great sorrow and sadness. Furthermore, it is not without reason that we should feel this way, when in our heart we remember the noble qualities and virtues which greatly honoured His Royal Highness. That was the reason why we loved him dearly, wishing that of all the princes in the world the Lord should make him prosper and extend his realm, with prolonged days of happiness until, at the end of his honourable old age, he left to you, his first-born, the governance of, and succession to, the kingdom in lasting peace with your neighbours.
>
> Since the Lord God, in Whose hands rests the power to bestow life as well as death upon each and every one of us, was pleased, in His mercy, to take him from this world, we bring our grief and sadness to a final end, finding consolation in the Lord who gives and deprives and takes away whensoever it pleases Him. The same One whom we firmly trust will grant a just reward and glory to the soul of the king, your father, in heaven on high, for whilst he lived in this world he strove to serve Him meritoriously and pleased Him with his honourable virtues.
>
> Accordingly, dearest son, we devoutly advise you to find consolation in the Lord God and to consider in your heart how to succeed to the governance established by your father who, setting an example of a life to lead, always showed himself to be a faithful Catholic. Therefore, we appeal to you in your kingly dignity always to live steadfastly in fear of the Lord God, respecting His Holy Church and being favourable towards ecclesiastic persons; to allow them at all times their rights and freedoms, as well as protecting and defending both widows and orphans; to take up the appeals of your subjects

---

[9] Pope Innocent VI.

so that no injustice is done against them; and, without favouring any person, always to honour and love justice, so that through your deeds you may be worthy to be called a king who rules well.

Be assured that if you act in this manner, you will always live your days in peace and happiness, with God there to help you; and His Holy Church will keep you in her prayers, being ready to act in your honour and for the fulfilment of your just requests. Dated in Avignon, etc.

The other letter, from the King of Aragon, stated the following:

Most high and most noble Dom Pedro, by the grace of God, King of Portugal and of the Algarve, we, En Pere by that same grace, King of Aragon and Valencia, King of Majorca, Sardinia and Corsica, and Count of Barcelona and Roussillon, send you greetings as a king, whom we regard as a brother we greatly love, esteem and trust, and upon whom we would wish much honour and good fortune, with a long life filled with good health, as we would wish for ourself.

Dear king and brother, we have received your letter, in which you have informed us of the death of the most high and most honourable King Afonso of Portugal, your father, whom God forgive, and that you, both as his first-born and heir to his realms, have been acclaimed King of Portugal.

In truth, dear king and brother, such news made us both sad and happy at the same time: sad at the death of the king, whom we knew loved us as his own son, and we him as our well-beloved father. But as no person is exempt from death, and as the king has now departed from the wretchedness of this world, we do grieve because of it, and if we could have done anything, we would have been only too ready to do so. However, we beseech God, Whose hand holds the life and death of each one of us, that He may receive his soul together with His saints in paradise, and we trust that He has done so.

Likewise, dear king and brother, we had great pleasure when we learned that you had been proclaimed King of Portugal and of the Algarve by the rights of succession which lawfully belong to you. Moreover, in believing this, be aware that just as we regarded King Afonso as our father, so we intend to regard you as our brother and to do for you everything that brings you honour, pleasure and benefits to your domain. Indeed, we do hope that you will act in the same way on our behalf and on behalf of our realms and lands.

Dear king and brother, inasmuch as, according to the contents of your letter, you wish to know about the state of health of our person and of the queen as well as of our children, may you be pleased to learn that we are all well in body and spirit, thanks be to God. We earnestly pray that in your letter you assure us of your good health and that of your royal household, and feel certain that it will give us immense pleasure. Dated in Saragossa, etc.

Chapter 4

How King Pedro dealt with judicial decisions in his house

Just as in the writings about this king we found that he was dearly loved by his people because he ruled according to the law and justice, as well as for the good governance he maintained in his kingdom, so it is fitting that we should say a little about each of these things, so that you can have an understanding of what olden ways were like.

In all the judicial decisions the king proceeded in this way: all the petitions that were given to him were handed to Gonçalo Vasques de Góis, his private secretary, who passed them on to a secretary of his choosing, who in turn was in charge of distributing and giving each one of them to the appropriate magistrate. As for the petitions that were common law cases, the magistrates through whom they had to pass immediately ordered their secretaries to draw up the charters, so that on the same day or the next the parties involved had their cases brought to a conclusion. The secretary who did not act in this way thereby lost the king's favour.

With regard to the other petitions that were subject to royal grace and favour, as they concerned the Crown estate, one of the comptrollers got his secretary to enter those petitions on a list. The secretary would also write out the petitions that the comptroller brought to him, describing whom they were from and what they were about. This document was held by the magistrate. When he later went over the petitions with the king, if he found more petitions to have been entered on the list than he had ordered to be included, according to the document in his power, then the magistrate would lose the king's favour for that mistake.

As soon as decisions had been reached with the king on the listed cases, the magistrates informed each person of the favour the king was granting them and they ordered their secretaries to write up the charters immediately. These had to be done the same day or no later than the following, or they suffered the penalty we have described.

If there were such obstinate people who would still harry the king, pestering him with other petitions after they had had a positive or negative judicial decision, or if they continued to linger at court, a man of standing would pay a forfeit in money and a low-born man would be given twenty lashes in the public square and then sent home. The king had with him informers who would report such men to him so that his verdict was meted out to them.

So as not to cause displeasure to the king with the favours he granted appearing twice, once on the list and the other on the charters, and in order that those who made the request had the judicial decisions on their cases issued more speedily, the procedure was as follows: whenever the king granted any favours to anyone, those who had to issue the judicial decision to that person would immediately write on the list, in the presence of the king, the manner in which it was granted to the person concerned. The king would put his signature on each charter, the chancellor being present whenever possible to see how the king reached his judicial decision. As soon as the magistrates had the charters drawn up and signed, they sent them to the chancellor with the list roll that the king had signed so as not to put any of them in doubt. They had to be sealed immediately that very day or the next by suppertime.

If the king went on a hunt, which might last more than four days, to avoid anyone being held back on account of him, those who were in charge of the petitions for grace were gathered together and they looked at what each person was requesting. If it was deemed inappropriate for the king to grant the request, they wrote to him setting out their reasons in detail. For those that they agreed should be granted, they likewise wrote their reasons, and they all signed the list. One of them then took it to the king, to inform him of the reasons that had led them to grant or reject each request. This way the people were given the appropriate judicial decision and the king was saved from much displeasure and harassment.

If town communities[10] had matters on which to confer with him in private, the king ordered that a closed and sealed charter be sent to him, by a courier, detailing all their needs. The king stipulated that 4 *soldos*[11] per day and no more be given to the courier. Once the king had seen what was requested, he gave the courier his reply immediately without further detaining him, as he deemed fit. If the matter were such that the town community required to be represented before him by some notable and learned men, the king

---

[10] The 'concelho' was a medieval municipality that often corresponded to a territory headed by a city or a small town. The 'concelho' after the 1340s was normally governed by a restricted number of more prominent and wealthier citizens, the 'good men' (Port. 'homens-bons'). From the 13th century, the 'concelhos' also sent their representatives to the Portuguese medieval parliaments or *Cortes*. As the social and economic importance of the cities grew, and the mechanisms of self-government became more closely controlled by the urban elites and regulated by the monarchs, the 'concelhos' also attained growing political clout.

[11] A *soldo* (Latin *solidus*) was a unit of account, based on the European system of *libras*, *soldos*, and *dinheiros*, adopted by Afonso III of Portugal in his *Regimento de Almotaçaria* (1253). This was similar to the British pound, shilling and pence before the UK adopted a decimal system. There were 20 *soldos* in a *libra*, and 12 *dinheiros* in a *soldo*; and so, 240 *dinheiros* in a *libra*. Of these, only the *dinheiro* was minted. See M. José Pimenta Ferro, 'Para o Estudo da Numária de D. Dinis', *Do Tempo e da História*, 5 (1972), 201–28, at pp. 201 and 210.

ordered that no more than one be sent, so as to cause the town community less expense, and he further ordered that this man should not receive more than 20 *soldos* per day.

Chapter 5

Concerning some of the things King Pedro ordered for the good of justice and for the benefit of his people

Just as King Pedro loved swift justice when it was clear that the people concerned deserved it, so he strove to ensure that civil cases were not protracted, while fully protecting the rights of each party. He felt that the proctors prolonged their cases unnecessarily and gave occasion to the lodging of deceitful pleas. What was even worse and most strange, they took payment from both parties, helping one against the other.

Consequently, he ordered that in his household and in his entire kingdom there should be no lawyers at all. Furthermore, he made it incumbent upon the judges and special jurisdiction magistrates not to be more biased in favour of one party than of the other. Nor should they be moved by any degree of covetousness and should not accept any gifts, thereby putting justice up for sale. Instead, they should work to resolve the cases quickly so that they were judicially concluded soon and rightfully, as they should be. Whenever he discovered that they were negligent in that respect, he would punish them with physical and pecuniary penalties and he would make them pay the parties for all the losses that might have been suffered as a result.

Having so ordained, the king found out shortly afterwards that one of his appellate judges, whom he greatly trusted, namely Master Gonçalo, an authority on canon law, had accepted a bribe from one of the parties who were in litigation before him and in favour of whom he had delivered his verdict and passed sentence. When the king found this out he was deeply aggrieved and immediately cast him out of favour forever, ordering that both he and his children should be banished to a distance of 10 leagues from wherever he, the king, might be. Yet all those who saw this said that the one from whom the bribe had been taken was right in that lawsuit.

Then the king ordered and prohibited anyone in his household and in his kingdom who had the power to administer justice from accepting any bribe from those who had lawsuits before them. Furthermore, if it were proved that a bribe had been accepted, the magistrate should die and forfeit his estate to the Crown. If such judges and officials took payment from any others who did not have lawsuits before them, they should lose his favour, except if the man concerned had no legal action in all of his territory – it being unlikely that such a man would be found. In addition, he ordered the Chief Justice and special jurisdiction magistrates not to get involved in any lawsuits, except when these were between such people concerning whom district judges were unable to reach a verdict, or save when they were dealing with a legal recourse or an appeal.

Likewise, the king was aware that some married men left their wives as well as the children they had, taking mistresses with whom they cohabited separately, and that there were other men who lived in their own homes with their mistresses together with their wives. Consequently, he ordered and established by law that any married man who lived with a mistress or kept her in his own home, were he a nobleman or a vassal who received a pension from the king or anyone else, should forfeit that pension. Furthermore, he regulated the monetary and exile penalties according to the social standing of people and even ordered that on the third count both men and women be whipped. When the king was told that many people complained of orders such as this, he replied that he considered them to be a service to God and to himself and for the benefit of all. He imposed the same orders and penalties on women who were the mistresses of clerics in major orders.

He banned, under law, women of any social standing from entering the Moorish quarter in Lisbon by day or by night, on pain of death by hanging. In addition, he ordered that any Jew or Moor found in the city after sunset be publicly whipped by its citizens.

One day, whilst talking about the administration of justice, the king said that it was and always had been his wish to ensure justice for the peoples of his kingdom and above all to act justly himself. Indeed, he felt that the greatest offence he and his sons, as well as certain other men in his domain, committed against the peoples of his land was to acquire food at a lower price than that at which it was normally sold. He therefore ordered that no one in his household, or in the household of the Royal Princes, or in that of anyone else who lived in his realm and was subject to his favours, being charged with the responsibility of acquiring fowls, should receive either chickens, ducks, kids, suckling pigs, or any other things they customarily took, unless they were bought in accordance with their owners' wishes.

On this matter, he imposed prison and monetary penalties on high-ranking people, while poultry farmers and lowly people were to be whipped in the place where they had acquired them as well as excluded from his favour. He also ordered his stablemen, those of his sons, and all in his land not to send anywhere for free straw unless there was a right to it. Instead, the muleteer who went to fetch it should be ordered to pay 3 *soldos* for a horse-load of straw or stubble and two for a donkey-load. The muleteer who went to fetch it and did not pay for it in this way would, the first time, be whipped and have his ears cut off, and on the second occasion he would be hanged. Another similar penalty was imposed on the farmer who did not gather in all the straw that he had.

When the king was told that he imposed great penalties for very small crimes, he replied in this manner: since the penalty that men most feared was death, if this did not restrain them from offending, even less would they pay attention to the other penalties, so it was good to hang one or two as a warning to all the others. He said that, as he understood it, this was a service to God and of benefit to all his people. He fixed the bread measures throughout the whole of Portugal and, to keep his land well provisioned and in profit, he gave orders concerning other things which we shall not go into at greater length, as we are unaware how it might please those hearing them.

Chapter 6

How the king had two of his *criados*[12] beheaded for robbing and killing a Jew

During his life, this King Pedro was devoted to administering justice impartially, being so fair in applying the law that he forgave no one for the errors they committed, whether or not they had been raised in his household or he held them in high esteem. If it is true that blessed is the king who himself investigates the harm and the violence done against the poor, then this is one such king, for he was glad to listen to them and rejoiced in ensuring that justice was done to them, so that everyone lived in peace.

He was, moreover, so zealous in meting out justice, especially to those who persistently sought to evade the law, that he subjected them to torture in his presence. Indeed, if they refused to confess, he would take off his royal robes and with his own hand would whip the miscreants. Although his counsellors

---

[12] The medieval word refers to 'criação' or *creatio*, the upbringing of a child or youngster put under the authority of a person unrelated to him or her by blood. This initiated a special bond of pseudo-kinship which could not be easily undone and marked the life of the 'criado' by obligations similar to family ties. In Lopes's chronicles the word is often used this way, especially in the case of the nobility. However, by the 15th century the semantic field of the word had evolved and it could already be applied also to paid domestic service. See 'Translators' note' above, p. xxvii.

and certain others greatly rebuked him for this, he became irritated at their words, and there was no way they could make him change his mind.

He ordered that no criminal case be brought to a conclusion except in his presence; and if he had information regarding some thief or offender in some place far away from where he happened to be, he spoke to one of his men whom he trusted, promising favours if he went to fetch the offender, instructing his man not to return until he could bring the wrongdoer over to him. So it was that prisoners were brought to him from the far ends of the realm and were delivered to him wherever he was. If they arrived at a time when he was eating, he would rise from the table in order to put them to torture immediately. He would lay hands on them himself whenever he saw that they were unwilling to confess, cruelly striking them until they did so.

Wherever the king went, one would always find ready with a whip the man charged with that task, so that as soon as some offender was brought to the king and the latter said, 'Let So-and-So bring the whip', the man came forward without further delay.

Since we have written that he was fair in applying the law in the governance of his people, you should hear two or three things so that you can see how he went about it. It happened that, while staying at the palace of Belas which he had built, two of his squires who had lived in his household for a long time and were close friends, decided to go and rob a Jew who used to travel through the countryside selling spices and other wares. So it was that they actually went to seek out that sordid plunder: they robbed him of all he had and, worse still, they killed him.

Their luck, which went against them, was such that they were arrested immediately and taken to where the king was lodging. The king, as soon as he saw them, was greatly pleased that they had been caught and began by asking them how it had all taken place. The squires, thinking that the long-standing protection and maintenance he had given them, and that their services to him would move him to feel somewhat kindly towards them, not as he was wont to treat other people, began to deny the incident, claiming that they knew nothing about it.

The king, who already knew what had happened, told them there was no point in further denials. They should either confess how they had killed the man or otherwise he would make them tell the truth by dint of cruel lashes. Amid their denials they realized that the king meant to put into action what he was expressing in words, and so they confessed everything just as it had taken place. Smiling, the king said that they had done well, because if they wanted to become professional thieves and to kill men on the highways, they should first practise on Jews, as Christians would come later.

While uttering those and other words, he paced up and down in front of them. Seemingly mindful of the care he had bestowed upon them, yet of how he wanted to have them put to death, at times tears came to his eyes. Then he turned on them abruptly, reprimanding them at length for what they had done. He carried on in this fashion for a very long time. Those who were there and witnessed it, fearing the worst from the way he spoke, strove hard to plead mercy for them, declaring that it was not right that such men should die for a miserable Jew. It was fitting that they should be punished by banishment or another form of punishment but not shown such immense cruelty for their first mistake, they who had been reared by the king. The king, listening to them all, constantly replied that after the Jews they would turn on the Christians. At the end of these and other arguments, he ordered them to be beheaded, and so it came to pass.

Chapter 7

How the king had wanted to subject a bishop to torture for sleeping with a married woman

Not only did the king employ justice against those he felt it was right to treat in that way, both secular and similar people, but his heart yearned so much to apply justice to wrongdoers that he refused to respect the clerics' right, both of minor and major orders, to their own jurisdiction. If he was asked to hand one over to the cleric's vicar, the king would say that the cleric should be sent to the gallows so that he could be handed over to Jesus Christ who was his Vicar, in order that justice should be done to him in the other world. The king wanted to punish and torture bad clerics in person, just as he had wanted to do to a bishop from Oporto, in the manner that we will describe to you.

The story is true, do not doubt it, that the king was leaving the region of the Minho on his way to the city of Oporto, when he was informed that the bishop of that place, who at the time was reputed to be a wealthy and honourable personage, was sleeping with the wife of one of the prominent men in that city. The man did not dare have a confrontation, fearful of the death threats to which the bishop had subjected him.

On hearing this, the king, wanting to find out more about what was happening, could not wait to question him. Then, having arrived at the city and eaten, without further ado the king called the bishop to the palace because he needed him with regard to matters of his concern. Before he arrived, the king instructed his ushers to throw everyone out of the palace, both the bishop's men and any others, once the bishop had entered the royal chamber. Even if someone from the Royal Council should come, they were not to allow anyone inside and they were to tell them to go to their lodgings because he had something to do and he did not want them to be present.

When the bishop came he went into the chamber where the king was. The ushers immediately made all the bishop's men and the others leave, so that not one of the men remained in the palace. Everybody had left.

When the king was alone with the bishop, he immediately took off his clothes except for a scarlet tunic. Then, with his own hands, he stripped the bishop of his clothes and began to demand that the bishop confess the truth about the evil deed of which he was guilty. As the king said this, he held in his hand a large whip to lash the bishop with.

The bishop's *criados*, when they first found themselves being ejected, just like all the others, and saw that no one dared to go in, knowing what the bishop had been doing and connecting it to the king's temperament and the way he behaved in such cases, immediately suspected that the king wanted to inflict some unpleasant trick on the bishop. They ran to the old count[13] and to the Master of the Order of Christ, Dom Nuno Freire, and to other members of the king's Royal Council, urging them to go at once to the bishop's aid. They rushed to where the king was but did not dare enter the chamber because of the prohibition order the king had imposed. The one exception was Gonçalo Vasques de Góis, his private secretary, who declared that he wanted to go in to show him letters from the King of Castile which had been hurriedly delivered.

With this stratagem and pretence they were able to gain entry to the chamber, where they found the king and the bishop arguing in the way we have described. They could not wrest the bishop from the king's hands and so they began to ask him to deign not to lay hands on the bishop, for by such a deed and by not respecting the bishop's jurisdiction, the Pope would be angry with him. They added that his people called him 'the Executioner' because he meted out justice to men in person, and this was not a fitting thing for him to do, however evil men might be.

With these and similar arguments the king's rage cooled down, and the bishop left his presence with a dismal countenance and a heavy heart.

---

13   João Afonso Telo (b. early in the 14th century), the Count of Barcelos, was then the only count in Portugal and not yet 'old' (a possible date for this event is 1360). Under King Fernando, in 1370, he received the title of Count of Ourém and his son inherited his previous title. From then on he was called the 'old count', to distinguish him from his son, the young one, and because of his age, after the latter died. Fernão Lopes is taking the expression from later sources.

Chapter 8

How the king had one of his squires castrated
for sleeping with a married woman

King Pedro was also very zealous in the protection of women in his household as well as those of his officials and all the other women among his people. He therefore bestowed great punishments on any men sleeping with married women, maidens, or nuns in orders.

It so happened that in his house there was a Chief Justice called Lourenço Gonçalves, a very intelligent and sensible man. He carried out everything the king ordered him to do and was never corrupted by false offers that interfere with men's judgements. Since the king considered him as loyal and very faithful, he put great trust in him and was very well disposed towards him. This Chief Justice was an important man and enjoyed a high status in his household, was very jovial and a good conversationalist. He was, at that time, in his middle age. His wife, Catalina Tosse by name, was a proud woman, beautiful and very elegant, graceful in manners and very refined.

At that time, there lived with the king a good and valiant squire whose name was Afonso Madeira. He was young, rich, distinguished then for his many remarkable qualities, a great jouster and horseman, a great hunter of large and small game, a fit and very dexterous fighter who had mastered all the skills and arts that every man of distinction is required to know. For all those reasons, the king loved him immensely and was very generous in the favours he granted to him.

This squire came to fall in love with Catalina Tosse and, not caring about the dangers that could befall him as a result of that affection, he plunged so deep in his love for her that he could not bear her to be out of his sight and was unable to restrain his desire, so besotted was he. But since neither place nor time was appropriate for him to speak to her as he would have liked and in order to have the opportunity to entice her into his knavish love relationship, he struck up such a great friendship with the herberger,[14] that wherever the king travelled, whether it was to a town or some village, Afonso Madeira would always be given lodgings next to or very near the Chief Justice. This practice of having lodgings allocated so that one was always near the other had already lasted for some time, during which he maintained a friendly

---

[14] Official responsible for the allocation of lodgings to members of the royal household.

attitude and manner of conversation with her husband so as to avoid giving rise to suspicion.

Afonso Madeira played an instrument and sang, apart from having the good looks and remarkable skills we have already described; and so, thanks to this continued proximity, together with long-standing affection and frequent conversations, there grew up between them a familiarity that bore fruit, and he saw his long-time desires satisfied.

Since such a deed is not the kind of thing that can easily be covered up, the king found out what was going on and he did not feel any less annoyed at it than if she had been his wife or daughter. Even though the king loved Afonso Madeira dearly, more than we ought to say here, he put aside all affection and had him seized in his chamber. He ordered those parts that men most prize to be cut off, so that there was no flesh left down to the bones, everything being cut away. Afonso Madeira's wound was dressed and he healed, but his legs and body grew very fat. He lived a few years more with his face wrinkled and beardless, dying in due course of his natural affliction.

Chapter 9

How the king ordered the wife of Afonso André to be burnt, and concerning other acts of justice he ordered to be carried out

Who has heard of the kind of punishment the king inflicted on the wife of Afonso André, an honourable merchant who lived in Lisbon?

It was customary, when kings visited cities, for the merchants and other citizens to joust with the men from the Royal Court as part of the festivities. Whilst Afonso André was jousting in the Rua Nova, the king, who was present, having been informed with certainty that Afonso André's wife was deceiving him, deemed that the time was right to find her and catch her while she was in the very act. With great stealth and the help of spies she was seized, together with the man who was incriminated with her. The king had her burnt and him beheaded.

Afonso André, who was still jousting, was told of this as soon as he finished and he made his way to the king to complain about what he had done to him. When the king saw him, and before Afonso André could speak, he asked to be rewarded by the latter for what he had ordered to be carried out, explaining that he had taken revenge against Afonso André's cheating wife and the one who cuckolded him, and furthermore he knew better what she was than Afonso André himself.

What are we to say of Maria Roussada, a married woman whose husband had forced her to sleep with him – an act which was at that time termed as *roussar* (to rape) – for which deed he deserved to die?

He already had sons and daughters by her, and they both loved each other dearly. When the king heard her being called by such a name, he asked why that was. So he found out how it had all been and that they had both agreed to get married in order to avoid that deed being made public. To enforce justice, the king had the husband hanged, and his wife and children followed behind wailing.

When the king was in Braga, the pleas of those that were with him were of no avail to save the life of Álvaro Rodrigues de Grade, an honourable and well-born squire from the Minho province, who had cut the hoops of a poor farmer's vat of wine. No sooner did the king find this out than he ordered his head to be cut off.

In addition, since one of his treasury registrars received 11½ *libras* without the knowledge of the treasurer, the king had him hanged. Neither the count[15] nor Beatriz Dias, the king's concubine, nor anyone else could save him.

Counting these two, eleven people, including thieves and miscreants, were put to death that day as a result of the application of justice.

A story that should not be left untold is that of an honourable squire, a nephew of João Lourenço Bubal, who was a confidant to the king, a member of his Royal Council, and the chief provincial governor of Lisbon. The squire lived honourably in Avis, where he kept good company. A courier was sent to his home to serve him with a distraint order issued by the judge and, on an impulse, he plucked the courier's beard and punched him.

The courier went to Abrantes, where the king was, and described all that had happened to him. As soon as he finished speaking, the king, who had listened to him in private, began calling to the Chief Justice, who was nearby, 'Help me, Lourenço Gonçalves, for a man has punched me in the face and has plucked my beard!' The Chief Justice and those who heard him were alarmed, wondering why he was saying this. The king promptly ordered the squire to be brought to him under arrest without the saving grace of any church sanctuary. So it was done. He was brought to Abrantes, where the king ordered him to be beheaded, saying, 'Ever since this man punched me and plucked my beard, I've always feared he'd stab me. But now I'm sure he'll never do that.'

---

[15] See Chapter 7, note 13 above.

Consequently, it can in fact be said of this King Pedro that the sayings of the philosopher Solon[16] and certain others were not found to be true in his time. According to them, the law and justice are just like a spider's web. Small mosquitoes, when they fall into one, are held there where they die, whilst big flies, being sturdier, when caught in one, break it and fly away. Therefore, they said, the law and justice were applied only to the poor, whereas other people, who had help and succour, when held by them, broke free and escaped. With King Pedro it was very much the opposite, for nobody, neither through pleas nor power, could escape a well-deserved sentence, with the result that everyone was afraid to break his law.

Chapter 10

How the king had ordered the admiral to be put to death, and concerning the letter which the Doge and the Council of Commoners of Genoa wrote pleading for him

King Pedro hated procuresses and witches, so that as a result of the punishments he inflicted upon them there were very few women who had such occupations. When he was in Beira, he found out that one by the name of Helena had procured a woman for Admiral Lançarote Pessanha and that he had slept with her. Her name was Violante Vasques. The king had the procuress burnt immediately and gave orders for the admiral to be beheaded. Although the members of his Royal Council strove to save the admiral from his wrath, they could never convince the king to agree, so the admiral fled. He was exiled and put from him for a long time, losing his royal allowance and all his benefits, as well as his position. Not knowing how to remedy this situation, the admiral decided to send a message to the Doge and the Council of Commoners of Genoa asking them to write to the king on his behalf, requesting him to grant the favour of a pardon. On seeing the admiral's message, the Genoese wrote to the king asking him to set aside his wrath. The letter from Gabriele Adorno, the Doge of Genoa, and the elders of that city's Council of Commoners read as follows:

> Prince and most noble lord, of great and royal majesty, when kindness is observed, very often the method and severity of justice is tempered by gentleness, and compassionate consideration always undertakes to renew

---

[16] Solon (c. 640–c. 559 BC) was a prominent lawgiver and poet in ancient Athens.

good friendships of yesteryear. If it is a good thing to make new friends and acquaintances, it is much better, as the wise man says, to renew and preserve old ones, for a new friend is neither equal nor similar to one of long-standing. Such reasoning leads us to trust that Your Supreme Highness will graciously listen to our humble entreaty, which now follows.

We have been informed of how the noble knight Lançarote Pessanha, your admiral, the son of the late illustrious nobleman Emanuele Pessagno,[17] worthy of happy memory, and our friend and citizen, has fallen victim to Your Royal Majesty's wrath. Apparently, as rumours have it, that situation was due more to the envy of some who did not speak well of him rather than due to other serious misdeeds that he may have been accused of. Indeed, it is incredible that someone brought up by and descended from forefathers who were always ennobled by virtuous and good habits should abandon the norm of honourable deeds. If he has erred in anything, your prudent gentleness should temper the harshness of your punishment, so as to revive the loyalty of his forebears through new benefits. While we expect this of Your Supreme Highness, we humbly implore you, as a result of what we have said and owing to our earnest pleas, to see fit to reinstate the admiral to the former grace of his honourable status. For this Your Royal Majesty will find us and our Council of Commoners ready and willing to do whatsoever is your pleasure. Dated, etc.

Despite this letter, no one could make the king set aside his wrath towards the admiral. However, after a long time the king forgave him, and he was restored to his favour.

Chapter 11

Concerning the coins that King Pedro had minted and the value of gold and silver at that time

No matter how measured one's praise of someone may be, those whose tongues are always wont to find fault will often discover matters which they can criticize. Therefore, since we have described this King Pedro as being generous and happy in giving and yet do not mention a number of generous acts deserving of such praise, it is possible that some will find fault with us,

---

[17] Emanuele Pessagno (or Pezagno), a capable seaman from Genoa, served King Dinis, Pedro's grandfather, who made him Admiral of the Portuguese Fleet. His son Lançarote served King Pedro in the same post (he is mentioned by Fernão Lopes again in Chapter 24) as well as Pedro's son, King Fernando.

saying that we are not writing history properly. This is not due to any failure on our part to acknowledge that the appropriate talent cannot be found to speak with authority about such highly praiseworthy acts. Rather, lest we deviate from those expressions of praise that the people from ancient times have recommended, we are presenting our narrative in accordance with the manner that they have laid down.

We know for sure that King Pedro never became annoyed whenever he was asked for gifts, and that he ordered up to 100 silver marks' worth in cups and goblets to give as New Year presents: he distributed them every year, along with other jewels, to whomsoever he thought fit. He added to the allowance given to his knights and vassals in the way we have said.[18] Before, a vassal's allowance amounted to only 75 *libras*, but King Pedro increased it to 100, namely some 15 crossed or Moorish *dobras*.[19] For this allowance the vassal was obliged to maintain a horse in good condition, as well as a hauberk[20] and mail coif;[21] on the vassal's death the horse and hauberk were to be left to the king by way of death duty. The king gave these items to whomsoever he chose, so that with the horse and the armour the allowance passed on to another vassal, with the result that the number of vassals remained unchanged and never diminished.

At the time of this king, the silver-alloy mark was worth 19 *libras*, and the Moorish *dobra* 3 *libras* and 15 *soldos*; the *escudo* 3 *libras* and 17 *soldos*; and the *moutão* 3 *libras* and 19 *soldos*.[22] King Pedro never devalued the coinage

---

[18] In Chapter 1 above.

[19] *Dobras mouriscas,* Moorish *dobras,* were coined by the Nasrid kings of Granada, but achieved a wider circulation in the Christian kingdoms of the Peninsula; *dobras cruzadas,* as the name suggests, were issued by Christian rulers and embodied Christian motifs in their design (see reference to 'Doña Blanca' *doblas* further down in the text). The *dobla* in all its forms, was a coin of much greater value than the *soldo* (the Spanish *sueldo*) and was usually struck in silver or gold. *Libras* and marks were internationally recognized denominations of account and weight for gold and silver.

[20] '*Louriga*' in the original. The Latin '*lorica*' most often refers to the 'hauberk' in medieval documents: a thighlength, or longer, shirt of mail often having an integral mail hood or 'coif', as the chronicle's wording implies. By the 14th century the hauberk was worn not just by knights but also by lower-ranking men-at-arms.

[21] '*Almofre*' in the original. It almost certainly describes the mail coif, lined with padded textile and permanently connected to the hauberk to protect the head and neck. Mail coifs remained common until the end of the 14th century, although after *c*. 1350 they were more characteristic of lower-ranking troops. The coif was often worn under an iron or steel helmet or over a close-fitting metal or hardened leather skull cap; it could also be worn on its own as the primary head protection.

[22] For further information on medieval Portuguese coins and respective images, see

out of any greed for temporal gain; rather, in his reign noble and unalloyed gold and silver coins were minted, that is to say *dobras* of very fine gold and of the same weight as the crossed *doblas* minted in Seville, known as 'Doña Blanca *doblas*'. Fifty of the *dobras* that King Pedro ordered to be minted were worth 1 mark. 100 others of smaller mintage were also the equivalent of 1 mark.

The *dobras* bore on the one side the fivefold shield of Portugal's coat of arms, whilst on the other they had the image of a bearded man, wearing a crown, seated on a throne, and holding a sword in his right hand. Around the coins were Latin inscriptions that in the vernacular meant 'Pedro, King of Portugal and the Algarve' on one side, and 'May God aid me and make me excel in vanquishing my enemies' on the other. The largest of these *dobras* was worth 4 *libras* and 2 *soldos*, the smallest 41 *soldos*.

Another silver coin was minted, known as the *tornês*; sixty-five of these were worth 1 mark, and their weight and alloy were identical to the *reales* of King Pedro of Castile. A smaller *tornês* was also minted; 130 of these equalled 1 mark. On one side appeared five shields, whilst on the other was displayed the head of a heavily bearded man with a crown on his head. The inscriptions on both sides were similar to those on the *dobras*. The larger *tornês* was worth 7 *soldos*, and the smaller one 3½ *soldos*. These coins were known respectively as a *dobra* and half a *dobra*, and as a *tornês* and half a *tornês*.

Another small coin was the Alphonsine *dinheiro*, the alloy and value of which was established by King Afonso [IV], King Pedro's father. With all these coins the realm was rich, well-off, and prosperous. Moreover, these kings amassed significant sums in their treasury, owing to the surplus in their revenue. How they went about building up and adding to the holdings in their treasury is described in the next chapter.

Cristina Mota Gomes, *Money with History: Collection of the Bank of Portugal* (Lisbon: Banco de Portugal, 2006). The mintings and values recorded in this chapter and elsewhere in Fernão Lopes do not figure among the sources cited in Peter Spufford's exhaustively-researched *Handbook of Medieval Exchange*.

Chapter 12

How kings went about accumulating wealth and adding to it

You have already heard about how much was done by former kings to cut back on both their own outlays and on those of the realm, establishing rules for themselves and their subjects in order to accumulate wealth and become rich. They maintained that, if the people were wealthy, then the king was wealthy also, and that a king who had wealth in his treasury was always able to defend his country and make war, whenever that were deemed necessary, and without causing any harm or detriment to his people. They considered that nobody could be so certain of remaining at peace as to be immune from unexpected adverse events.

To accumulate great wealth they all acted in the following way: every year the kings were informed by their comptrollers of finance of all the expenditure that they had incurred, not only in embassies but also in all other actions that it was necessary to accomplish. The comptrollers told them of what, over and above that amount, still remained from their revenues and the levying of duties, both in money and in other forms of income. The order was then issued for the purchase, from these sources, of quantities of gold and silver to be placed in the castle in Lisbon in a tower built for the purpose and known as the Torre Albarrã or Outer Tower. This tower was greatly fortified, though its construction was never completed. It was located over the main gate of the castle, and in it was stored most of the wealth which the kings had amassed in gold, silver and coins. The keys to the tower were held, one by a custodian of the Monastery of São Francisco, another by a prior of the Monastery of São Domingos, and the third by a member of the chapter of the city's cathedral.

The kings had the following method of amassing gold and silver. In all the large and small towns of the realm that were suitable for this purpose, the kings had their money-changers who bought silver and gold from anyone wanting to sell: they alone were authorized to make such purchases. At the end of the year each one took what he had bought to the designated place where it was to be deposited in the treasury. The money-changers received a portion of the value of each item of gold that they had bought and they also deposited the remaining coinage in the treasury.

There was another tower in the castle of Santarém, where there was similarly an immense treasury in which coins and other items were held, in so vast a quantity that it had to be powerfully braced in advance to prevent it from collapsing owing to the great weight of what was deposited in it. There was similar provision in Oporto, Coimbra, and other places, and there, every year, the surplus gold, silver and coins arising from the purchases made by order of the kings were deposited.

Whenever a king died and a homily was delivered to honour his noble deeds in however many years he had reigned in justice and according to the rule of law, this wealth was counted as one of his great and honourable actions. He would earn immense praise when they said, 'This king, who reigned for such a number of years, deposited in the treasury towers such a quantity of gold, silver and coins.' The greater the amount each king deposited in the towers, the greater was the honour that they considered his achievement deserved.

When King Pedro began his reign it seemed to some that he was disinclined to order any increase in the wealth that earlier kings had so carefully begun to amass. Observing this, one of his confidential courtiers, João Esteves by name, viewed the situation as being very grave and decided to draw the matter to the king's attention. One day, when the king was conversing with him in a jocular mood, he spoke as follows:

> Sire, it seems to me, should this meet with your favour, that it would be appropriate to provide for your own finances and to see what can be spent. From the surplus you could begin to determine how to add something to the wealth which you have inherited from your father and forefathers, in order to do what the other kings did and to have enough to undertake more abundant expenditure if it were to become necessary to do so. It will be more honourable for you to undertake expenditure after increasing the amount in your treasury than to spend what the earlier kings have bequeathed to you, without depositing anything therein.

In answer to this and to similar reasoning the king declared that João Esteves had spoken well and requested him to put in writing how much his levied duties would amount to, as well as the expenditure to which it was subject. After a few days his courtier brought to him in writing everything that the king had requested of him. After they had both separately inspected the document, they found that, after deducting the expenditure that kings customarily had to undertake, the king could deposit annually in his treasury, in the castle tower in Lisbon alone, a sum of up to 15,000 *dobras*.

At once the king ordered that each year everything that was left over from his revenue should be deposited in gold, silver and coins in those places where the kings customarily deposited their wealth. That is why the king stated that it was no trivial matter for a king to conserve the wealth that others had bequeathed to him and to live off the levied duties that he received from his kingdom, without causing any detriment to his people or taking anything from them that was theirs. That was how he proceeded, never spending any of the wealth that he inherited. On his death it all passed on to his son, King Fernando, who spent it as he saw fit, as you will hear in due course.

Chapter 13

How King Pedro of Castile began to amass a vast fortune

K ing Pedro of Castile amassed a very great fortune in quite a different way, without altering the currency or inflicting special charges on his people. Consider the manner in which he operated, though we are describing matters outside our own country.

It happened that King Pedro was in the village of Morales, a league away from Toro, and that one day he was playing dice with a group of his knights. One of his keepers of the wardrobe stood nearby in charge of a number of small caskets containing silver and *doblas*, amounting in all to a sum of around 20,000 *doblas*. The king said that this sum was all he held in his treasury and that he did not possess any other money. On that very same evening, when the king was in his chamber, his chief treasurer, Don Samuel Leví, in the presence of everyone, addressed him as follows:

> Sire, today it pleased you to announce to those who were here present that the amount held in your treasury was no more than 20,000 *doblas* and that you used it for gaming and for pleasurable pursuits. I concluded, Sire, that you said this to humiliate me as your chief treasurer and to imply that I do not look after your financial affairs properly. However, Sire, you are well aware that I have been your treasurer since the beginning of your reign till now, that is, for some seven years. In that time, your kingdom has always been subject to such an unceasing series of troubles as have led your rent collectors to dare to do things they ought not to have done. As a result, I have been unable to control the situation as peaceably as it required. Now, however, if you will grant me authority over two castles of my choosing, I shall in a very short time garner into them for you such a large sum as to enable you to say that you have amassed more than 20,000 *doblas*.

The king was greatly pleased at these words and gave his treasurer charge of the castles of Trujillo and Hita. Don Samuel installed in them men whom he could trust and sent letters throughout the kingdom to all those who had been and still were royal rent collectors since the beginning of the king's reign, commanding them to come and submit their accounts which he received from them in the following way.

Payments were made by the king [via the rent collectors] to a knight or some other person of about 1,000 *maravedís* by way of allowance or otherwise. Don Samuel summoned to him all those who had received any money from the individual whose accounts he was checking. He required each one to swear by the Gospels how much money he had received on every occasion from the rent collector in question and how much money he had left with him as an inducement in order to avoid delays. Each of those to whom such monies were given [by the king] duly declared that he had not received more than a certain amount and that the remaining monies had been given by him to the collector as an inducement because he had been led to understand that he could not be paid in any other way. Then, if the collector could not show the exact place where everything was paid to him, Don Samuel ordered that half of what he had embezzled in that way should go to the king's treasury and half to the one whom he had swindled.

All those who received such payments were only too happy to tell the truth in order to recover what they had lost. Thus, in less than a year, Don Samuel garnered into those castles a sum so vast that it was a wonder to behold. Such was the beginning of the huge amount that King Pedro went on to amass in his treasury, as we shall go on to relate in due course.

Chapter 14

How King Pedro of Portugal made João Afonso Telo a count and dubbed him a knight, and the great feast that he gave for him

We consider that there were three matters to which King Pedro of Portugal devoted most of his time. Those were justice and the affairs of the realm, hunting both large and small game, which he relished, and dancing and feasting as practised in those days, in which he took very great pleasure to an extent difficult to imagine today. These dances of his were performed to the music of long trumpets which were played at that time; indeed, he had no liking whatsoever for other instruments, even if available. If somebody ever did want to play another instrument for him, he soon got tired of it, declared that the devil should take it, and sent for the trumpeters again.

Let us now set aside our description of the games and festivities that the king ordered to pass the time and to which he devoted himself night and day in endless dancing. Consider, however, just how pleasurable it would be: he was wont to sail across from Almada to Lisbon in small boats, and the citizens and all the craftsmen came out to greet him, dancing and tumbling as was the custom then. He then left the boats, came ashore and danced with them all the way to the palace.

Consider indeed the pleasure he took when one night he lay in bed in Lisbon, unable to sleep: he roused all the servants and all those who were sleeping in the palace and sent for João Mateus and Lourenço Palos, ordering them to bring their silver trumpets. He had torches lit and set off with all the others [from the palace], dancing through the city. Wrested from their sleep, people went to their windows to see what kind of festivity it could all be and why. When they saw the king dancing, they were delighted to see him so happy. The king spent most of the night in this fashion, then danced back to the palace, requested wine and fruit, and lay down to sleep.

Without talking further about these amusements, we come to when the king ordered that João Afonso Telo be made a count and dubbed a knight: he was the brother of Martim Afonso Telo and received from the king the greatest honour in a celebration that up to that time had never before been vouchsafed by any king to any subject. Indeed, the king ordered that 600 *arrobas*[23] of wax be used to make 5,000 ceremonial candles and torches. From the Lisbon area, where the king then was, there came forth 5,000 oarsmen from the rowing crews to carry the candles.

When the time came for the count to spend his vigil as knight in the Monastery of São Domingos in Lisbon, the king ordered that from the monastery, all along the route to the palace (a considerable distance), all these men should stand motionless, each holding a burning candle, thus creating an immense blaze of light. The king and many noblemen and knights passed among them, dancing, enjoying themselves, and spending much of the night in this way.

The following day, large pavilions were erected in the Rossio close to the monastery.[24] In these were great mounds of baked bread and huge casks filled with wine and ready for drinking. Outside whole cows were roasting on the spits; all those wanting to eat the meat had it freely available, and nobody was turned away. That was how they continued while the feast lasted, in which others were dubbed knights and whose names we shall not trouble to mention.

---

[23] An *arroba* is a former measure of weight, roughly equivalent to 15 kg or 33 lb.

[24] The word *rossio* means 'square' but it was the name given (at that time, as it is today) to the large square in the centre of Lisbon.

Chapter 15

The pacts that the King of Castile and King Pedro of Portugal signed and how the King of Portugal promised to support him against Aragon

A number of historians have written in praise of King Pedro [of Portugal], relating that he reigned in peace throughout his lifetime and that it was not in vain that fortune saw fit to guide his reign, at its beginning, middle, and end, through peace and unbroken calm. When he came to power on the death of his father, King Afonso, he found the kingdom free of any dissension likely to lead to conflict with any king, whether of Spain[25] or of some more distant land. In addition, when he became king, he immediately sent Aires Gomes da Silva and Gonçalo Eanes de Beja to his nephew, the King of Castile, with a message, and a nobleman by the name of Fernán López de Estúñiga, representing the king, travelled from Castile to see King Pedro. It was duly agreed that the two kings would be true and loyal friends, and their mutual friendship was signed and sealed at that time.

A year later, when King Pedro was in Évora, a group of messengers arrived from the King of Castile, namely Don Samuel Leví, his chief treasurer, along with García Gutiérrez Tello, the chief magistrate of Seville, and Gómez Fernández de Soria, the governor of that city; these men negotiated a more binding truce between the two kings than the previous one.

On this occasion it was also decided that Prince Fernando, the eldest son of the King of Portugal and heir to the throne, was to marry Princess Beatriz, the daughter of the King of Castile, and that their betrothal should be carried out by their proctors between the middle of the coming February and the last day of March; then the marriage would take place on the last day of April. Moreover, as his daughter's dowry, the King of Castile should give the same amount of money as King Afonso of Portugal had given his daughter Maria when she married his father, King Alfonso. The King of Portugal was to give Princess Beatriz, as dowry and bond, the same amount of money that his father, King Afonso, had given Princess Constanza[26] when she was married to him.

In addition, it was agreed that Princess Constanza, the daughter of King Pedro of Castile, was to marry Prince João, and the other daughter, who was

---

[25] 'Spain' was the name then given to the whole of the Iberian Peninsula, being derived from the Latin *Hispania*, the name given to the Peninsula by the Romans.

[26] Constanza Manuel, the daughter of Don Juan Manuel, was princess consort to Prince Pedro of Portugal, whom she married in 1340.

called Princess Isabel, should marry Prince Dinis.[27] It was agreed that the betrothals and marriages of these princes and princesses should be concluded six years later, and that the King of Castile should give to each of his daughters towns capable of providing them with a rent of 90,000 *maravedís*. For his part, the King of Portugal would give to each of his sons towns which would yield 10,000 Portuguese *libras* per year.

It was also settled that the King of Castile was to be his ally and the enemy of his enemies, and the two of them would come to each other's aid, on land and at sea, whenever it was necessary; furthermore, the King of Castile was not to make peace with the King of Aragon, against whom he was seeking Pedro of Portugal's aid at the time, nor indeed with any other lord or king, without informing him first.

It should be pointed out that this support that the King of Castile requested of King Pedro of Portugal had in the past been sought by him of the father of the latter, King Afonso [IV], when King Pedro of Castile went to war against Pere III[28] of Aragon, which was during the last year of the reign of King Afonso, as you shall see presently. This support was to be in the form of mounted troops on land, and a number of galleys at sea.

In response to his grandson's request, King Afonso said that he was fully aware of the pacts and agreements that had been made between his father, King Dinis, Pedro's grandfather, King Fernando,[29] and King Jaume of Aragon, which all three had signed, in their own name and that of their successors. For this reason, after consulting with all the important men in his Royal Council, who had been summoned to discuss the situation, King Afonso decided that he could not justifiably supply the aid requested of him.

When the King of Castile received this response he never asked for his support ever again. When King Afonso of Portugal died and his son, Dom Pedro, became king, the King of Castile made contact with him, asking for his support, on land and sea, in the war in which he was engaged against the King of Aragon, saying that he would be happy to do the same for him if it became necessary.

In reply to this the King of Portugal said that he should be well aware of the strong and close ties that had always existed between the kings of Portugal and Aragon, and because of these bonds, he could quite rightly be exempted from saying or doing anything which might be prejudicial to the King of Aragon or to his kingdom. Furthermore, his father, King Afonso, and Pere, the King of Aragon, who was then on the throne, had signed pacts and

27 João and Dinis were the sons of King Pedro and Dona Inês de Castro.
28 En Pere III, the Ceremonious, reigned from 1336 to 1387.
29 Fernando IV was the father of Alfonso XI, Pedro of Castile's father.

alliances, promising to befriend and support each other, particularly against King Alfonso, the father of the King of Castile. This had already been brought to Pedro of Portugal's attention several times, ever since the old enmity had flared up again between the King of Castile and the King of Aragon.

However, in spite of all these reasons, he believed that there were enough close ties between him and the King of Castile and just as many sound reasons why they both ought to do whatever they could for the honour and benefit of each other. This is what he intended to do in this hour of need, and whenever it was necessary.

Accordingly, in order to strengthen the friendship and family bonds between them, he was willing to support him in this war which the King of Castile had instigated. However, since, God be praised, he had plenty of troops, more than the King of Aragon had, whereas some of his galleys had been destroyed, he could therefore manage without help on land more easily than at sea. Therefore, although this was more costly for him, the King of Portugal was very willing to send him support in the form of ten large galleys, financed for three months, which he would have fully equipped when he sent for them.

Indeed, King Pedro of Portugal did send him aid, twice at sea, and twice on land, providing brave and well-armed horsemen, during the course of the long and hard-fought war between King Pedro of Castile and King Pere of Aragon.

When some people hear about this, they will want to know more about this war, why it began in the first place, and why it went on for so long. We could be excused for not getting involved in this matter, as these are events that concern Castile, and not Portugal. However, we shall grant their wish, as it seems to us, moreover, that if they do not know about the deeds and atrocities of this king, Don Pedro of Castile, it will be impossible to understand the reason why he later fled his kingdom and came to Portugal, seeking aid and support, and the circumstances in which, after his death, several towns in Castile went over to King Fernando and became his.

For all these reasons, we shall give a brief account of how these things came about. We shall begin with the events which happened early in his reign, at the time when King Afonso of Portugal, his grandfather, was still alive, and then we shall describe later events, which took place during the reign of his uncle, King Pedro [of Portugal]. It seems to us that this is the most appropriate place to relate these events, combining his deeds with the account of the war.

We shall start with what he did before the war began, so that you will know exactly how things happened.

Chapter 16

Concerning certain people the King of Castile had put to death, and how he married Princess Blanche of Bourbon and then abandoned her

According to the testimony of a number of authors who have written about the deeds of this King of Castile, he was very good at giving free rein to whatever his wild, unruly nature demanded of him, to such an extent that we could well be criticized for not being more discreet in our narration of other people's ill deeds, particularly those which cast upon them a wicked and shameful reputation, if we were to record in detail every ugly thing that could be said of him. Therefore, we shall leave aside many such deeds about which others have written and mention only the most important ones.

This king did not have any of the virtues and qualities which it is fitting for good kings to possess. People say that he was very lascivious, so much so that when a woman took his fancy, whether they were noblewomen, wives of knights, or even nuns or of any other state, he showed no respect for any of them. He greatly coveted what others had to the point of derangement, and only wanted in his Royal Council men who would praise his ideas and his actions. He had many good, honourable people put to death, some for foolish reasons, simply for giving him good advice, and others for no good reason, on the slightest suspicion, so that many worthy men avoided him, fearing for their lives. No man was safe in his presence, even if he had served him well and had been treated by him with honour and great generosity. Leaving aside the false accusations he brought against his victims in order to kill them, we shall speak briefly only of the executions and nothing else.

During the second year of his reign Doña Leonor Núñez de Guzmán was put to death. She had in the past been the mistress of his father and was the mother of Count Enrique [de Trastámara], who was later to become king. Although some people claim that this had come about on the order of King Pedro's mother, Queen Maria, it is certain that she would not have given an order of that nature without the consent of her son. The king gave all the possessions of Leonor Núñez to his mother. He ordered the death of Garci Lasso de la Vega, an illustrious Castilian nobleman who had many distinguished sons-in-law, kinsmen, and friends, just because he felt suspicious of him. He ordered the execution of three eminent citizens of Burgos, namely Pedro Fernández de Medina, the scribe Juan Fernández, and Alfonso García de Camargo. In a similar fashion he besieged Don Alfonso Fernández Coronel in the town of Aguilar, which he took by force. He then ordered his execution, as well as that of Pedro Coronel, who was Don Alfonso's nephew, Juan González de Deza, Ponce Díaz de Quesada, Rodrigo Íñiguez de Biedma, and Juan Alfonso Carrillo, a brave knight.

The king sent a message to the King of France, requesting him to give one of the daughters of his cousin, the Duke of Bourbon, to him in marriage. Out of his six daughters the emissaries chose one called Princess Blanche, a very attractive young lady of eighteen, and they received her on behalf of the king. When King Pedro heard about this, he ordered that she should be brought to him immediately. The King of France arranged for the Viscount of Cardona[30] and a number of other knights from his country to escort her with all due honour. With the bride, King Pedro received from the King of France a very substantial dowry of gold, silver and other riches. It was at this time that the *doblas* known as 'Doña Blanca' and the Castilian *reales* of King Pedro were struck. While the emissaries were gone to arrange the wedding, the king took María de Padilla as his mistress. At the time she was a maiden in the house of Doña Isabel de Meneses, the daughter of Don Tello de Meneses and wife of Dom João Afonso de Albuquerque, who had brought her up. The king felt so passionate towards her that when Princess Blanche arrived he no longer had any intention of marrying her, already having a daughter, Beatriz, by his mistress.

However, following the advice of Dom João Afonso de Albuquerque, and very much against his wishes, the king decided that the marriage should take place in Valladolid. It took place on a Monday, and then, on Tuesday, the following day, an hour after eating, the king abandoned his wife. Nothing could stop him, not even the tears and pleas of his mother, Queen Maria,[31] nor those of his aunt, the Queen of Aragon.[32] He rode off so swiftly that he arrived that evening at the village of Pajares, 16 leagues from Valladolid, where he spent the night, and the next day he arrived in Montalbán, where Doña María de Padilla was staying.

When the king left, he and some of the men accompanying him had mules waiting for them in specific places, but only three of them arrived with him, and this caused a commotion amongst the great lords and nobles of the land

---

[30] Pero López de Ayala, one of Lope's main sources, says it was the Viscount of Narbonne. Indeed, it seems more likely that the king of France would rely on one of his vassals for this mission. See *Cronica de Don Pedro Primero*, in *Cronicas*, ed. José-Luis Martín (Barcelona, 1991), Year 4, ch. 3, p. 65.

[31] Queen Maria was the daughter of Afonso IV of Portugal, as mentioned at the beginning of Chapter 2.

[32] Leonor of Castile, second wife of Alfons III of Aragon, and sister of Alfonso XI of Castile.

who were there. Some of them at once took leave of the king. Later, yielding to pressure, the king returned to Valladolid where he spent two days with his wife, after which it was impossible to persuade him to stay any longer, and he left and never wished to see her again. The viscount and the other noblemen who accompanied Princess Blanche departed without even speaking to the king.

While Queen Blanche was still alive, less than a year after the king had married her, the king was smitten by Doña Juana de Castro, the daughter of Don Pedro [Fernández] de Castro, who was nicknamed 'Don Pedro of the War'; she was the widow of Don Diego de Haro, and via a third party he asked her to marry him. When she refused his proposal, since the king was already married, he replied that he had reasons why this was not the case. He then ordered the Bishops of Ávila and Salamanca[33] to pronounce that it was permissible for him to marry. Out of fear they complied with his wish, and the king and Doña Juana were received in the church of Cuéllar with all due solemnity by the Bishop of Salamanca, who performed the marriage ceremony. The next day the king departed and he never saw Doña Juana again. She always called herself queen, although this displeased the king.

Queen Maria went to Tordesillas, taking her daughter-in-law [Queen Blanche] with her. But the king had Queen Blanche moved from there to Arévalo, where she was kept in seclusion so that neither his mother nor anyone else could see her. Later, he had her imprisoned in Medina Sidonia, and there he ordered her to be put to death. Queen Blanche was then twenty-five, a very wise and virtuous lady.

The king had ordered the death of Alvar González Morán and Don Álvaro Pérez de Castro, the brother of Dona Inês, who was the mother of Dom João and Dom Dinis, the sons of King Pedro of Portugal, then a prince: but they were warned by Doña María de Padilla, who sent to tell them, and so they escaped death. One day in Medina del Campo, in the early afternoon in his palace, he ordered the execution of Pedro Rodríguez de Villegas, the Chief Provincial Governor of Castile, and, likewise, of Sancho Rodríguez de Rojas. A squire of Pedro Rodríguez was also killed.

The king ordered twenty-two worthy local men in Toledo to be put to death for having planned an uprising in the city against the [expected] murder of Queen Blanche, which everyone believed was due to take place there. Amongst these men there was an eighty-year-old goldsmith whom he ordered to be killed. Just as he was about to be executed, the old man's eighteen-year-old son begged the king kindly to permit him to be killed in place of his father, and the king agreed to this. But everyone present would have preferred the king

33   Sancho Blázquez Dávila, Bishop of Ávila (1312–1355) and Juan Lucero, Bishop of Salamanca (1339–1361).

to spare them both. He had four gallant knights of the city, namely Gonzalo Méndez, Lope de Velasco, Tello González Palomeque, and his brother, Lope Rodríguez, put to death.

When the king entered the town of Toro where his mother, the queen, was living, he ordered her to leave the alcazar and come to his presence. Then he ordered the execution of Don Pedro Estebáñez [Carpenteyro], who called himself Master of Calatrava, and who was accompanying the queen, of Ruy González de Castañeda, who was escorting her by the arm, along with Alonso Téllez Girón and Martim Afonso Telo, all four surrounding the queen. When she witnessed them being killed so close to her, she fell to the ground in a deathly faint, and as she was being lifted up she shouted and cursed her son.

A few days after this she asked him to send her to Portugal, to her father, King Afonso, and he agreed. She died there some time later, as you have heard. The king went on to order the death of Gómez Manrique de Uruñuela and others. Then he organized a tournament in Tordesillas, with fifty men on each side, planning that his brother, Don Fadrique, the Master of Santiago, who would be jousting, would be killed. However, the king did not want to disclose this plan of his to anyone, so it was not carried out that day.

Chapter 17

How the quarrel first began between King Pedro of Castile and his brother, Count Enrique [de Trastámara], and why the count left the kingdom

As further on we shall speak of the war and the deep quarrel that was later to arise between Count Enrique and his brother, King Pedro, we need to relate first how this dissension began and how the count came to leave the kingdom. This must be done before we go on to talk about the war between Castile and the King of Aragon, to whose aid the count was later to go.[34]

It is important you should know that, when King Alfonso [XI] died in the siege of Gibraltar in March 1350, after which his elder son, Prince Pedro, who was in Seville at the time, had been proclaimed king at the age of fifteen years and seven months, many of the nobles and great lords who were there with the king left the encampment, bearing his body, so that he could be laid to rest in Castile. Amongst these were Prince Ferran, the son of the King

---

[34] In exile he aided Pere III of Aragon against Pedro of Castile from 1356 to 1361.

of Aragon, and Marquis of Tortosa, who was the nephew of the aforemen-
tioned King Alfonso, being the son of his sister, Queen Leonor; Don Enrique,
Count of Trastámara; his brother, Don Fadrique, Master of Santiago (both of
them being sons of Leonor Núñez[35] and King Alfonso); Dom João Afonso
de Albuquerque; as well as a number of other great lords, masters of Orders,
and members of the nobility.

Just as the body of the king was approaching the town of Medina Sidonia,
which belonged to Leonor Núñez, she entered the town, because Alfonso
Fernández Coronel, who had been governing it in her name, told her he no
longer wished to do so. As Leonor Núñez made her entry, there was much
rumour amongst the great lords and knights bearing the king's body, as they
feared she was taking residence there to lend support to her sons and relatives
who were with her.

When Dom João Afonso de Albuquerque saw that Doña Leonor's sons and
relatives were making a stop in this well-fortified town along with her, he
arranged with some of the others that Count Enrique and Don Fadrique, his
brother, be held in the town as prisoners. Leonor Núñez found this out and
was very frightened. However, negotiations were opened with her in which
she was assured of her safety, namely by Don Juan Núñez de Lara, whose
daughter was married to Don Tello, Doña Leonor's son, as he was convinced
that such an assurance could be relied upon.

Doña Leonor left the town, together with her sons and Don Pedro Ponce de
León, Don Fernán Pérez Ponce, the Master of Alcántara, who was his brother,
Don Alvar Pérez de Guzmán, and other family members. They all agreed to
keep out of King Pedro's reach, greatly fearing to go to Seville where he was,
and be taken prisoner. Consequently, they left Medina the same day and went
to Morón, a town with a well-fortified castle close to Moorish territory. But,
since they still did not feel secure there, they moved on to Algeciras, which
belonged to Don Pedro Ponce; as for Don Fadrique, he returned to the lands
of the Order of Santiago.

Queen Maria, her son King Pedro, and all those who were in Seville went
outside the city boundary to receive the king's body. His mortal remains were
given all due respect and ceremony, and he was then laid to rest in the royal
chapel in the church of Santa María.

When the king heard about the departure of his brothers and the other
nobles, and that they were in Algeciras, he arranged to be secretly informed
about what they were doing and found out that they were trying their utmost
to take possession of the town. He then sent armed galleys, with Gutierre
Fernández de Toledo as captain. Count Enrique and the others, realizing that

---

[35] See Chapter 16.

no good would come to them by remaining there, went back to Morón, which was where Don Fernán Pérez[36] Ponce was.

At that point Doña Leonor Núñez went to Seville and, in spite of the reassurances she had been given, the king placed her under arrest in the alcazar. Discussions then took place between representatives of the king and Count Enrique and the other great lords, and finally it was decided that they should all go to Seville to join the king. There the count went every day to see his mother, who was accompanied by his betrothed, Doña Juana, the daughter of Don Juan Manuel.

The count agreed to his mother's plea that the marriage should take place, so that the pledge would not be broken, as was rumoured it might be. So they did marry, to the great displeasure of the king, the queen mother, and many other people, and the king decided to forbid anyone to visit Doña Leonor. She was taken from there to Carmona, and Count Enrique fled to Asturias when he heard that the king had ordered his arrest. After that, his mother, Doña Leonor, was taken to Talavera, and there, through Alfonso Fernández de Olmedo, her secretary, Queen Maria ordered her to be put to death, as you already know.[37]

While Count Enrique was in Asturias, he heard how the king had ordered his mother and then Garci Lasso, the Provincial Governor of Castile, to be killed. Consequently, he did not dare stay there any longer and headed for Portugal, to be with King Afonso. When King Pedro went to see his grandfather in Ciudad Rodrigo, as we have already mentioned,[38] King Afonso begged his grandson to forgive the count. King Pedro agreed, but the count returned to Asturias, as he did not dare go anywhere near the king.

The king found out that, in Asturias, the count was reinforcing the defence of Gijón. Accordingly, he went there and laid siege to the town, which was where the count's wife, Doña Juana, was to be found. In fact, the count did not risk staying there and took refuge on an inaccessible mountain called Montoyo. The people of Gijón negotiated with the king, begging him to forgive the count if he promised that he would not wage war against the king from any of his townships. The king agreed and left.

When the time came for the marriage of the king to Princess Blanche in Valladolid, as we have said, Count Enrique arrived there with his brother, Don Tello, with 600 men on horseback and 1,500 foot soldiers. When they reached Cigales, which was 2 leagues from where the king was staying, the count sent word to the king that he would only risk entering the town with

---

[36] The name given in the Portuguese text, by mistake, is Fernán Rodríguez Ponce.

[37] See Chapter 16 above, where the story is told in a slightly different way.

[38] This was in 1351. Lopes is referring to his account of Afonso IV's reign. See Prologue above.

his entire escort, as he was greatly afraid of a number of men at Court. The king sent a message to reassure him. They were, however, wary of the king's assurances and were forced to fight against the king, who went out to meet them with his troops. But they eventually reached an agreement and became dependent on his favours.

The king married Blanche of Bourbon and abandoned her the next day, returning to Doña María de Padilla. Dom João Afonso de Albuquerque, who managed the king's Royal Household, quarrelled with the king because of this departure. In due course, it was agreed that Dom João Afonso could go and live in Portugal if he so wished, and that his castles and possessions in Castile would be secured. That is what the king promised him, but after Dom João Afonso went to Portugal, he laid siege to the town of Medellín, took it, and destroyed it. Later he besieged Alburquerque but when he did not succeed in seizing it, he departed, leaving Count Enrique and his brother, the Master of Santiago, Don Fadrique, in Badajoz, as lords of the marches.

After the king left, the count sent a message to Dom João Afonso, proposing that the three of them should join forces and raid Castile together. This idea sounded very attractive to Dom João Afonso, and they signed a pact, agreeing that this is what they would do. They enlisted the support of Don Fernando de Castro, who was in Galicia, and they began their attack on Castile, wreaking destruction along the way.

At this point King Pedro sent his chief chamberlain, Juan Fernández de Henestrosa, to Arévalo where his wife, Queen Blanche, was staying, in order to take her to the alcazar in Toledo. As he was escorting her through the town, the queen said she wished to go first to the Church of Santa María to pray. But once inside the church, she refused to leave, fearing that she would be killed or put in prison. Juan Fernández did not dare force her to leave the church against her will, and he returned to the king.

The people of Toledo discussed the situation and felt pity for the queen; they resolved not to allow her to be taken prisoner or to be put to death in their city, vowing to defend her with their lives and all they possessed. They began by sending for Don Fadrique, the Master of Santiago, and housed him and his troops within the town. Then they sent letters to Count Enrique, Dom João Afonso de Albuquerque, and Don Fernando [Ruíz] de Castro to let them know their intentions.

Moreover, in addition to Toledo, the towns of Córdoba and Cuenca also supported the queen, as did the bishopric of Jaén and Talavera. It is only right to add that the princes, Ferran and Joan,[39] the king's cousins, as well as many

---

[39] Princes Ferran and Joan were the sons of Queen Leonor of Aragon, Alfonso XI's sister.

great lords and knights, left the king to uphold the cause of the other side, with the result that he was left with no more than 600 horsemen.

All these noblemen sent messages to him saying that they were prepared to serve him and do his bidding on the condition that he would live with his wife and not rule his kingdom through María de Padilla's relatives, nor make them his favourites. However, the king refused to comply with these conditions.

About this time, Dom João Afonso de Albuquerque fell ill, and the king arranged to speak in secret to the physician who was caring for him, promising to reward him and asking him to give his patient something which would make him die. The physician complied with the king's wishes, which came to light later. The vassals of Dom João Afonso vowed that they would not bury him until this quarrel was settled, for such were the instructions he had left in his will. Whenever these nobles assembled to discuss what they should do, Ruy Diaz Cabeza de Vaca, who had been his chief steward, spoke on Dom João Afonso's behalf, and their combined troops came to as many as 5,000 men on horseback and a substantial number of foot soldiers.

Finally, seeing that he was losing men by acting in this way, the king decided to yield to his adversaries in the town of Toro. There, without more ado, they shared out the offices of the kingdom and of the Royal Household between them, in a manner which did not please the king. Then they went off to bury Dom João Afonso's body, thinking that the dispute was over.

The king, feeling like a prisoner because of the way they were treating him, pretended he wanted to go hunting, and one morning, very early, he rode off to Segovia. The princes of Aragon joined him with a view to reaching a compact with him. Thus, the company formed by all those who had come together began to disband. Count Enrique and his brothers, Don Tello and Don Fadrique, constituted a single party, and their total number would be as many as 1,200 men on horseback as well as many foot soldiers. They succeeded in entering Toledo, but the king made his way there and regained control of the city, with the result that they left it and rode off.

Then Queen Maria sent a message to them, requesting them to go to Toro, where she was at the time, because she was afraid of her son, the king. The count and his brothers went there, but the king arrived with his troops and fighting broke out at the gates of the town. However, owing to a lack of water, the king could not remain there and left.

After the king's departure Count Enrique left for Galicia, and some people said that he had gone to join Don Fernando de Castro, while others maintained that it was to avoid being besieged. The king had thought of going after him, but then decided to take the town of Toro first, and laid siege to it again. He negotiated with Don Fadrique, who was his brother as well as Count Enrique's, and who had remained in the town to defend it, urging him to go over to him, which he agreed to do.

Next day the king seized the town, after entering through a gate which had been left open for him. He arrested Doña Juana, the wife of Count Enrique, and ordered a number of local men to be executed, as well as the knights attending his mother, the queen, as we have already mentioned.[40]

When Count Enrique learnt that the king had seized the town of Toro and slaughtered the men who had been on his side, and discovered that his brother, Don Fadrique, had now joined the king's ranks, he realised that it was not prudent to carry on fighting or to stay any longer in the kingdom. Consequently, he asked the king to grant him safe conduct so that he could travel to France. The king agreed to this and granted his request.

Count Enrique found out later that the king had ordered Prince Joan, Diego Pérez Sarmiento, his chief provincial governor, and all the other knights and officials in the districts he thought the count would be travelling through, to waylay him and kill him, just as he was later to order the death of all the great lords and noblemen who had been part of the group that had risen against him, over the matter of Queen Blanche.

The count left Galicia and headed for Asturias, which had not received these orders from the king, as he had considered it extremely unlikely that the count would take that route. The count travelled swiftly through Asturias and then headed for Vizcaya, where his brother Don Tello was, and from there he sailed to La Rochelle, where he joined the King of France, who was fighting against the English, and served under him.

This was how the feud between him and his brother, King Pedro, came about, as well as his flight from the kingdom of Castile. Furthermore, all these quarrels you have heard about in this chapter went on for over seven years.

Chapter 18

How and why the war between Castile and Aragon began

In 1356, when King Pedro of Castile had been on the throne for almost seven years, while in Seville he ordered a galley to be equipped for a leisure trip to go and view the tunny-fishing grounds. He sailed to Sanlúcar de Barrameda and saw, there in the harbour, ten Catalan galleys and one large

40 In Chapter 16 above.

vessel the captain of which was an Aragonese knight named Messer Francesc del Perelló. The ships were going to support the King of France against the King of England, by order of the King of Aragon.

When the captain came into port to take on supplies he found two vessels from Piacenza, loaded with oils, bound for Alexandria, whereupon he seized them, declaring that they were the property of the Genoese, with whom the Catalans were at war at the time. The king sent word to him to say that, since these vessels were in a port which belonged to his kingdom, he was not to seize them, at least out of respect for the king's presence. The captain replied that those people were enemies of the King of Aragon and therefore he had every right to do so. The king sent word to him a second time, saying that, if he did not relinquish them, he would have all the Catalan merchants who were in Seville put in prison there and all their possessions confiscated.

In spite of all this, the commander of the galleys did not wish to obey the king's instructions and sold the vessels there and then for 700 *doblas*. He then went on his way without another word to the king. The king was greatly displeased by this and with good reason, but the vengeance he wrought was out of all proportion, for, just as a tiny spark can start a huge fire if the right materials are to hand, so it was that, simply to take his revenge on Aragon for this incident, King Pedro, mad with rage, instigated a cruel and bloody war against Aragon, which was to last for many years, as you will hear presently.

First of all, he ordered all the Catalan merchants who were in Seville to be seized and all their possessions confiscated. The following day, he made a swift departure from the city by land, put all the Catalan merchants in chains and then sold off everything they had. Very soon after this, he sent a message to the King of Aragon, complaining about the conduct of Messer Francesc, because of the lack of respect that the captain had shown towards him, even though he, the king, had sent him the command twice; accordingly, he was asking the King of Aragon to hand the captain over to him, so as to exact due retribution from him.

In addition, he requested that Don Pedro Muñiz de Godoy, a man he disliked, should be stripped of the commandery[41] the King of Aragon had bestowed on him. If the King of Aragon failed to do these things, he could rest assured that he would certainly wage war on him. The King of Aragon replied that he regretted the insult suffered by the King, and that as soon as the aforesaid knight returned to his kingdom he would attend to the case himself and see that justice was done in a way that would be pleasing to the King of Castile.

---

[41] Benefit or estate bestowed on someone as a reward for services rendered.

As for the matter of the commandery bestowed on Don Pedro Muñiz, he would find a different favour to extend to him rather than the one which so much displeased the King of Castile. But until he decided what to do instead, he could not deprive him of the commandery without bringing shame upon himself. The messenger, who was well aware of King Pedro's intentions, was by no means satisfied by this response and immediately challenged the King of Aragon and his kingdom to go to war. The King of Aragon replied by saying that the King of Castile had no valid reason to act in this way and he would leave the matter for God to judge. Without further ado, he ordered his kingdom to prepare for war.

Chapter 19

How the King of Castile entered the kingdom of Aragon, and what he did that year

Meanwhile, fired by a desire for vengeance, the King of Castile, after sending to Aragon the message that you have heard about, and before receiving any response, ordered seven galleys and six *naos*[42] to be made ready immediately. The king sailed in one of these, thinking he might come across the aforesaid knight somewhere along the Portuguese coast. He arrived at Tavira and, having learned that he had in fact passed that way, returned to Seville. Then the king sent the galleys off in the direction of Ibiza, and war broke out all over that area.

---

[42] *Naos* were usually one- or two-masted ships with a capacity of up to 200 tons and features specifically Iberian in comparison to the north European 'cog' and the 'hulk' of the Hanseatic League. These are the ships that eventually evolved into and coexisted with the much larger 'carracks', and that were used both for commerce and warfare. At the end of the 14th century, shipbuilding technology was undergoing a process of evolution whereby different types of vessels were favoured by different regions in Europe, though all subject to cross-influences, including from the Mediterranean, in an effort to improve capacity, speed, and manoeuvrability. For this reason, it has proved impossible to find an English word that can accurately represent the Portuguese and Castilian *naos*, frequently mentioned by Fernão Lopes in his chronicles. See the 'Translators' note' (pp. xxvii–xxviii) for the decision to maintain the original *nao* and *naos* for these Portuguese ships and their counterparts from other Peninsular kingdoms. See: Filipe Castro, 'In Search of Unique Iberian Ship Design Concepts', *Historical Archaeology*, 42:2 (2008), 63–87.

This was at the beginning of 1357, around the time of the death of King Afonso of Portugal, whose aid had been sought by this grandson of his, King Pedro, in this war, as we have already related. The King of Aragon, well aware of the hostile attitude of the King of Castile towards him, informed Count Enrique and a number of Castilian knights who were in France at that time, out of fear of King Pedro. The count went with them to join him, and the king received them warmly, bestowing on the count a number of castles in which to house his men and enough money to maintain 800 horsemen.

When the King of Castile heard about this, he left Seville and made for Aragon, where he seized several castles, and then returned to Deza, a town belonging to him, close to the Aragonese border. As the fighting was spreading with increasing intensity, Cardinal Guillaume [de la Jugie], a legate of Pope Innocent [VI] travelled to Deza to speak to the king and to try to establish a pact between the two monarchs. He was not entirely successful in putting an end to the fighting because of the huge demands that King Pedro was making of the King of Aragon. He did, however, achieve a truce which lasted for two weeks, during which King Pedro took the town of Tarazona. The cardinal was furious with the king and said that King Pedro had seized the town while he was on his way to talk to the King of Aragon, when the truce was still in operation.

The king kept saying that the truce had already been over by then, whereas the cardinal declared that this was untrue: the fact remains that the king left the town well provided with men. After this second incursion of the king into Aragon and the seizing of Tarazona, many men from his kingdoms, as well as a number of English soldiers, went to join him, so that there were 7,000 mounted soldiers and 2,000 light horsemen, as well as many foot soldiers.

When the cardinal understood that it was impossible to negotiate a lasting truce between the two kings, he decreed that they were to keep a year-long truce, and this was proclaimed on Monday, 10 May, that same year. The King of Castile then went off to Seville to order galleys to be built and to make preparations to have a fleet ready for the following year, as soon as the truce expired.

Meanwhile, while the treaty was still in place, Pedro Carrillo, who was with Count Enrique, came to an agreement with King Pedro, arranging that the king would give him land in his kingdom, and in return he would join forces with the king. The king was all in favour of this idea, and that is what happened. When Pedro Carrillo had been there for a few days without coming to any harm, he tried to find a way to rescue Doña Juana, who had been imprisoned ever since the king had taken the town of Toro,[43] and take her back to her

---

[43] In Chapter 17 above.

husband, Count Enrique. Indeed, he did rescue her, and this is how the count got his wife back. King Pedro was very angry when he found out that she had been rescued in this way.

Chapter 20

How King Pedro had his brother Don Fadrique, the Master of Santiago, put to death in the alcazar of Seville

If it is said that the person who harms another person has his action inscribed in dust, and that the victim has his inscribed in marble, then this was certainly true in the case of King Pedro.

The king was driven by an overwhelming rage against his brothers and other subjects of his kingdom who had supported the cause of Queen Blanche, and opposed that of Doña María de Padilla's family, as you have heard. Indeed, these events had already taken place more than three years before, as it was by this time 1358. Now, whilst staying in Seville, he decided to have his brother, Don Fadrique, killed. When Don Fadrique was on his way back from war, after taking the town of Jumilla, in the kingdom of Murcia, in his brother's service, the king summoned him.

On the day that Don Fadrique was due to arrive in the town, the king sent for his cousin, Prince Joan. After making him swear on the Cross and the Gospels, he told him that he wished to have Don Fadrique killed, and asked for his help in the matter, saying he would see that he was well rewarded. He added that after the death of the Master of Santiago he planned to go to Vizcaya to kill his other brother, Don Tello, and then he would give him his lands. Prince Joan replied by saying he felt greatly honoured that King Pedro saw fit to confide his secrets to him, adding that he was happy to carry out what the king had in mind.

Accordingly, on Tuesday, 29 May, Don Fadrique arrived late in the morning. The moment he arrived he went to see the king, who was in the alcazar, playing backgammon. He kissed the king's hand, and several other knights did the same. The king gave him a warm welcome and treated him in a friendly manner, asking him where he had travelled from and enquiring about his lodgings. The master replied that he had set out from Cantillana, about 5 leagues away and said that he thought the lodgings would be satisfactory. As quite a lot of men had entered with Don Fadrique, the king told him to go to his quarters and settle in, and to come back and join him later.

The master left and went to see Doña María de Padilla and his nieces, who were in another part of the palace. He then went out into the yard where he had left the horses, but there were none to be seen there, because the guards had been instructed to take them away. While Don Fadrique was wondering if he should go back to the king or what he ought to do, one of his men, suspecting that such an action did not bode well, advised him to escape through the wicket-gate in the yard, which was open, as once he was out there he would find plenty of horses.

While he was deciding what he should do, someone came and told him that the king wished to speak to him. He therefore set off to see the king, but he was suspicious and felt frightened. As he made his way through the doors of the halls and state rooms, the people accompanying him were dwindling in number, so that when he finally reached the part of the castle where the king was, there was nobody else accompanying him but the Master of Calatrava.[44] They both stood outside the door, but no one opened it to let them in. Although all these signs were a presage of death, knowing that he had done nothing he could be blamed for, the Master of Santiago managed to summon up a degree of courage.

At this point someone opened the door of the room where the king was and he ordered the chief crossbowman, Pedro López de Padilla, to seize the master. 'Which one, Sire?' he asked, to which the king replied, 'The Master of Santiago'. Pedro López then laid hands on the master, saying, 'You're under arrest'. The master was terrified but, when he heard the king repeat the order of execution to the crossbowmen, who were bearing maces, he managed to break free from Pedro López, who was holding him, and ran out into the courtyard. He tried to unsheathe his sword, which he was carrying suspended from his neck. But as bad luck would have it, he could not manage to do this, because the tabard he was wearing got in the way. As he darted swiftly this way and that, the crossbowmen were unable to reach him with their maces, but finally they managed to strike him, and he fell to the ground apparently dead.

When the king saw the master lying on the ground, he searched all over the alcazar, hoping to find some of the master's men in order to slay them. He did not find any, however, as they had fled and gone into hiding. In the chamber where María de Padilla was he found Sancho Rodríguez de Villegas, the master's chief chamberlain, who had sought refuge there when he heard that they were killing him. He seized Princess Beatriz, the king's daughter, hoping to escape with his life by so doing. But the king forced him to let her

---

[44] Diego García de Padilla, brother of María de Padilla. He was appointed by Pedro I of Castile, against the will of many members of this military order and ruled from 1355 to 1365.

go and struck him dead with a club he was carrying. He then returned to the place where the master was lying and, when he saw that he was not quite dead, he ordered one of his attendants of the bedchamber to kill him; then he went and sat down to eat.

On that very same day he issued the order for the following people also to be put to death: in Córdoba, Pero Cabrera, a knight who lived there, and a juror by the name of Fernán Alfonso de Gahete; he ordered the death of Don Lope Sánchez de Bendaña, Grand Commander of Castile; and, in Salamanca, they killed Alfonso Jofré Tenorio, in Toro, Alfonso Pérez Fermosino and in Mora, Gonzalo Menéndez de Toledo. The king declared that he was ordering these men to be put to death because they had been allies of Queen Blanche. Moreover, although the king had previously pardoned them, he ordered them all to be beheaded, regardless of his promises.

Chapter 21

How the king departed from Seville to seize his brother, Don Tello, intending to kill him, and how he killed his cousin, Prince Joan

Whilst the king was still eating, he sent for his cousin, Prince Joan, and told him in secret that, as soon as he finished his meal, he wished to leave for Vizcaya in order to kill his brother Don Tello, and that he wanted Prince Joan to go with him because he would then hand over that land to him. In spite of the fact that he was married to Doña Isabel, the sister of Don Tello's wife, the prince was very pleased to hear this and kissed the king's hands in gratitude, not suspecting in the least what the king's intentions towards him were.

The king left forthwith, accompanied by the prince, and in seven days he reached Aguilar de Campóo, where Don Tello was staying. On that day Don Tello was out hunting and, when one of his squires saw the king, he went immediately to warn his master, who fled the minute he heard this news and reached Bermeo, a town on the coast which belonged to him. He boarded a pinnace[45] that belonged to some fishermen and headed for Bayonne, an English possession. Eager to catch Don Tello, the king followed the route he had taken.

---

[45] A small boat, typically with sails or several oars, often forming part of the equipment of a warship or other large vessel. See Ian Friel, *The Good Ship: Ships, Shipbuilding and Technology in England, 1200–1520* (Baltimore, MD: The Johns Hopkins University Press, 1995), p. 143.

The day that Don Tello arrived in Bermeo and took to sea was the same day that the king arrived there and boarded another boat, in the hope of catching up with him. The sea was quite rough, which made the king angry, and he stopped pursuing Don Tello, as he was a good distance ahead. The king returned to land and seized Don Tello's wife, Doña Juana.

When Prince Joan learnt that Don Tello had escaped in this way, he reminded the king of what he had said in Seville about his plans to have Don Tello killed and then hand over Vizcaya, Don Tello's land, to him. Therefore, he said, as Don Tello had fled the kingdom in exile without his permission, the king should now honour his promise and give the land of Vizcaya to him. The king replied that he would order the Vizcayans to assemble in their customary manner and that he would go there himself and command them to accept the prince as their liege lord. At this, the prince kissed both the king's hands, well pleased and full of gratitude as he was at the prospect of acquiring the land.

When the Vizcayans came to assemble in their usual place, the king consulted with their leaders and told them in secret that, when he spoke of his intention of giving the land to Prince Joan, they should reply by saying that they would accept no one but the king as their liege lord. They agreed to do as he wished.

With more than 10,000 Vizcayans gathered together, the king pleaded the case of his cousin, the prince, at some length, making the point that the land of Vizcaya did belong to him by right, as a result of his marriage,[46] and he begged them, even ordered them, to accept the prince as their master. But they replied that they would never accept any other liege lord but the King of Castile, and that nothing would make them change their minds. The king then said to the prince that he could see for himself what these people wanted, and that they certainly had no wish to have him as their liege lord. He would, however, go to Bilbao and speak again to the Vizcayans to try to persuade them to accept the prince as their lord.

The prince began to realize that all this was a trick on the part of the king and became distressed. Once the king reached Bilbao he sent for the prince the following day. He arrived there and entered the chamber unaccompanied, though two of his men remained by the door. Then the men who were party to the plot to kill him began to tease him, trying to remove a small dagger that he had with him, and in this they succeeded. Martin López, the king's lord chamberlain, put his arms round the prince firmly, a crossbowman struck

---

[46] Prince Joan was married to Doña Isabel de Lara, the daughter of Don Juan Núñez de Lara, who had become the Lord of Vizcaya via his marriage to Doña María Díaz de Haro. Doña Juana, the wife of Don Tello, was Doña Isabel's sister.

him on the head with a mace, and others followed suit, with the result that he fell down dead.

This incident took place on a Tuesday, two weeks after Don Fadrique had been killed in Seville. The king ordered the prince's body to be thrown from a window of the house where he was staying and declared to the assembled crowd of Vizcayans, 'Here's your Lord of Vizcaya, who wanted you to be his subjects!' Then, immediately afterwards, the king commanded Juan Fernández de Henestrosa to travel to Roa, where his aunt, the Queen of Aragon, who was the prince's mother, and his wife, Doña Isabel, were at the time, the mother knowing nothing of her son's fate and the wife knowing nothing of her husband's.

The ladies were taken as prisoners and the very next day, the king arrived at Roa. He ordered all their possessions to be seized and imprisoned them in Castrojeriz. Then he left and made for Burgos, where he stayed about a week. While he was there he took delivery of the heads of the men he had put to death all over the kingdom, after the murder of the Master of Santiago, Don Fadrique, which you have heard about.

Chapter 22

How the year-long truce between the kings came to be broken, and how King Pedro assembled a fleet to wage war on Aragon

We have told you about the deaths of the Master Don Fadrique and Prince Joan, which you have just heard about, not because we take any pleasure in relating cruel deeds. Rather, we have presented them at some length and in greater detail than the deaths of others, because they were very important people, and in order to enable you to see exactly how the king had them killed.

For this reason, although the year's truce that the cardinal had brought about between King Pedro [of Castile] and the King of Aragon was still in force, when Count Enrique heard about the death of his brother, Don Fadrique, and when Prince Ferran, the Marquis of Tortosa, was told of the death of his brother, Prince Joan, they decided to join forces and entered Castile.

The count entered via Soria and arrived at the town of Serón, which he plundered; he then made an assault on the castle of Alcázar, with a view to seizing it.[47] Then he returned to Aragon. As for Prince Ferran, he entered via

---

[47] Pero López de Ayala, Lopes's main source for Castilian history, tells us that

the kingdom of Murcia and caused severe damage there. The king learnt of this while he was in Valladolid and immediately sent troops to protect the borders with Aragon. Then he went to Seville where he ordered twelve galleys to be built post-haste for war. While this was being done, six Genoese galleys arrived (the Genoese were at the time at war against the Catalans). The king was delighted to see these and commissioned them for 1,000 crossed *doblas* each per month.

With these eighteen galleys the king duly arrived at a town called Guardamar, which belonged to Prince Ferran, and on the morning of 17 August he ordered a substantial number of troops to leave the galleys and attack the town. He took it by force, even though it was well protected by its ramparts, and many of the townspeople took refuge in the castle.

Then, about midday, amidst all the fighting, as frequently happens in this region, a mighty onshore wind began to rage.[48] As the galleys were unmanned the wind blew them all ashore. Only two escaped this fate because they were further out to sea, one belonging to the king and one to the Genoese. The king ordered the sixteen other vessels to be burnt as it would be impossible to repair them. Very little in the way of oars and other equipment could be salvaged, and this was put in a *nao* from Laredo which happened to be there.

The king and the patrons of the galleys left on horses belonging to the soldiers of Gutierre Gómez de Toledo, who had arrived there himself, along with a number of others, to lend them support, with 600 men on horseback. The king rode away, extremely distressed by this most unfortunate event, whilst the sailors from the galleys followed on foot, very dejected.

The king reached Murcia, and the Genoese took ship to their own land, sailing from Cartagena. Immediately the king gave the order for more galleys to be built with all haste in Seville, and in eight months twelve new galleys had been constructed. Fifteen others, which had been in the dockyards, were repaired. He also ordered many weapons to be made and a large arsenal to be built, and he ordered all the ships in the kingdom to be given instructions not to convey any cargoes anywhere. The king then departed from Murcia and, returning to the Aragonese border, seized several castles in Aragon before travelling back to Seville. This was the fourth raid King Pedro made into Aragon.

---

the count did not succeed in seizing Alcázar. See *Cronica de Don Pedro Primero*, ed. José-Luis Martín (Barcelona, 1991), Year 9, ch. 8, p. 196.

[48] The town of Guardamar, located on the coast to the east of Murcia, is regularly battered by the east wind.

Chapter 23

How the Cardinal of Boulogne came to make peace between the King of Castile and the King of Aragon but could not get them to agree

While the King of Castile was in Seville he learned that Cardinal Guy of Boulogne was in the town of Almazán in order to make peace between him and the King of Aragon. The cardinal sent to ask the king if he wanted him to come to his presence in Seville or if he should wait where he was (if the king by chance happened to be coming to that region). The king had already left Seville for the Aragonese frontier when this message reached him in Villa Real; he said that he was very pleased at the cardinal's arrival and asked to meet him in Almazán to which he was directly headed.

Thus it was that the king arrived there after a few days, and the cardinal told him in the presence of his Royal Council all that the Pope had asked him to say concerning his grief over the war between him and the King of Aragon, and about the pleasure he would feel to see them at peace. The king answered that the war with the King of Aragon was very much the latter's fault. He told the cardinal what had happened with the captain of the Aragonese galleys at the mouth of the Barrameda (as you have heard),[49] and how he had complained to the King of Aragon who had never dealt with it as he ought to have done and had asked all the King of Castile's enemies in France to wage war on him.

The cardinal said he wanted to go and speak to the King of Aragon about this. The King of Castile said that this would please him and that he would gladly make peace, as long as the King of Aragon did the following: firstly, he should hand over the knight [who had been involved in the Barrameda incident], so that justice could be done to him where he, the King of Castile, wished it; secondly, the King of Aragon should expel his own brother Prince Ferran, the Marquis of Tortosa, as well as Count Enrique and all the others who had come to help in the war; thirdly, he should hand over the castles of Orihuela and Alicante, as well as other places that had formerly belonged to Castile; and finally, he should pay the 500,000 florins that the war had cost him.

Although the cardinal thought these demands were unreasonable, he said it would be his duty and pleasure to go and speak to the King of Aragon about them. He arrived in Aragon and told the king in detail all the things that the King of Castile had said. The King of Aragon replied in the following way:

---

[49] In Chapter 18 above.

Eminence, my friend, you can see that if he really desired to make peace with me he would not demand the things he sent you to require from me. As for the knight, it is not right for me to hand him over to be summarily executed, because he does not deserve it. But this is what I will do: let him charge the man legally and, if it is found that he deserves death, I will hand him over as a prisoner so that he can be executed in Castile.

As for what he says about expelling from my kingdom his brothers and enemies Count Enrique, Don Tello and Don Sancho, I declare that I will be pleased to do this if we reach an agreement. However, to exile my own legitimate brother Prince Ferran from the kingdom seems a strange thing to ask.

About the places he requires me to hand back to him, I see no reason to do it, as they were judged to belong to Aragon by decree of King Dinis of Portugal and Prince Juan of Castile[50] in the presence of many nobles of his kingdom; both he and I have documents proving how they were partitioned.

I am not bound to pay him the costs that he has incurred in waging war because it was not my wish to go to war; rather, it troubled me and still troubles me to have such discord between us. This is what I will do for him if we make peace: if he finds himself at war with the Emir of Granada or with the Marinids of Morocco, I am willing to offer ten galleys for six years armed for four whole months at my expense and, if the Moors invade and it suits him to go into battle, I will offer myself and my men to be with him on the day of the battle. If he does not accept these terms, tell him that I entreat him on behalf of God not to wage war on me because he does not have a just cause. If he acts differently, I leave all to the command and justice of God.

The cardinal returned to the King of Castile and told him what you have just heard. The king started to complain, saying that the King of Aragon did not respect the war nor did he want to reach an agreement with him, but that this time it would be proven how much each of them was worth. However, so that the King of Aragon would understand how much he wanted to have peace, he would ignore all the other things he had demanded as long as the King of Aragon handed over the five places that he had requested and expelled his brothers and the people with them from his kingdom.

The cardinal was very happy with this, believing that, as the king had given up on what he had at first said, he might succeed in brokering a treaty. He went to Calatayud, where the King of Aragon was to be found and told him how, in the interests of peace, the King of Castile only wanted those two things.

The King of Aragon consulted his Royal Council and declared that all the people and troops mentioned would be expelled, but that he did not intend to

---

[50] Son of Alfonso X and brother to Sancho IV.

give up a single town or castle belonging to his kingdom. He added that the King of Castile should be perfectly content with his first answer.

When the cardinal returned with this message, King Pedro was very angry, declaring that all this was just to distract him from preparing his fleet. He begged the cardinal to excuse him but he did not intend to say more about this and would continue to wage war as much as he could. This answer troubled the cardinal a great deal but, unable to do anything else, he said no more about it. Infuriated, the king then wanted to take some immediate form of revenge and passed sentence on his cousin Prince Ferran, on Count Enrique and on many other knights, which made them his enemies once and for all. Indeed, the worst part was that he ordered the murders of his aunt Queen Leonor, the mother of Prince Ferran, and of Doña Juana de Lara, the wife of his brother, Don Tello. In this his wish was fulfilled, but it did not bring him much benefit. After issuing these and other commands, he posted officers of the marches on the border with Aragon and left Almazán for Seville.

Chapter 24

How the King of Castile asked for help in the form of galleys from the King of Portugal and then left with his fleet to make war on Aragon

The King of Castile, being in such disagreement with the King of Aragon in the year 1359, was keen to build a great armada with which to attack his kingdom. Although he had quite a big fleet, comprising both *naos* and galleys, he was not yet satisfied with it. Consequently, he sent his lord chamberlain Juan Fernández de Henestrosa to his uncle the King of Portugal to ask that the ten galleys which he had been promised in aid against Aragon be made ready, as he was in great need of them.

The King of Portugal was happy to do this and immediately ordered ten galleys and a galliot[51] to be equipped with good men, with his admiral Master Lançarote on board. When the King of Castile received word that the ten Portuguese galleys were ready, he left Seville in the middle of the month of April with his whole armada made up of eighty *naos* with forecastle, twenty-eight galleys of his own, two galliots and four smaller vessels, plus

---

[51] A smaller galley.

three galleys belonging to the Emir of Granada, which he had sent in aid at the king's request.

The king waited for the Portuguese galleys in Algeciras for fifteen days, but when he saw they were not coming, he left for Cartagena and waited there for all his ships to arrive. He then attacked Guardamar, taking the town and the castle. From there he made his way along the coast, attacking a number of places, but without success. He arrived at the River Ebro near Tortosa, a town belonging to Aragon, where the ten Portuguese galleys also arrived, sent in aid by his uncle the King of Portugal. The King of Castile and his whole fleet were very pleased at this. The king then had in total forty-one galleys, as well as the small foists.[52]

The king left there with the whole armada and arrived on the eve of Easter[53] at Barcelona where the King of Aragon was living. There were twelve armed galleys there that could not be captured because they were positioned alongside the city, from where they were defended with many crossbows and cannons.[54] The king spent three days at Barcelona with his whole fleet and then went to the island of Ibiza and besieged a fine town of the same name.

Having set up his siege with engines and siege towers, he learned that the King of Aragon had forty armed galleys off the island of Majorca and was keen to fight him. When the King of Castile heard this, he said that it was not worthwhile to remain on land or to bother with the siege of Ibiza, since the whole war would be decided in the coming [sea] battle in which both kings were going to be present.

The king immediately had all his people brought back to the fleet and he himself boarded an uxel that had belonged to the Moors and could transport forty horses under cover. He ordered three wooden castles to be built on it: one at the stern, one in the bows and one amidships, and put on board 160 men-at-arms and 120 crossbowmen.

The king then left Ibiza with his entire fleet and reached a place known as Calpe. There his *naos* and galleys were anchored close to land behind a high rock that stands there in such a way that they could not be seen unless from close at hand.

The Aragonese galleys sailed into view about 2 leagues further out to sea. There were forty of them but no other vessels. The King of Aragon was not with them; he had remained in Majorca because his advisers had not wanted

---

[52] A light galley with the oars in close pairs, but which could also have sails. See Björn Landström, *The Ship* (London: Allen & Unwin, 1976) p. 127.

[53] That is to say, on Holy Saturday.

[54] Cannons and other artillery devices were already being used in Europe since the 1330s.

him to be present. The galleys could not see the Castilian fleet owing to the great rock that hid them. They sailed in the following order: in the middle were two large galleys with castles made for fighting, in one of which was the Count of Cardona, whilst in the other was Bernat de Cabrera, the Admiral of Aragon; in the vanguard there were two galleys a considerable distance ahead of the others with many foot soldiers and horsemen following on land to help in the fight if necessary.

When the two leading galleys saw the Castilian *naos* and their whole fleet, they furled their sails and took up their oars. On seeing this, all the others immediately did the same so that they could manoeuvre more easily. However, once aware of the [Castilian] ships, they feared them so much that they dared not attack at sea, and all of them entered the River Denia that evening at the hour of vespers.

Straightaway King Pedro made sure that all his troops were ready, expecting to have to fight a battle the next day. However, there was so little wind that they could not use the *naos*, and, having consulted his advisers, whose opinions varied, he decided that, since the enemy's fleet lay in such a narrow river, he could not fight them; rather, he would go to Alicante to see if they were willing to fight him there. The king left with his fleet and the Aragonese galleys dashed to Calpe where the Castilian fleet had previously lain.

Chapter 25

How the Admiral of Portugal left with the ten galleys, how King Pedro disbanded his fleet, and other matters

After having spent six days at Alicante and seeing that the Aragonese fleet was not going to appear, the King of Castile left and headed back to Cartagena. There, the Admiral of Portugal told the king that his liege lord, the King of Portugal, had ordered him to attend with his ten galleys for three months, going wherever he sent him. As the three months were now up, he dared stay no longer and would not disobey his liege lord's command. The King of Castile was greatly troubled when he heard this, because he did not want the admiral to leave so suddenly, but he gave him permission to leave as he could not keep him there.

When the Portuguese galleys left, the king decided to leave the fleet and go overland to Castile. He sent all the galleys to Seville, allowed the *naos* to depart and headed for Tordesillas where Doña María de Padilla, the mother of his children, was staying. When the Aragonese galleys found out that the

King of Castile had disbanded his fleet, they did the same to thirty galleys, leaving ten to patrol the sea and attack any Portuguese or Castilian ships. Indeed, they attacked a number of ships but only small vessels.

Around this time in the month of September, Count Enrique, Don Tello his brother and a number of nobles and knights of Aragon (up to 800 horsemen) entered Castile by way of Ágreda. Don Fernando [Ruiz] de Castro, Juan Fernández de Henestrosa and others who were at the frontier bordering on the Almazán district came out to meet them with around 1,500 horsemen.

It came about that they fought a battle near Moncayo, and Don Fernando de Castro was defeated. Juan Fernández de Henestrosa was killed, as were other fine nobles, and, along with others, Íñigo López de Orozco was taken prisoner. This distressed King Pedro a great deal, and his enemies gained much encouragement from it.

That year the King of Castile ordered the deaths in Carmona (where they were prisoners) of his brothers Don Juan and Don Pedro, who were the sons of his father King Alfonso and Leonor Núñez de Guzmán. Don Pedro was fourteen years old and Don Juan was nineteen, innocent boys who never did him any harm. Everybody so hated and feared King Pedro because of these murders and of many others that you have heard about, that at the slightest excuse they left him to go to Aragon to join Count Enrique. That is what Diego Pérez Sarmiento and Pedro Fernández de Velasco did, as well as others, bringing with them many of their men.

The point was reached where the count told the King of Aragon that, if it was his wish to deploy a goodly company of soldiers, he would enter Castile with them and he believed he would not find anybody to oppose him. The king had a good mind to do this but wanted his brother Prince Ferran to lead them. Count Enrique refused, so there was no expedition on that occasion.

Chapter 26

How the Cardinal of Boulogne wanted to make peace between the kings but could not, and how King Pedro's men fought the count and defeated him

The Cardinal of Boulogne, who was in Aragon in order to reconcile these kings, saw how King Pedro had lost part of his army in the battle between Count Enrique and Don Fernando de Castro, and that some of his knights had left him to go to Aragon. He thought that for these reasons and others, he might wish to reach some kind of peace agreement with the King of

Aragon. He sent word to both kings asking them if they would like to speak further about this, and both agreed to do so. The cardinal therefore came to Tudela in the kingdom of Navarre where he met Gutierre Fernández de Toledo, who was the King of Castile's proctor, and Bernat de Cabrera, the proctor of the King of Aragon. They spent several days there but failed to come to an agreement.

Learning about this failure, King Pedro left Seville for León when he was told that Count Enrique, Don Tello and some Aragonese lords were joining together to invade Castile. From there he left for Valladolid, knowing that these troops had already entered his kingdom, had killed the Jews of Nájera and other places, and were pillaging the Jewish quarters of these towns.

The count arrived at Pancorbo, staying there for some days, and afterwards left for Nájera. The king went there with his forces and camped in a place called Azofra. A cleric from Santo Domingo de la Calzada came to him there and told him that Saint Dominic had appeared to him in dreams telling him to tell the king to be sure that if he did not guard himself against Count Enrique, the latter would kill him with his own hand. The king believed that the cleric had been persuaded to say this by others, but though the cleric denied it, the king had him burnt in his very presence.

The king left on a Friday for Nájera where the count was to be found outside the town with 800 horsemen and 2,000 foot soldiers, having ordered his tent and a banner to be placed before the town on a hill. The king's vanguard fought the count and defeated him, taking the tent and banner and killing part of his army. The king left in the evening for Azofra where his camp lay.

The next day, on his way to fight the count at Nájera, the king met a squire who was mourning for an uncle whom they had killed. The king took it as an ill omen and decided not to continue, returning to Santo Domingo de la Calzada. He was told there, two days later, that the count had left for Aragon, taking the Navarre road. The king had wanted to follow him, but the cardinal advised him against it for it was quite enough that they had abandoned his towns and left. The king ordered his men to halt and from there he assigned his officers of the marches to the appropriate locations before leaving for Seville.

While he was there he learned how an Aragonese knight called Mateu Mercer was patrolling the sea with four galleys, attacking Castilian and Portuguese ships. The king armed five galleys and sent one of his crossbowmen called Zorzo from Tartary with orders to take them and go in search of the pirate. He found him off the Barbary Coast, where he fought and overwhelmed him, bringing his galleys and him as prisoner back to Seville. The king commanded that the pirate and many who were with him be put to death.

But now let us leave the king in Seville killing and imprisoning people, of whom we shall speak later, and let us mention a number of other things that happened in Portugal that year, and that we think you should know about.

Chapter 27

How King Pedro of Portugal said that Dona Inês had been his acknowledged wife, and the manner in which the marriage took place

You have already heard at length, when we spoke of the death of Dona Inês,[55] the reason why King Afonso had her killed and the great conflict that it caused between him and King Pedro, then still a prince. It so happens that never, prior to this point in time, while Dona Inês was alive, nor after her death, nor during his father's reign, nor after he himself became king, did King Pedro name her as his wife. Rather, it is said that King Afonso often sent someone to ask him if he had married her, for in that case he would honour her as his son's wife, and he had always answered that he had not done so and that she was not his wife.

About four years after becoming king, while staying at Cantanhede in the month of June, the king decided to announce publicly that she had indeed been his wife. Present before him were Dom João Afonso, who was the Count of Barcelos his chief steward; Vasco Martins de Sousa, his chancellor; Master Afonso das Leis and João Esteves, his counsellors; Martim Vasques, the Lord of Góis; Gonçalo Mendes de Vasconcelos and his brother, João Mendes; Álvaro Pereira and Gonçalo Pereira; Diogo Gomes and Vasco Gomes de Abreu; and many others whom we do not care to mention. The king then summoned a notary and before all of them swore to the truth of the following, while touching the Gospels.

Around seven years earlier more or less, his father being still alive and he a prince (though he was unable to remember the exact day and month), while staying in Bragança, he had taken as his legitimate wife by *verba de praesenti*,[56] as Holy Church commands, Dona Inês de Castro, the daughter of Don Pedro Fernández de Castro. Dona Inês had in turn taken him as her husband using similar words. After the ceremony he always viewed her as

---

[55] Dona Inês died in 1355. Lopes must have dealt with this in his chronicle of Afonso IV (1291–1357). See note 2 of the Prologue about this chronicle.

[56] That is, by mutual declaration of assent before witnesses.

his wife until the time of her death, living together with her and behaving as a married couple should.

King Pedro then added that since this marriage was neither publicized nor made known to his whole household during the life of his father, owing to the fear and anxiety he caused him, he now wished to unburden his conscience and tell the truth. In order that there could be no doubt in the eyes of those who were suspicious about whether the marriage really had taken place, he was bearing faithful and truthful witness that what he had said had truly happened.[57] He ordered the notary who was present to provide documentation of what he had said to any person who asked for it. Nothing more was done at that time.

Chapter 28

Concerning the testimony given by a number of people about the marriage of Dona Inês and concerning the arguments delivered by Count João Afonso in that regard

Three days after this took place Dom João Afonso, who was the Count of Barcelos, Vasco Martins de Sousa and Master Afonso das Leis arrived in Coimbra. In the palace where canon law was studied, the university being in this city at that time, they called two witnesses into the presence of a notary: Dom Gil, who was then the Bishop of Guarda, and Estêvão Lobato, a *criado* of the king. They were told that having sworn on the Gospels they were to speak truthfully about the marriage between King Pedro and Dona Inês.

Each witness was questioned separately. The bishop said first that, while travelling with Dom Pedro and Dona Inês, and being then the Dean of Guarda and the king still a prince, in the town of Bragança the prince summoned him one day to his chamber, Dona Inês also being there. Dom Pedro told him that he wanted to take her as his wife. Without further delay the said lord placed his hand in the dean's hands, as did Dona Inês, and he married them both by *verba de praesenti* as Holy Church commands. He also said that he saw them live afterwards as man and wife until Dona Inês's death, and that these

---

[57] While discussing the text with the translators, Teresa Amado noted the similarity between the reported words of the king in this chapter and those of Count João Afonso in the next, 'dramatised' in direct speech, considering this an obvious indication that Fernão Lopes used the same documentary source. See also *CKJ1*, Chapter 186, especially the words of João das Regras referring back to King Pedro's public statement.

events could have taken place around seven years previously more or less, but he did not remember which day or month. More about this he did not say.

Similarly, Estêvão Lobato was questioned. He said that the king, while still a prince and during a stay in Bragança, summoned him to his chamber and told him that he had called him because he wished to marry Dona Inês, who was present, and he would like him to be a witness. The Dean of Guarda was already there and, nobody else being present, he took the said lord by one hand and her by another, and married them with those words that are customary at such weddings. He added that he saw them live together until the time of her death. Finally, he said that this happened on the first day of January about seven years earlier, more or less.

As soon as they had been questioned and what they said had been recorded in writing, according to what you have just heard, Dom Lourenço the Bishop of Lisbon, Dom Afonso the Bishop of Oporto, Dom João the Bishop of Viseu, and Dom Afonso the Prior of Santa Cruz in Coimbra, were brought in, having already been prepared for this earlier, along with all the nobles previously named, as well as many others whose names we shall not mention. The vicars, clergy and many other people, both laity and churchmen, were also all brought together for this occasion. Silence was called for so that everybody could hear properly. Then Count João Afonso began to speak:

> My friends, you should know that a little over seven years ago, the king who now reigns, while still a prince during the lifetime of his father King Afonso, was in the town of Bragança and took as his legitimate wife by *verba de praesenti* Dona Inês de Castro, the daughter of Pedro Fernández de Castro, and she also took him as her husband. He always afterwards held her to be his wife, living with her as married couples should until the time of her death.
>
> This ceremony and the marriage were not made public to everybody in the kingdom during the lifetime of King Afonso because of his son's fear and anxiety over marrying without his consent. For this reason, in order to unburden his soul and speak the truth to allay the doubts in some people's minds as to whether this marriage, about which they had known nothing, really happened, the king, our liege lord, swore on the Holy Gospels and bore faithful and truthful witness that it happened in the manner that I have just described. You can see an account of it in a document drawn up by Gonçalo Peres, the notary who is here present. Moreover, you can see the testimony of the Bishop of Guarda and Estêvão Lobato, who were present at the marriage and who are also here present.[58]

---

[58] See Chapter 27, note 57 above.

He then had the notary read at length the entire testimony of both men, before adding:

> It is the will of the king, our liege lord, that this should no longer be covered up. Rather, it pleases him that everybody should know about it: in order to prevent any possibility of some great doubt about this springing up again in the future, he has commanded me to inform you of all this to remove suspicion from your hearts and to make it clearly known to all.
>
> However, despite all that I have said and that has now been read out and declared to you here, some might say that all this would not be enough if there were no papal dispensation allowing them to marry, owing to the close kinship between them: Dona Inês being a niece of the king our liege lord, a daughter of his first cousin.[59]
>
> The king has, therefore, ordered me to provide you with proof by showing you this papal bull that he received while still a prince, in which the Pope gave him a dispensation so that he could marry any woman even if she were as closely related to him as Dona Inês, or indeed even more closely related.

Then a letter from Pope John XXII was read out in the presence of everyone. It proclaimed:

> Greetings and apostolic blessing from John, Bishop, servant of the servants of God, to the much beloved son in Christ Prince Pedro, the eldest son of our much beloved son in Christ, Afonso, the noble King of Portugal and the Algarve: If the rigour of Holy Canon Law places a ban and interdict on the consummation of a marriage, desiring, for the protection of public decency, that it not be done between those who are linked through some close kinship, nevertheless sometimes the Bishop of Rome, by issuing a dispensation through the absolute power that he has in God's place, can by special grace temper such rigour.
>
> Therefore, out of special favour to you, we are persuaded by reasons that we hope will henceforth bring peace and harmony to those kingdoms, just as we are desirous of yielding to requests from you and your father King Afonso, who in his letters to us humbly supplicated on your behalf that you be allowed to marry legally any noble woman whose devotion was to the Holy Church of Rome whom you would join in marriage, even if laterally related in the second degree on one side and in the third degree on the other, and even if barred by kinship or marriage to the fourth degree owing to two other collateral lines.
>
> Accordingly, with the special grace of our apostolic authority, we remove and take away all these impediments, dispensing you and any woman whom

---

[59] The word 'sobrinha', as in the original Portuguese, often refers to the daughter of a cousin, not necessarily a niece as it is understood today.

you thus marry by our apostolic power, so that the children born to you both shall be legitimate without further impediment. May no man therefore dare, in his presumption, to go against this our dispensation. If any man so do, may he be sure to incur the anger and wrath of Almighty God and the blessed apostles, Saints Peter and Paul.

Dated in Avignon, on the 12th Kalends of March, in the ninth year of our pontificate.

After this letter had been read out, the count declared in everyone's presence that for their protection and in the name of Prince João, Prince Dinis and Princess Beatriz, who were the children of the said noble couple, he wanted documents to be drawn up for each of them and required the notary to deliver them. They all then left for their lodgings, none of them lacking reasons to go on talking about this story.

Chapter 29

Reasons against the foregoing advanced by a number of those who were there and who doubted this marriage very much

After the arguments you have heard, given in the presence of men of learning as well as of many common people, those of poor and simple understanding easily believed it and decided that all they had heard was the truth, as they were not able to unravel the thread of such an intricate story. Others, who were more sophisticated in their understanding, educated and very discerning, scrutinized the facts minutely to see if what they had heard could be true or not, and found them mentally unacceptable, thinking it was totally against reason.

Whether one believes something that one hears depends on one's reason and not on one's wishes. Therefore, the prudent man who hears something that his reason cannot accept will then wonder at it and become very doubtful. This is why there were plenty of people amongst those present who were not very happy with such a story, since they saw that what was presented to them had no basis in reason. If anybody wishes to ask why they thought all these things to be sheer pretence, let this question be answered by their reasons, which to us appear very clear.

Those who said the opposite to those who defended it as a true story explained themselves as follows. They argued that the Ancients, especially that shining light of philosophy, Aristotle, who wrote a brief treatise on this topic,[60] could not accept the idea that a reasonable man in good health and fully in command of his senses could be so overcome by forgetfulness that he would be unable to remember any important thing that happened in the past.

As nobody has a memory of present or future events, they therefore of necessity remember past things that have already happened. Memory is when the image of something seen or heard in the external world is always present in the capacity for remembrance. Recollection is when something done or heard has left the capacity for remembrance but is remembered again on seeing another similar thing.

Thus, if I got married, or a great favour was done to me, or I was called to a great council on a certain Easter Day, or on 1 January, or on another important day of the year, I might later forget what happened, not retaining it always in my memory, but later, being at another wedding, or at an event of the same kind as the others, which occurred on a similar day, I would then remember that I had got married on Easter Day, or that something else had happened to me, having seen something similar or being questioned about it. For it is normal that I should remember the day and the event, even if I forget how long ago it happened.

Those with doubts also said that a different way of remembering is if I got married on an Easter Day and then after some years my wife died on the same day; or I felt great joy one Christmas Day and later great grief on the same day. I would necessarily remember those initial pleasures, even if I did not remember the number of days since it took place, because the passage of time is something that does not get deposited in the memory. Yet the precise day on which such a thing happened to me would never be so erased that I could not recall it completely, because such a day is part of the essence of remembering, but the passage of time is not. Therefore, a man in full health cannot possibly forget an important event, even if he forgets the number of days since it happened, as this is fleeting and not essential to remembrance.

Consequently, they argued, how could human understanding attempt to explain that a marriage as important as this one with so many reasons for it to be remembered should have been forgotten in such a short space of time both by the man who had got married and those who had witnessed it, not remembering the day or the month? Certainly, by searching for the truth of what happened, reason cannot accept it.

---

[60] 'On Memory and Reminiscense'. See D. Bloch, *Aristotle on Memory and Recollection: Text, Translation, Interpretation and Reception in Western Scholasticism* (Leiden: Brill, 2007).

Leaving aside all the reasons for which the king should have remembered when it was: such as his decision to live with Dona Inês and the great quarrel he had with his father because of it, the long time it took him to get married, the important decision that led him to do it and the secrecy imposed on those who say they were present; leaving aside all of this, just the fact that it happened on the first day of January, the first day of the year, according to what Estêvão Lobato said, a festival, moreover, that was particularly celebrated in the prince's palace and throughout the kingdom, should have been quite enough for the day of the marriage to have been remembered, even if it had happened many years before.

Those arguing that all that they had heard seemed to be pretence also noted that, if the king had said in his testimony that he had not dared to reveal the marriage in his father's lifetime, owing to the fear and anxiety he caused him, who, then, prevented him after his father's death from proclaiming it immediately, seeing that he was free to do so, if he wanted so much for it to be known?

They said that it seemed to be like the case of King Pedro of Castile. That king had ordered his wife, Queen Blanche, to be slain in the lifetime of Doña María de Padilla, whom he kept as his mistress, but while Doña María lived he was never heard to say that she was his wife. After she died he declared publicly at *Cortes*[61] held in Seville that he had married her before he had married Queen Blanche, naming four witnesses who were present, who at once swore under oath that it had happened as he had said. From then on he commanded them to call her queen, even though she had already died, and to call their children princes and princesses. He made them all pay immediate homage to a son of theirs called Don Alfonso and ordered them to adopt him as their king after his death.

Nevertheless, those who thus talked secretly among themselves about these and other questions, said that the truth, which does not seek to hide, was greatly concealed in this event. Since understanding is always predisposed to obey reason, many who heard these things stopped believing what they had believed before and adhered to the arguments advanced here.

However, it is not up to us to determine whether what they said happened or not. All we wanted to do was to note briefly what the Ancients said in their writings, including here some of their reasoning, leaving it up to the readers of these words to choose whichever opinion they want to follow.

[61] A consultative assembly in which the towns were represented and which by the 19th century was to evolve into a parliament.

Chapter 30

How the Kings of Portugal and Castile agreed to hand over to each other several people who thought they were living in safety in their kingdoms

Since it is said that the principal fruit of the soul is truth, by which all things should be firmly set – and which has to be clear and without pretence, especially in kings and great lords, in whom any virtue shines most brightly, or its opposite seems most ugly – people were appalled by the much abhorred exchange that took place this year [1360] between the Kings of Portugal and Castile. It was so appalling that, although we have found it written that the King of Portugal was true to everyone, we intend to praise him no longer because he consented against his sworn word to such an ugly thing as this.

It happened, as we have said, that after the murder of Dona Inês, whom King Afonso, the father of King Pedro, ordered to be killed in Coimbra while the latter was a prince, the prince greatly blamed Diogo Lopes Pacheco, Pero Coelho and Álvaro Gonçalves, his chief bailiff. He blamed many others too but was most determined in his bitterness against these three.

To speak the truth, Álvaro Gonçalves and Pero Coelho were very much guilty of this deed, but Diogo Lopes was not because he tried to warn the prince many times, through his counsellor Gonçalo Vasques, that he should protect that woman against the wrath of his father. Yet afterwards the king and his son reached an agreement, the prince pardoning these men and others whom he suspected, and the king likewise waiving all complaints that he had against the prince's men. Great oaths and promises were made about this, as you have heard at length.[62]

Thus, Diogo Lopes and the others lived in safety in the kingdom for as long as King Afonso lived. While the king was sick in Lisbon from his final illness, he called for Diogo Lopes Pacheco and the others to come to him and told them that he knew that Prince Pedro his son harboured ill will towards them despite the oaths and the pardon that he had granted and of which they were well aware. He said that, as he felt himself to be closer to death than to life, they ought to place themselves in safety outside the kingdom because he no longer had any time left to be able to defend them against his son, should he want to do them harm.

They immediately left Lisbon and went to Castile, Prince Pedro then being out hunting on the southern side of the Tagus on a riverbank known as Canha which is 8 leagues from the city. The King of Castile received them well,

---

[62] See Prologue, note 2 above.

and they received grace and favour from him, living in his kingdom safely and without fear.

After King Pedro ascended the throne he issued a sentence of treason against them, saying that they had done things against him and his estate that they ought not to have done. He granted the possessions of Pero Coelho to Vasco Martins de Sousa, a rich noble and his chancellor of the great seal, and those of Álvaro Gonçalves and Diogo Lopes to other people as he saw fit. The king created so many grants out of these possessions and divided others into so many parcels that after he died those to whom they had belonged could never manage to retrieve them or recover them from those to whom they had been given.

Similarly, at this time, the following [nobles] fled from Castile, out of fear of their king, who had ordered them to be killed: Don Pedro Núñez de Guzmán, who was the Chief Provincial Governor of León,[63] Men Rodríguez Tenorio, Fernán Gudiel de Toledo and Fernán Sánchez Calderón. These Castilians lived in Portugal in the favour of King Pedro, believing there to be no danger, just as the [fugitive] Portuguese in Castile did, because confidence, founded in reason, had driven them to find hazardous shelter with the guarantee of security.

The kings, however, did not honour such confidence, secretly making an agreement that the King of Portugal would hand over as prisoners to the King of Castile the nobles who lived in his kingdom, and that he in turn would hand over Diogo Lopes and both the other men who were living in Castile. They ordered that they would all be taken as prisoners on the same day so that their capture would not be a warning to the others, and that those who brought the Castilian prisoners to the borders of Portugal would receive the Portuguese captives brought from Castile.

Chapter 31

How Diogo Lopes Pacheco avoided being captured, and how the others were handed over and forthwith cruelly put to death

After this agreement had been reached in the way that we have described, the nobles whom we have mentioned were captured in Portugal. On the very day when the order of the King of Castile for the arrest of Diogo Lopes

---

[63] The former kingdom of León had been finally united with Castile in the year 1230.

and the others reached the town where they were to be found, it so happened that very early that morning Diogo Lopes had gone out to hunt partridges. Pero Coelho and Álvaro Gonçalves were both arrested, but when they went to fetch Diogo Lopes it was discovered that he was no longer there and had gone out hunting that morning. The gates of the town were shut lest anyone should try to send a message to warn him, and the guards then waited in order to arrest him on his return.

There was a lame beggar to whom Diogo Lopes was always charitable in his home at mealtimes and who sometimes shared a joke with him: aware of the steps that were being taken, he decided to warn him on his way back before he reached the town. He secretly found out the direction that Diogo Lopes had taken. Approaching the guards at the gates, he asked their permission to go out. Failing to suspect such a man, they opened the gates and let him through. He walked as far as he could in the direction in which he thought Diogo Lopes would be returning and found him already on his way back, along with his squires, quite unaware of the news that the pauper was bringing.

When the beggar told him that he wished to speak with him, Diogo Lopes showed no inclination to listen, little suspecting that he was bringing such a message. Nevertheless, the beggar insisted that he should hear what he had to say and told him privately that the King of Castile had sent a large detachment of guards who, having captured the other two, had arrived at his palace to capture him also. He also told him how the gates of the town were guarded to prevent anyone from getting out to warn him. On hearing this, Diogo Lopes fully grasped the situation: gripped by the fear of death, he fell into deep thought. Seeing him in such a state, the beggar then added: 'Take my advice: it will be to your advantage. Separate yourself from your people and come with me to a valley not far from here. Once there, I'll tell you how you can get to safety.'

Diogo Lopes then told his squires to carry on hunting nearby, for he wished to go with the pauper to a valley where the latter had told him that many partridges were to be found. His men did as he asked, while the two of them made their way to the valley. Once there, the pauper told him that, if he wanted to escape, he should put on his own tattered garments and make his way on foot, as fast as he could, as far as the road to Aragon. Then he should seek employment from the very first muleteers[64] that he would meet and should accompany them on their way back home. Either this way, or clad in a friar's habit, if he were able later to acquire one, he should seek safety in Aragon because he was bound to be hunted in Castile.

---

[64] These would be muleteers heading back to Aragon.

Diogo Lopes took his advice and set off on foot. The pauper, meanwhile, avoided returning immediately to the town. Diogo Lopes's squires waited for him for a long time but, as he failed to come back, they set off looking for him in the direction that he had taken. On searching for him they came upon his horse wandering on its own. Thinking that he must have fallen off it or that it had bolted away from him, they looked for him even more carefully. The delay caused by this took so long that night was coming on. Realizing that they would not be able to find him, they took his horse and returned to the town, not knowing what to think about these events.

When they reached the town, having spotted how the guards were lying in wait for him and then learning of the arrest of the other two, they were very frightened, realizing that he had fled. On being questioned about him, they stated that while hunting on his own he lost track of them, and that when they had gone to look for him they had found only his horse; the search had occupied them until then, and they did not know what to think, save that he must be lying dead somewhere. Those who had been charged with his capture set out looking for him in various townships. As to what happened to him on his way, how he reached Aragon and went onward to France to join Count Enrique, how the latter had him steal precious metals from Avignon, and other events that befell him, we shall not dwell thereon any further, as that is not our concern.

When the King of Castile learned that Diogo Lopes had not been captured, he was very angry but could do nothing further. He then sent Álvaro Gonçalves and Pero Coelho, captive under strong guard, to his uncle, the King of Portugal, as had been agreed between them. When they reached the frontier, there they found Men Rodríguez Tenorio and the other Castilians whom King Pedro was sending [to the King of Castile]. It was there, said Diogo Lopes, when relating this episode later, that donkeys for donkeys were exchanged. These nobles were taken to Seville, where the King [of Castile] was at that time, and there they were all put to death.

Álvaro Gonçalves and Pero Coelho were brought to Portugal and arrived at Santarém, where King Pedro was at the time. Pleased at their arrival, though troubled by the flight of Diogo Lopes, the king went out to meet them and in a cruel and pitiless rage he tortured them by his own hand, seeking to get them to confess the names of those guilty of the death of Dona Inês and to disclose what his own father had plotted against him when they were at odds because of her death. Neither of them replied to the king's questions with an answer that could satisfy him. It is said that in his anger he struck Pero Coelho across the face with his whip; the latter then gave vent to unseemly and vile words against the king, calling him a traitor, a perjurer, executioner and butcher of men. The king ordered onions and vinegar to be brought for the rabbit,[65] and then, getting weary of them, gave the command for their execution.

The details of the manner of their death would make a very strange and cruel tale: the king ordered Pero Coelho's heart to be torn out through his chest and that of Álvaro Gonçalves to be torn out through his back. The words that he uttered, as well as those uttered by the man who tore out their hearts and who was unaccustomed to this task, would be truly terrible to hear. Finally, the king ordered them to be burnt; the entire exercise was carried out in front of the palace where he was staying, so that, while eating, he was able to behold everything that he had commanded to be done.

The king lost much of his good reputation as a result of this exchange [of prisoners], which was seen as great infamy, both in Portugal and in Castile. All the noblemen who heard of it declared that both kings had made a very grave mistake in going against their word, given that these nobles had been granted sanctuary in their respective kingdoms.

Chapter 32

Concerning a number of things which King Pedro of Castile ordered to be done, and how he made peace with the King of Aragon after invading his kingdom

Before these events, we left King Pedro of Castile in Seville,[66] capturing and killing as he pleased, and we related the deaths of a number of people whom he killed later, as well as certain events which took place in Portugal in the year 1360.

After the ignoble exchange of knights between the two kingdoms, of which you have already heard, King Pedro of Castile ordered the cruel death of one of them, namely Don Pedro Núñez de Guzmán, the Chief Provincial Governor of León. Next he ordered the killing of Gutierre Fernández de Toledo, his keeper of the great wardrobe, whose head was brought to him, and of Gómez Carrillo, the son of Pero Rodríguez Carrillo who had sailed off happily aboard a galley on which the king had dispatched him under the pretence that he was to be handed the town of Algeciras to act as its officer of the marches. Instead, the patron of the galley cut off his head, which he delivered to the

---

[65] *Coelho* is Portuguese for rabbit.
[66] At the end of Chapter 26 above.

king, and cast his body into the sea. The wife and sons of the said Gómez
Carrillo were taken prisoner.

The king also ordered the killing of a Castilian knight named Diego Gutiérrez
de Závalos and expelled from his kingdom Don Vasco, the Archbishop of
Toledo, after killing his brother Gutierre Fernández. He commanded the
confiscation of all the archbishop's belongings, so that he was unable to take
a single book with him and took only the clothes which he was wearing at
the time. The archbishop fled to Portugal and died in Coimbra. On a single
day the king ordered the arrest of Don Samuel Leví, his chief treasurer and a
prominent member of his Royal Council, as well as of all the latter's relatives
throughout the kingdom. He confiscated from him, as from all the others,
whatever belongings he found them to possess, subjected him to cruel torture
and cast him as a prisoner into the dockyard of Seville, where he died.

That year, King Pedro decided to wage war on the Red Emir of Granada,
who was said to have sided with the King of Aragon. The Red Emir had
expelled Emir Mohammed from his realm but quickly arrived at an agreement
with King Pedro whereby he should not interfere in his hostilities against his
own enemy, the Emir Mohammed. On the contrary, he should be extremely
angry at him because he had wanted to wage war on him in the past.

Having settled this, in January 1361 the king made his way to Almazán, bent
on invading the kingdom of Aragon, taking with him large numbers of troops,
and on this occasion he was assisted by 600 Portuguese. Their captain was the
Master of Avis, Dom Martim de Avelar, a valiant and honourable nobleman,
and all of them were very pleased to serve under him. The King of Castile
seized a number of Aragonese townships on this occasion.

The Cardinal of Boulogne, the Papal legate, spoke to the king urging him
to avoid spilling as much blood as he was prepared to do, because the King
of Aragon was ready with all his forces to join battle with him, as he realized
that in a prolonged war he was not his equal, because at that time the King
of Castile had 6,000 horsemen and many foot soldiers at his disposal. Owing
to his fear that the Emir of Granada, who, they told him, was in league with
the King of Aragon, would wage war against him if the strife between them
were to last much longer, for this would run counter to his own plans, the
King of Castile grudgingly made an insincere peace with the King of Aragon.

The terms of the peace were as follows: the King of Aragon would expel
from his realm Count Enrique, his brothers Don Tello and Don Sancho, as
well as the Castilian knights and squires, who were with them in Aragon;
the King of Castile, in turn, would restore to the King of Aragon all the
townships in his realm which he had seized; thenceforth they should become
allies. Documents were accordingly drawn up, and the peace was proclaimed

throughout the encampment, to the great joy of all those present, for the war in which they were engaged was much against their wishes.

Chapter 33

Concerning a number of incursions which the King of Castile made that year into the emirate of Granada and how, after the Red Emir had sought his protection, believing himself to be safe, the king had him killed

When the king came back from Aragon and arrived in Seville, he assembled his forces in order to wage war against the Red Emir of Granada, declaring that he wished to go to the aid of Emir Mohammed and that it was on account of the Red Emir that he had made peace with Aragon against his true wishes. Emir Mohammed went to the king with a force of 400 horsemen and allied himself to him. The king reached Antequera but did not succeed in reducing it and withdrew. He ordered his men to make their way onto the plain of Granada. Comprising 6,000 horsemen, the Christians won two battles there, and numbers of the Moors were killed and taken captive. In another battle the Christians were defeated, some of them were killed, and the Master of Calatrava,[67] together with Sancho Pérez de Ayala and others, was taken prisoner.

Thinking that he would please King Pedro, the Red Emir gave a warm welcome to the Master and to the other men, with the aim of softening the king's ill will towards him. He released the master and a number of the other knights, giving them some of his jewellery, and sent them back to the king. The king showed very little gratitude to him for so great a present; rather, a few days later, he made another incursion, won four Moorish townships, placing a garrison in each of them, and returned to Seville.

The Moors attacked one of the townships, Sagra by name, breaching its wall and forcing their way in. Fernán Delgadillo, its governor, came to an agreement with them, was given safe conduct and made his way to the king, who promptly had him killed. The king then made another raid on Granada, captured a number of townships and returned again to Seville.

The Moors were all aggrieved at this and told the Red Emir that, owing to the conflict which he, the Red Emir, had with Emir Mohammed, the king had

---

[67] Diego García de Padilla, Master of Calatrava (1355–1365).

now invaded their territory three times, and that the emirate of Granada was being laid waste. The emir was startled by this and, realizing that he could not accomplish what he had begun, decided to go and place himself in the power of the King of Castile and be dependent on his favour, believing that, once the king saw him, he would take pity on him and would treat him well. He left Granada at once with 400 horsemen and 200 foot soldiers. They reached the alcazar of Seville, where the king was lodging. They bowed most reverently before him, and the king gave them a good welcome.

Then one of the Moors spoke up on behalf of the Emir of Granada, declaring among other matters that he could defend himself well against Emir Mohammed, his adversary, but against King Pedro, who was his king and liege lord, and to whom he owed obeisance, he could not defend himself. After his emir had thought deeply and heard others on these matters, the best decision he could come to was that he should place himself in the king's power and be dependent on his favour. That favour was what he now sought, pleading that he might take the matter in hand and judge it favourably. However, were he to wish otherwise, the emir begged the boon that he and his men be dispatched overseas to Moorish territory.

The king answered the Moor, declaring that he was greatly pleased at the arrival of the emir and his men and that in regard to the conflict which he had with Emir Mohammed he would take steps to release him from it. The Red Emir and his men then bowed to the king with great reverence on this account, deeming that their concerns were being handled well, and went away very cheerfully to the lodgings which the king had commanded they be given in the Jewish quarter of the city.

Greed, which is the root of all evil, led the king to discover at once that the Red Emir was carrying with him such a great hoard of seed-pearls, precious stones and other gems that he felt a huge urge to seize it all. He commanded the Master of Santiago to invite the emir to dinner on the following day, along with the principal figures of note among his entourage. Some fifty of them accompanied him to the dinner.

Once dinner was over, when they all felt safe and none had risen from the table, Martín López[68] arrived with a body of armed men and arrested the emir and all the others. The emir was at once searched, and he was found to be carrying three large bright rose-red rubies. On the belt of a young Moor they found 730 rubies, whilst on one of his pages they discovered fifty seed-pearls as big as shelled hazel-nuts. Another youth was found to be in possession of such a quantity of seed-pearls, as big as chick-peas, as to make possibly as

---

[68] Martín López de Córdoba, lord chamberlain to King Pedro of Castile.

much as a gallon, while some were carrying seed-pearls and others precious stones. Everything was brought to the king.

Meanwhile, other men-at-arms went to the Jewish quarter and arrested all the other Moors. All the *doblas* and gems which they found on them were also brought to the king. The emir and all his men were imprisoned in the dockyard. Two days later the emir and thirty-seven Moorish knights were taken out to a field known as the Tablada, and there the king had them all put to death. With his lance King Pedro was the first to attack the Red Emir, who was sitting astride an ass, dressed in a tunic of scarlet[69], and cried out, 'Take that for making me agree to such a wretched treaty with the King of Aragon.' To this the Moor retorted in his native Arabic, 'Your little raid didn't turn out so badly.'

King Pedro then sent the heads of the Red Emir and his thirty-seven knights to Emir Mohammed of Granada, who returned to him a number of prisoners. Yet, though King Pedro uttered many reasons to justify this deed, in order to demonstrate that he had not gone against his own conscience, all his men deemed it to be a great wrong and would have been glad for it not to be so.

Chapter 34

Concerning the agreements which the King of Castile reached with the King of Aragon when he invaded his kingdom, and how he later came to disregard them

King Pedro was keen to return to war against Aragon, declaring that the peace which he had reached had been against his will, owing to his fears about the Red Emir. He therefore formed an alliance with the King of Navarre,[70] whereby they agreed to become allies and help each other, and then commanded his forces to be in readiness. No one, however, thought that he planned to attack Aragon, owing to the peace which existed between them. Secretly, before the King of Aragon could find out, and in order to seize a number of townships in the meantime, he invaded Aragon and captured six castles and surrounded the town of Calatayud. While laying siege to it, he seized thirteen castles in that region.

The King of Aragon, who was at the other end of his kingdom, was astounded when he heard what had taken place. He appealed for help from Provence,

---

[69] 'Scarlet' was a fine, high-quality woollen cloth.
[70] Carlos II of Navarre.

where Count Enrique, his brothers and the other exiled Castilian noblemen were at war, undertaking to grant them great rewards when in his kingdom.

Meanwhile, the town of Calatayud endured so harsh a siege that it was easy for King Pedro to take it through negotiation. He left a garrison there and made his way back to Seville. As he feared the wrath of the King of France,[71] owing to the death of his wife Queen Blanche, whom he had ordered to be killed, he now entered into a very firm alliance with King Edward of England and with the Prince of Wales his son,[72] according to which they would help one another against all others.

He immediately went back into Aragon, reached the town of Calatayud, which was already on his side, and seized seven villages around it. When he forced his way into Cariñena, he ordered the killing of all the inhabitants, till there was not a single one left. It is said that he ordered them all to be killed because, after he had laid siege to it and found that he could not capture it, he had raised the siege, whereupon the inhabitants, seeing his men leaving, began, much as they pleased, to shout all manner of insults and curses from the ramparts. The king was infuriated at this and commanded his troops to make their way back to the town. He attacked it with such violence that he at once forced a way in, and that was the reason for the massacre.

He also surrounded the township of Tarazona and took it. While he was laying siege to it, there arrived Dom Gil Fernandes de Carvalho, the Master of Santiago in Portugal, with 500 knights and squires, all of them ready to come to his aid, and sent by his uncle King Pedro of Portugal. Among them were Martim Vasques de Góis, Gonçalo Mendes de Vasconcelos, Martim Afonso de Melo, Álvaro Gonçalves de Moura, Nuno Viegas the Elder, Rui Vasques Ribeiro and many other noble and valiant knights.

The king then set out and captured Teruel and eleven other townships. He went on to take the town of Segorbe and the village of Murviedro,[73] before arriving at the city of Valencia. Having laid siege to it for a week, the king then learnt that the King of Aragon, Prince Ferran his brother,[74] Count Enrique, Don Tello, Don Sancho and the other forces which the King of Aragon had summoned, including 3,000 horsemen, were all assembled ready to do battle against him. But King Pedro, who had no wish to go into battle against them, left Valencia for Murviedro. The King of Aragon advanced to within 2 leagues

---

[71] Jean II of France.

[72] That is, Edward III (1312–1377) and Edward the Black Prince (1330–1376).

[73] Also known as Monviedro, this ancient township is known nowadays by its even older name of Sagunto.

[74] One of the princes of Aragon (see Chapter 17 above) and brother to Pere III of Aragon.

of that place and drew up his battle line but, finding nobody against whom to fight, he turned back. From the river bank at Murviedro King Pedro was greatly aggrieved to see four of his galleys being taken away by six Aragonese galleys, which had captured them.

It was there that the Kings of Aragon and Castile began to strike a deal, namely that King Pedro would marry Princess Joana, the daughter of the King of Aragon, and that Joan, the eldest son of the King of Aragon, would espouse Princess Beatriz, the daughter of King Pedro. This was subject to certain conditions. When they came together to sign the treaty, King Pedro was asked about his intentions and answered that he would not be party to it and that they should not press him further. He then made his way back to Seville. King Pedro declared [to his household] that during the negotiations it had been secretly planned that, as he was to marry the daughter of the King of Aragon and was thereby to establish such a close family bond with him, the King of Aragon should first capture or kill Prince Ferran, his brother, and Count Enrique, who were both King Pedro's enemies, but, as he had not done so, he was not interested in the agreement any more.

It would appear that this was true, because a few days later the King of Aragon ordered the arrest of Prince Ferran, his brother, after the meal to which he had been invited only that day, because, it was said, he intended to go with his army to take part in the war in France. As he resisted arrest, he was at once slain, as were Luis Manuel and Diego Pérez Sarmiento also. All his subjects deemed this to have been a great wrong, for Prince Ferran was his brother and a very noble lord to boot.

The King of Aragon then conspired with the King of Navarre to kill Count Enrique. They pretended that all three of them should meet in a certain castle to discuss a separate matter. However, Don Juan Ramírez de Arellano, who was the lord chamberlain of the King of Aragon and chosen by Count Enrique to keep the castle as a secure place for their discussions, refused to consent to such a killing, and that was why the count escaped being put to death on that day.

Chapter 35

How King Pedro again invaded Aragon, this time with a fleet of ships and galleys, and what he did there

The King of Castile left Seville once more, at the beginning of 1364 in the fifteenth year of his reign, invading Aragon via the kingdom of Valencia and capturing Alicante and other townships. On arriving at Burriana, he noticed a number of galleys and other ships bringing to [the city of] Valencia provisions which were desperately needed. He therefore deviated from his journey in order to prevent their arrival and pitched his camp at a place known as the Grao, which is next to the sea and half a league from the city. There, every day, he awaited his fleet and the Portuguese galleys which were due to come to his aid. They were all in Cartagena already, but the weather had not yet allowed them to depart.

While King Pedro was without news of the King of Aragon, a squire arrived to inform him that the King of Aragon and Count Enrique, along with all the other great lords and armies, which probably amounted to 3,000 horsemen, as well as many foot soldiers, were approaching in great secrecy and were intent on doing battle with him before he left that place. Moreover, keeping pace with them at sea were a dozen galleys and other ships bringing supplies; to avoid discovery, they had not lit any fires for three nights and on the following day they would confront him.

On hearing this, the king left at once and went to Murviedro, which lay 4 leagues away. On the morning of the following day the King of Aragon arrived with all his men. They set up camp between Murviedro and the sea, at a league away from the town, whilst their galleys and ships lay close at hand [as they travelled down the coast to Valencia].[75] In that way the city received aid both by land and by sea.

After twelve days the King of Castile's fleet arrived, comprising twenty of his own galleys and forty *naos*, as well as ten galleys from Portugal, sent by his uncle to help him. The Aragonese fleet, on seeing the Castilian vessels, were stricken with fear and headed up the River Cullera. King Pedro went aboard his fleet at once and stationed them at the mouth of the river, planning to seize the Aragonese galleys. But while he was there, the east wind, blowing on shore along that stretch of coast, coupled with a ferocious sea, caused everyone to believe that the galleys would be smashed against the shore.

The King of Aragon and all his forces waited for them on land, convinced that the galleys would be utterly destroyed by the wind, which was blowing with ever greater intensity. King Pedro's galley had already lost three anchor

---

[75] Fernão Lopes follows Pero López de Ayala's *Crónica de Don Pedro Primero*, quite closely at this point. See José-Luis Martín's edition (1991), Year 15, chs. 1–3, pp. 299–302. However, Lopes's version lacks a short sentence clarifying that after stopping 1 league away from Murviedro, the King of Aragon made his way down to Valencia by land while his fleet accompanied him by sea. This probably explains why the armies of Aragon and Castile were so close at this point, though there was no confrontation, as the King of Castile was still waiting for his own fleet, far more powerful than Aragon's, and did not want to risk an attack without its support.

chains and their anchors, and his whole enterprise depended on the fourth. The storm abated at sunset, and the king, who had endured very great danger, left behind his officers of the marches and headed back to Castile. Then the King of Aragon surrounded Murviedro but failed to take it. He too departed and went back to his kingdom.

Meanwhile, the King of Castile turned round once again, set out from Seville, entered Aragon and captured a number of townships. Fearing that they would be besieged, the inhabitants of Orihuela informed their king. The King of Aragon approached with his forces to a point 2 leagues away from where the King of Castile was and supplied the township with the food which it lacked. King Pedro avoided fighting a battle with him but stayed in that area for a few more days before going back to Seville.

On receiving news that galleys of his, which were out at sea, had captured five Aragonese galleys, he left at once for Cartagena, where these five galleys lay, and ordered that all their crews be put to death, so that not a single one escaped, except for those who knew how to make oars, because he had need of them. From there King Pedro left for Murcia. Knowing that the King of Aragon had surrounded Murviedro, he in turn laid siege to Orihuela, capturing the township and its castle and returning again to Seville.

As for the inhabitants of Murviedro, since they were suffering greatly from the siege and were very short of food, they sent frequent messages to King Pedro, begging him to go and help them. But the king, since the only way in which he could help them was by a pitched battle, dared not do so, as he wished to avoid a battle with the King of Aragon, owing to his fear of his own men whom he did not fully trust. He therefore sought other ways of waging war than in battle, for King Pedro did not dare to take the field, owing to the large numbers which he had ordered to be killed and to those in his kingdom whom he knew to be dissatisfied with him and to hate him.

The inhabitants of Murviedro, who were so short of food that they were eating rats and their very beasts of burden, made a pact with the King of Aragon and surrendered their township to him. The defenders inside the township numbered 600 men-at-arms, not counting foot soldiers and cross-bowmen. The great majority of them sided with Count Enrique owing to their fear of King Pedro, not because of his failure to go to their aid.

Chapter 36

How Count Enrique invaded Castile with numerous companies and was proclaimed king, and how King Pedro ordered the abandonment of all the Aragonese townships which he had captured

After the King of Aragon had taken Murviedro, he left for Barcelona. At his summons, a number of captains from the companies which he had summoned arrived there and signed with him an agreement whereby they undertook to present themselves the following February in order to invade Castile with Count Enrique. On learning of this, King Pedro made his way to Burgos, where he had ordered his army to assemble. While he was there, he learned that Count Enrique had been joined by the companies and that they had left Saragossa in order to invade Castile. They included captains from Aragon, namely the Count of Denia and Don Felipe de Castro, along with other knights; from France came Sir Bertrand du Guesclin, the Count de la Marche, the Lord of Beaujeu, the Marshal d'Audrehem, who was the Marshal of France, and others; from England came Sir Hugh Calveley, Sir Eustace [d'Ambreticourt], Sir Matthew Gournay,[76] Sir William Allamant and Sir John Devereux, as well as numerous other knights and men-at-arms from England, Guyenne, Gascony and other countries.

They all reached the township of Alfaro but did not care to attack it and journeyed the next day to Calahorra, which was not a fortified town. Its inhabitants negotiated with the count, welcomed both him and his forces into the town and informed them that King Pedro was in Burgos and anxious to avoid doing battle with them. They then took the decision to tell Count Enrique that, since so many noble people were happy to support him in this campaign, he should proclaim himself King of Castile.

At first he began by refusing. However, as being a king brings no little enjoyment, he agreed without much argument that it would please him greatly, and so he was proclaimed king. Those who accompanied him then requested big favours and positions in his kingdom, and he was very happy to grant them everything, apportioning what he had already captured and promising what was still to be taken, as at that time it behoved him to do so. These events took place in the year 1366.

---

[76] Although Fernão Lopes writes 'Martim de Gorimai', this is, in fact, Sir Matthew Gournay.

King Enrique then headed for Burgos, where King Pedro lay, and reached Navarrete, which surrendered to him without waiting to be attacked. He then laid siege to Briviesca and took it. Having received news of this, it was early in the morning on the eve of Palm Sunday that King Pedro ordered the killing of Juan Fernández de Tovar, owing to the rancour he felt towards his brother.[77] Then, without saying anything to his own men, he mounted his horse with the object of leaving at once, whereupon the leading burgesses of the city [of Burgos] approached him, begging him not to abandon them, because the count stood just 8 leagues away. Without heeding their arguments, he relieved them of their fealty to him and immediately departed. He left accompanied by a number of knights and 600 Moorish horsemen which the Emir of Granada had sent to help him in his war, but many of his men remained behind in Burgos, pleased at this turn of events. As it was, those who had deserted him never dared return to him. On the day of his departure he sent letters to all the garrisons in the Aragonese fortresses which he had seized, ordering them to abandon them, to destroy them if they were able and to rejoin him. This they did, but many of them went over to King Enrique.

Thus the Aragonese war came fully to an end, having lasted a good eleven years. It is certain that the kingdom of Aragon would have been utterly laid waste if the life of King Pedro had not been so swiftly cut short by fate, for he had invaded Aragon eleven times, capturing fifty-two townships of which we have spoken here, not to mention many which we have not named.

King Pedro reached Toledo, left a garrison in the city and left for Seville. The inhabitants of Burgos, realizing that they could not hold out against King Enrique, sent messages to him and welcomed him into the city. There he was crowned king, and many proctors travelled to him from towns and cities all over the realm, acclaiming him as their liege lord, with the result that twenty-five days after his coronation the entire kingdom accepted his sovereignty. He received them all very graciously and to no one did he fail to grant what he requested. King Enrique made many land grants to the great lords and knights who had accompanied him, both foreigners and natives of his own land. He sent to Aragon for his wife and children, and she was welcomed with great honour. He then left Burgos and headed for Toledo, where there was a great uprising as to whether they should welcome him or not, because some people were very pleased by that idea, whilst others were utterly opposed to it. In the end, however, the decision was taken to welcome him in, and he was joyfully received.

---

[77] That is, Don Fernán Sánchez [de Tovar], who had welcomed King Enrique to Calahorra.

Chapter 37

How the King of Castile sent a daughter of his to Portugal, and how he left Seville out of fear of the people of the city

While King Pedro was in Seville, he heard news of all these events, and after much thought he agreed with his followers to ask for help from the King of Portugal, his uncle. To give the latter weightier reasons to be moved to grant him this help, he sent word to remind him that he was well aware that a marriage had been arranged between his own daughter, Princess Beatriz, and Prince Fernando, the first-born son of the King of Portugal; therefore he was sending him the princess and all the dowry that had been agreed she would receive at the time of the marriage. Moreover, he declared that Princess Beatriz would inherit the kingdoms of Castile and León. He sent her immediately away from Seville, and with her Martín López de Trujillo, a man in whom he had a great deal of trust, and also a certain quantity of *doblas* that had been left to the princess by her mother, María de Padilla, along with jewels, seed-pearls and other things.

After Princess Beatriz had left Seville for Portugal, King Pedro had news that King Enrique was heading towards Seville from Toledo. Consequently, he decided to send for the treasure that he kept in the castle of Almodóvar, which was all in gold and silver coins. He ordered a galley to be fitted out and in it he placed this treasure, as well as all the wealth he had in the city. He gave command of the galley to his treasurer Martín Yáñez, ordering him to go to Tavira, a town in Portugal in the kingdom of the Algarve, and to watch over the galley until he arrived there. He also had many pack-mules loaded with all his wealth, and took with him a very great amount of gold and precious stones and pearls, both those he had taken from the Red Emir and his people and much other wealth that he had gathered, along with as much of the silver as he could take along.

When the king was thus prepared to leave Seville, he was told that the citizens were rising up against him and meant to rob him there where he was. Fear-stricken, he left at once for Portugal. He took with him his daughters the Princesses Constanza and Isabel, for he had already sent away the eldest, Princess Beatriz, as we have said. With King Pedro there went Martín López de Córdoba, who was [now] the Master of Alcántara, Diego Gómez de Castañeda, Pedro Fernández Cabeza de Vaca and others.

According to some written accounts, when the king left Seville, there were some among those who were accompanying the pack-mules with his wealth who, seeing that the king was fleeing from the kingdom in that way, returned to the city with what they were carrying, whilst others, issuing from the town, robbed him of part of his wealth.

In Seville, Master Egidio Boccanegra,[78] King Pedro's admiral, who was Genoese, equipped a galley and other vessels and set forth to capture the treasure galley in which Martín Yáñez was making his way to Tavira, and did so on the River Guadalquivir, for he had not yet sailed any further than that. The wealth that was in the galley consisted of 36 *quintais*[79] of gold and many jewels, of which afterwards King Enrique received the greater part.

Chapter 38

How the King of Castile informed his uncle that he had entered his kingdom, and how the latter excused himself from seeing him and giving him aid

A t this time the King of Portugal was staying in the palace of Valada, which is near a town called Santarém; this was in the month of May. By the time King Pedro [of Castile] sent his daughter Princess Beatriz to marry Prince Fernando, as you have heard a little earlier, with the purpose of getting better aid from his uncle the King of Portugal, news had previously arrived in Valada, where the King of Portugal was staying, that the King of Castile was sending him two of his daughters who were already in Alcáçovas, 20 leagues away. But no one could say with certainty why the king was sending them or with what intention. The King of Portugal, who had not heard that the king his nephew was in such a predicament, supposed that the princesses were coming for a different reason, even though there was no other reason besides that one, and ordered suitable lodgings to be made ready in his palace.

The King of Castile left his kingdom, and made such haste along the way, without stopping anywhere, that before his daughter Princess Beatriz could come to where the King of Portugal was, he caught up with her on the road along which she was travelling. King Pedro [of Castile] came to Serpa, and from there to Beja, and from there to Coruche, which was 6 leagues from the

---

[78] The brother of Simone Boccanegra, the first Doge of Genoa.

[79] The Seville *quintal* (plural *quintais*) was a measure of weight, roughly equivalent to 110.7 lbs (*c.* 50.796 kg). See Luís Seabra Lopes, 'Sistemas Legais de Medidas de Peso e Capacidade, do Condado Portucalense ao Século XVI', *Portugalia*, New Series, 24 (2003), 119–20.

place where his uncle the King of Portugal was staying. From there he sent word to him that he was coming, with a message about the aid and support that he needed from him, and also about the marriage of his daughter to Prince Fernando, his son. When he learned of this, the King of Portugal was perplexed, and sent to tell King Pedro not to come any further and to remain where he was until he received a message from him.

The King of Portugal summoned his son Prince Fernando, who was not there, and discussed the matter with him and his counsellors. Some said that he should see King Pedro, give him shelter in his kingdom and help him to recover his lands. But thinking further about it, they realized that the king could not do this without considerable inconvenience and expense, and very great harm to his kingdom, especially as there were no good reasons to expect such a plan ever to be fulfilled, because King Enrique, King Pedro's brother, already had all of Castile in his power, except for such a small number of towns as not to be worth considering.

Moreover, King Pedro was much hated by all those in the kingdom, both of high rank and low, so that one had to wonder how much they would all do to get even with him. For whoever might try to drive King Enrique and all those of his party out of Castile, whether by battle or war of attrition, must have great military power. Furthermore, if it did not turn out according to King Pedro's wish, he would be left in a position of enmity and at war with King Enrique. On the other hand, to receive King Pedro into his kingdom, and not make an effort to help him, would bring the King of Portugal great dishonour and shame. Indeed, he could not excuse himself from helping him if he saw him and spoke with him. Thus they agreed that the safest course of action would be that neither he nor his son the prince should see King Pedro, seeking some plausible reason so that it might appear that he was avoiding it legitimately.

Then Count João Afonso Telo went to Coruche, where the King of Castile was awaiting the reply from his uncle, expecting to be given lodgings in Santarém. The count told him that the King of Portugal had received his message and learned of the manner of his coming, and that he would willingly receive him in his kingdom and help him to recover his lands as was just and right, but that he was not in a position to do so, because on those other occasions when he had given him help, both by sea and by land, the nobles of his kingdom had returned extremely discontented and outraged with him and his men. In addition, there were those in King Pedro's company with whom some Portuguese had had quarrels, and it was inevitable that among them there were notorious divisions and rows, which would be ill-suited to the interests of them both. Moreover, King Pedro was well aware that his son Prince Fernando was the nephew of Queen Juana (the sister of his mother

Princess Consort Constanza, and daughter of Don Juan Manuel), who had just recently entered Castile and that he did not expect he could convince him to give his agreement to such help.

Indeed this was the case, according to some written accounts, for the prince stood strongly against it, but in a well-argued way. With these and other reasons the count excused the king his liege lord, saying that at that time he could not see King Pedro nor offer him more help than he had already given him, whereupon the count took his leave of King Pedro, and departed for his own lodgings.

Chapter 39

How the King of Castile departed from Coruche and left Portugal, and concerning those who were sent to accompany him

Despite the arguments we have put forward and many other words that were spoken between the King of Castile and the count concerning his affairs, King Pedro understood very well that the outcome of all his statements was that his uncle the King of Portugal had no wish to receive him in his realm or to help him in any way. He was so aggrieved by this that he could not refrain from giving some expression to his anger. After the count spoke with him, took his leave and went back to his lodgings, King Pedro was sad and deeply vexed, and with a perturbed mien he took some *doblas* that he had in his hand and threw them over a porch of the house where he was staying. A knight of his company, seeing what the king was doing, asked him in jest why he was throwing away those *doblas* in such a fashion, as it would be better to give them to some of his men, to whom they might be useful. The king answered him, saying: 'Never mind that, for he who sows them will come to reap them later,' meaning by this that, if he were not so much younger than the King of Portugal, he would willingly make war on him for not receiving any aid from him then, nor any welcome.

He then made up his mind to go to Alburquerque and there leave his daughters and all that he was bringing with him. When he arrived at the town they refused to let him in; rather, some of those who were in his company took refuge inside. The king, seeing that his affairs were going from bad to worse, sent a message to his uncle the King of Portugal, saying that, since he did not wish to help him in any other way, he asked to be given a letter of safe conduct to enable him to pass through his kingdom. He did this out of fear of Prince Fernando of Portugal, on account of his being the nephew of the wife of King Enrique, as was mentioned earlier.

The King of Portugal gave his full agreement, and sent him the Count of Barcelos,[80] of whom you have heard, and Álvaro Pérez de Castro to go with him through the kingdom and leave him in safety in Galicia. They went to join him and set off on their journey. When they arrived in Guarda, according to some, they told the king that they wished to turn back and that they could go no further with him for they feared Prince Fernando, who had sent them threats on account of their travelling in his company. They say that the king then gave them 6,000 *doblas*, two silver belts and two tucks so that they would go with him as far as Galicia. If this indeed happened, what they are reported to have said was fabricated, for the prince had no reason to send any such message to them, since it had been decided in the Royal Council, and with his agreement, that they should accompany King Pedro until he was out of the kingdom. It is said that they got as far as Lamego with him, and no further.

On parting, the count stole from the king a daughter of King Enrique, his brother, whom he was taking along with him as a captive, a fourteen-year-old girl called Doña Leonor of the Lions. That was because King Pedro, owing to the grievance he had against her father,[81] when this girl was under the care of her nurse, not many months after her birth, had her abducted with great cruelty. Indeed, he ordered that she be cast, clad only in her shift, into the enclosure where he kept a number of lions, which had been starved throughout the previous day. It was done just as he had ordered. The lions came and approached her, and it pleased God that they did her no harm, but rather, as if they took pity on her, they came up to her without injuring her in any way. This was reported to the king by some of his men, and he ordered her to be taken out of the lions' den and handed over to those who were raising her. She was, however, placed under such a strict guard that her father could never rescue her. King Pedro had taken her along with him at the time, the count brought her to the King of Portugal, and later she was handed over to King Enrique, her father.

[80] Count João Afonso Telo.

[81] At the time, King Pedro's annoyance against his half-brother came from the fact that he had married Juana Manuel, who had been the prospective wife to the king himself.

Chapter 40

How King Pedro arrived in Galicia, killed the Archbishop of Santiago and departed for England

The King of Castile left Lamego, quite defenceless and with very few followers, for there were no more than about 200 horsemen riding with him. He arrived in Monterrey, a town in Galicia, and from there he wrote messages to Logroño, to Soria and to Zamora, all of which were on his side, urging them to hold on, for he would bring them help. He informed the King of Navarre and the Prince of Wales that he was in Galicia and wished to know what support he could expect from them. There he waited for the Archbishop of Santiago and for Don Fernando de Castro, his standard-bearer and Provincial Governor of the provinces of León and Asturias, who prior to this had come to Galicia in answer to his command. He spoke with all the prelates, knights and squires, as well as with representatives of the cities, towns and fortresses, with the result that all of them took his side.

For three weeks they remained in council, deliberating whether it was better to go on to Zamora and from there to Logroño, since King Enrique and his forces were in Seville, or to go to Bayonne in England[82] to make a personal plea for aid from the Prince of Wales. The king preferred the advice to go to England rather than to return once more to his kingdom, for he trusted as little in those who had expressed their support for him as in those others who were not on his side. He left Monterrey and went to spend the Feast of Saint John[83] in Santiago [de Compostela] in Galicia; there he agreed with his followers to kill the archbishop and seize his strongholds.

Don Suero [the Archbishop] came trustingly on his command on the Feast of Saint Peter,[84] for the king had sent to summon him to the council. However, as he was coming in through the city he was slain at the door of the Cathedral of Santiago by Fernán Pérez Turrichao and Gonzalo Gómez Gallinato, two knights who hated him and whom the king had ordered to kill him. They also killed Pero Álvarez, the Dean of Santiago, a man of great learning and wisdom. The king was watching from the top of the church while all this was done.

The king took all the wealth that the archbishop kept in the castle of Rocha, gave the strongholds to Don Fernando de Castro and made him the Count of Trastámara, Lemos and Sarria (where King Enrique had himself once been the count), making him the hereditary lord of the said county in perpetuity,

---

[82] Meaning 'Bayonne, an English possession', as referred to in Chapter 21.
[83] 24 June.
[84] 29 June.

granting it to him and all his legitimately-born heirs. However, Álvaro Pérez his brother and Andrés Sánchez de Gres, who were coming to see the king, returned in fear to their own lands when they learned of the death of the archbishop, and swore fealty to King Enrique.

The king left Santiago and went to La Coruña,[85] a place where he received a message from the Prince of Wales, saying that he should go to the English domain and that the prince would help him to recover his kingdom. The king left La Coruña, and took with him 22 *naos*, as well as a galley and a carrack; he left Don Fernando de Castro in Galicia and handed over all his authority to him. The king sailed in the carrack with all three of his daughters and all of the wealth he had with him, which was 36,000 *doblas* in coined gold, because he had left all the rest of his treasure in the galley that Martín Yáñez was to take to Tavira. He also carried with him many pieces of gold jewellery, seed-pearls and precious stones. Crossing the sea, he reached Bayonne. Let us leave him there looking after his affairs, about which we do not wish to say any more at present.

Chapter 41

How King Enrique arrived in Seville, and concerning the alliance he made with the King of Portugal

King Enrique departed from Toledo knowing all that had happened to King Pedro in Seville and likewise in Portugal, and how he had gone afterwards to Galicia. He arrived in Córdoba, where he was received with great pleasure, and from there he went on his way to Seville, knowing that the city supported him. There he was received with such great rejoicing that, although the king arrived near the city early in the morning, it was after midday when he entered his palace.

The king distributed rewards to his followers and to those troops who were travelling with him, in such a fashion that all of them were most contented, and he sent them back to their own lands. But Sir Bertrand du Guesclin and other great lords remained with him, along with some Englishmen and Bretons, some 1,500 lances in all.

The king stayed in Seville for four months. Before he left there, he wrote to King Pedro of Portugal to declare how he wished to have peace and friendship

---

[85] This port is also referred to in English as 'Corunna', particularly after the Peninsular War battle fought there on 16 January 1809.

with him. He said that he would send to the border such men as he trusted to represent him, and asked King Pedro also to send envoys to the border so that they might reach an agreement on their plans.

Thus it was that King Enrique sent Don Juan, who was the Bishop of Badajoz, and Diego Gómez de Toledo, a knight. In turn, the King of Portugal sent Dom João, who was the Bishop of Évora, and Dom Álvaro Gonçalves [Pereira], who was the Prior of the Order of the Knights Hospitaller. They all met together on the banks of the [river] Caya on the border between the two kingdoms. There they agreed on behalf of the two kings that they should be loyal friends to each other and maintain peace and concord.

It was also decided that the King of Castile should try as hard as he could to induce the King of Aragon to be the friend of the King of Portugal, as he himself was, and to intercede with the King of Aragon to allow Princess Maria, daughter of the aforesaid King Pedro of Portugal, to come to Portugal with all of her belongings, or to live in whatever country she might prefer, she who had been the wife of Prince Ferran, the Marquess of Tortosa. They praised and ratified the agreements that had been made previously in Ágreda between King Fernando and King Dinis, the grandfathers of the present kings. Likewise, Mohammed, the Emir of Granada, immediately concluded a treaty of friendship with King Enrique and became his ally.

The king departed from Seville and went to Galicia. In Lugo he besieged Don Fernando de Castro, who was loyal to King Pedro of Castile; but he could not take the town. Don Fernando arranged with King Enrique that, if King Pedro did not come to his aid within five months, he would leave the realm and hand over to him all his strongholds. But, if he then wished to stay under King Enrique's authority, the king would give him the township of Castrojeriz, from which his family derived the name of Castro, and he obtained the title of count after receiving the said town from King Pedro. They also agreed that during this five-month period the two factions should not attack each other, a bargain which was very badly kept by Don Fernando.[86]

King Enrique was pleased with this, and returned to Burgos, where he summoned *Cortes*, in which the greatest men of the land were present. As they were quite sure that King Pedro intended to carry out an invasion, King Enrique was promised aid towards the costs of the war and offered their personal service, as he could clearly see. The king, meanwhile, was sending

---

[86] According to López de Ayala in his *Crónica del Rey Don Pedro*, Year 1366, Chapter 18, Fernando de Castro immediately started to fight Enrique's followers in several different spots. Enrique, however, did not have time to be concerned, because the Prince of Wales was already on his way to Castile to be with King Pedro in the coming battle against his brother.

for men who kept on coming to him every day, whom he rewarded generously and treated with great honour.

Since no more of the deeds of both of these kings happened during the era of King Pedro of Portugal, we will cease to speak further of them. While they are gathering their men for the battle of which you will hear later,[87] we shall record other matters, as the plan of this work requires. But before we speak of them, hear this which I found written, *scilicet*, that on Thursday, 22 October 1366, there was a commotion in the sky from midnight onwards, which happened in this manner: all the stars raced from east to west, and after they had all come together, they began to race away, some here, others there. After that, they started to explode as they fell from the sky, so many and so thickly, that as they loomed low in the air they seemed like great bonfires, and the skies and air appeared to be ablaze, and the earth to be about to burn up. Indeed, the sky seemed to be split into many pieces where there were no stars.

There was no man who, on seeing this, was not terribly frightened. So great was the fear that all those who saw this believed that they were going to die, and it lasted for a very long time. We have written this so that you will not think it a novelty when another similar event occurs, and also as a reminder of the wonders that God brings to pass.[88]

Chapter 42

How the King of Portugal sent his ambassadors to the house of the Prince of Wales to defend himself against the charges King Pedro was making against him

The great vexation that King Pedro of Castile felt on account of the poor reception he had encountered in Portugal caused him at times to be unable, when speaking, not to express his anger about it. Sometimes, when there were

---

[87] The Battle of Nájera, in April 1367, as recorded by Lopes in *CKF*, Chapters 5–9.

[88] Indeed, this was the sighting of a Leonid meteor shower, a phenomenon caused by the Tempel-Tuttle comet on crossing the Earth's orbit periodically, about every 33–34 years. The visibility of the phenomenon, however, may vary each time in intensity as well as geographically. See John W. Mason, 'Leonid Meteors and Comet 55P/Tempel-Tuttle', *British Astronomical Association*, 105, 5 (1995), 228 and 230.

many men around the Prince [of Wales], he complained of the poor reception he had found from his uncle the king, when he was hoping to find the opposite. He said that he did not mind it as much for his own sake as for that of the princesses his daughters, whom the King of Portugal should have welcomed and protected at his request. Speaking of the matter at great length, he gave many indications through his gestures and facial expressions that he had a great desire to take revenge.

This was spoken in such a way and in such words that inevitably someone wrote to the King of Portugal about it. Being familiar with King Pedro's twisted disposition, and foreseeing what could come of this, he arranged to send someone to defend him before the prince, to show that the fault had not lain with him, both in his reception of King Pedro and regarding the hospitality to his daughters. He sent the Bishop of Évora and Gomes Lourenço do Avelar, who arrived in Gascony, where King Pedro and the prince were staying at the time. Once they arrived, the prince decreed a day and time for them to deliver their message, which they laid before him in the presence of the King of Castile. They began by relating in detail everything that certain people were saying in Portugal regarding the grievances of which King Pedro was complaining, blaming the king his uncle, but they stated that they had come to prove that he was blameless, as His Highness would be able to see clearly.

The King of Castile replied to this, saying that it was just as they had said, that he did feel much aggrieved because the King of Portugal had not welcomed him into his kingdom and given him refuge as was right, since he was his uncle, the brother of his mother. He said further that he felt greater vexation at his daughters not being given shelter than at the harshness that he had shown towards him. He explained that if the king his uncle had taken them in and given them protection in his realm, along with some belongings that he was carrying, where it was certain that they would be safe, then he would have been free of the burden and could have gone back to recover his kingdom. He claimed that many had risen up against him who would not have done so if he had been present, but, he explained, this was made impossible by the responsibility that he had for his daughters, which had obliged him to flee with them, not having any safe place where he could leave them. Indeed, at that time, when he would have liked to leave them in some castle in his land, he trusted none sufficiently to dare to do so.

On this matter many words went back and forth between King Pedro and the ambassadors, until they asked the prince to question the king as to whether, at the time when he had written to his uncle that he was in his kingdom, he had made him aware in his letter that he wanted to leave his daughters with him, and also the treasure he was bringing along, as he had just been saying in the prince's presence. The prince then asked him this, and he said that he had not mentioned anything about his daughters or about the wealth he was bringing with him. 'Well then,' said the prince, 'your uncle could not be expected to guess what you had in mind!'

Then they informed the prince of the aid King Pedro had received from Portugal, both by sea and by land, and how all the great lords and noblemen who had gone to join him had returned very ill-contented and outraged both by him and his men. They said that this had been one of the reasons why the king his uncle had not wanted to have him in his realm, so that feuds, quarrels and killings would not arise between them. They spoke until they wearied of it; the prince, in full knowledge of the facts, said that he did not consider the King of Portugal to be at fault, as he had done previously. Regarding the *nao* and wealth, concerning which the King of Portugal sent the prince a message claiming they were being detained wrongfully in England, he said that he would have them released at once, as the friend that he was and wished to be. This in fact he did, so that within a few days they were sent back.

Chapter 43

How Dom João, the son of King Pedro of Portugal, was made the Master of Avis

You have heard in the first chapter of this story how, after the death of Dona Inês, the king, while he was a prince, never wanted to marry, nor would he take a wife after he came to the throne, but he did have a son by another woman. His name was Dom João. The king entrusted this boy to Nuno Freire, the Master of the Order of Christ, who raised him and cared for him. It so happened that, when the boy reached the age of seven, Martim de Avelar, the Master of [the Order of] Avis passed away. The Master of the Order of Christ, as soon as he learned of this, went at once to King Pedro, who was staying in Chamusca at the time, and requested the title of Master [of Avis] for that son of the king, whom he had brought with him. The king was very pleased at this request, and even more pleased to grant it to him.

Then the master held the boy in his arms, and while he was holding him the king buckled on his sword and dubbed him a knight and kissed him on the mouth, giving him his blessing. He wished that God might make him grow from good to better and give him as much honour in deeds of chivalry as He had given to his grandfathers; this blessing was well fulfilled in him, as you will hear later. Then the king declared to the master:

Let the boy have this for the time being, for I know that he is destined to rise higher, if this is the son João of whom I have heard tell on several occasions, although I should have preferred the prophecies to be fulfilled in my son Prince João[89] rather than in him. The truth is, I was told that I have a son named João who is destined to rise very high, and through whom the kingdom of Portugal will win great honour. Since I do not know which João it will be, and no one can know for certain, I will arrange that these sons of mine, both having the same name, will always be attended upon to an equal degree. Let God choose one of them for this destiny, according to His grace. Nevertheless, I strongly suspect that it will be this one, and not the other, because I dreamed one night the strangest dream anyone has ever had. It seemed to me that, as I was sleeping, I saw all Portugal in flames, so that the entire kingdom seemed like a bonfire. As I was looking at this sight in shock, this son of mine, João, came with a staff in his hand, and with it he put out the whole fire. I reported this dream to certain people who understand such matters, and they told me that it could mean nothing but that some great deeds would be done by his hand.

Now that is indeed what came to pass afterwards, as we have said. Once this was done,[90] the Master of the Order of Christ returned to the town of Tomar and sent a message to the commanders of the Order of Avis, bidding them to come there at once to speak of things pertaining to the service of God and to the benefit of the Order. The master did this because the Orders of Avis and of Christ are both subject to the rule of the Order of Saint Benedict. Those summoned by his letters and commands came at once to that town.

The master then spoke with the grand commander [of the Order of Avis] and with Fernão Soares and Vasco Peres regarding the will of the king, after which he sat in chapter with them, as was the custom of his Order. The grand commander offered a proposition to the master, in his name and in that of the other commanders, saying that he knew well how their liege lord, Martim de Avelar, the Master of Avis, had died, and that they had no master to rule over them as befitted the service of God, as their Order required; nor did they intend to elect any other than the one that he might give them. Since he followed the same rule and was in a position to do it, they asked of him as a boon, for the service of God and the good of the Order, to give them a master who could govern them as their rule required.

The master replied that they had spoken very well, as honourable knights and sensible men. Moreover, since it was his duty to do and command everything that might be of service to God and for the good of their Order, he therefore

---

[89] The son of King Pedro and Inês de Castro.

[90] That is to say, the granting of the title of Master of the Order of Avis.

wished to accept the task of giving them a master who would govern them as their rule demanded. To be their master, he was giving them Dom João, the son of King Pedro, whom he was raising, and whom he believed to be a liege lord who would govern them as befitted the service of God and the good of the Order. The grand commander and the others then said that they were very grateful to him for giving them such an honourable lord as their master.

Dom João was immediately summoned, his secular garments were removed, and he was clothed in the habit of the Order of Avis. Upon this, the grand commander and the others kissed his hand as their master and liege lord. When this had been done, he was taken away to the headquarters of the Order of Avis of which he was the Master.

There he was raised for several years, until the time came when he began to bloom in his skills, virtues and acts of chivalry, as the story will recount later, each being told in its place. If some wish to say that his youth and illegitimate birth made him ineligible to be the Master, the response to them will be that the Pope gave him a dispensation, declaring that, although he had been appointed at a young age and born outside legitimate matrimony, his good conduct and the honourable benefit that would come to the Order from him made up for all that, and that he confirmed him in his post.

Chapter 44

How Dona Inês was translated to the Monastery of Alcobaça, and concerning the death of King Pedro

Such a love as the one that King Pedro had for Dona Inês has rarely been found in anyone. In this respect the Ancients have said that no one is so truly loved as one whose death the long passage of time is incapable of erasing from the memory. If anyone should say that there have been many who loved as much as he or more, such as Ariadne and Dido and others whom we do not name, as can be read in their letters,[91] the response is that we are not speaking of invented lives, which some authors, well-supplied with eloquence and flourishing in rhetorical skill, set forth any way they liked, uttering in the names of such people things that none of them ever thought of; rather, we

---

[91] Lopes is referring to Ovid's *Heroides*, a well-known and much cited work in literary circles in the late medieval period.

are speaking of those loves that are told of and read in historical accounts, whose basis lies in the truth.

King Pedro had this true love for Dona Inês from the moment when he fell in love with her, being married[92] and still the Crown Prince, so that although at the beginning he was unable to see and talk to her, as they were apart from each other, which is the main reason for love to be lost, he never stopped sending her messages, as you have heard in its place.[93] How much he strove thereafter to be with her, and what he did because of her death, and what punishments he dealt out to those who were guilty of it, going against his oath, all clearly prove what we are saying. Being mindful of honouring her remains, since he could no longer do anything else for her, he ordered the fashioning of a tomb of white stone, all very skilfully wrought, on top of which was her image with a crown on her head, as if she had been a queen.

He had this tomb placed in the Monastery of Alcobaça, not at the entrance where the kings are laid to rest, but inside the church to the right, near the chancel. He had her body brought from the Monastery of Santa Clara in Coimbra, where it was lying, with as much honour as could be shown. She was transported in a litter, very fittingly adorned for that time, which was borne by high-ranking knights and accompanied by great noblemen, many other people, ladies and maidens, and many of the clergy. Along the road stood many men holding cierges, so marshalled that her body made the entire journey between lighted cierges. In that fashion they arrived at the aforesaid monastery, which was 17 leagues away, where with many Masses and great solemnity the body was placed in the tomb. This was the most honourable translation that had ever been seen in Portugal until that time.

Likewise, the king had another equally well-wrought tomb prepared for himself, and had it placed next to hers, so that when he died they might lay him in it.

While in Estremoz, he fell ill from his final sickness. As he lay ailing, he remembered how, after the death of Álvaro Gonçalves and Pero Coelho, he had ascertained that Diogo Lopes Pacheco had not been to blame for the death of Dona Inês, and he set aside all cause of complaint he had against him. He also ordered all his property to be restored to him. Afterwards, his

---

[92] To Constanza Manuel, the daughter of Juan Manuel, who was one of the most important Castilian noblemen of his time. The marriage took place in 1340, when Pedro was 20 years old. Constanza gave birth to a daughter, Maria, and two sons, the elder of whom, Luís, died in infancy, and the other became King Fernando, born in 1345. She died in that same year or in 1349.

[93] In the *Chronicle of Afonso IV*, Pedro's father. See Chapter 30, note 62 above, and also Prologue, note 2.

son King Fernando carried this out, had all his property returned to him, and commuted the sentence that his father the king had passed upon him, to the extent that he could lawfully do so.

The king ordered in his will that there be each year in perpetuity in the monastery six chaplains to sing and say Mass for him every day, and have processions for him with the Cross and holy water. King Fernando, his son, so as better to fulfil this and have the Masses sung, gave afterwards to the monastery as a permanent gift the town called Paredes, in the area of Leiria, with all the income and property rights therein.

King Pedro left in his will certain legacies, *scilicet,* 100,000 *libras* to his daughter Princess Beatriz for her dowry, and 20,000 *libras* to his son Prince João, and another 20,000 to Prince Dinis, and likewise to other people. King Pedro died in the early morning hours of Monday, 18 January 1367, having reigned for ten years, seven months and twenty days, at the age of forty-seven years, nine months and eight days. He left orders that he be taken to the monastery we have mentioned and placed in his tomb, next to that of Dona Inês. Since Prince Fernando, his eldest son, was not there at the time, the king's body remained there and was not immediately borne away, until the prince came, and on the Wednesday he was placed in the tomb. People used to say that there had never been ten years in Portugal like the ones in which King Pedro had ruled.

BIBLIOGRAPHY OF WORKS CITED

For a comprehensive bibliography including all chronicles see volume 5.

Amado, Teresa, 'Fiction as Rhetoric: A Study of Fernão Lopes's *Crónica de D. João I*', *The Medieval Chronicle*, 5 (2008), 35–46

——'Time and Memory in Three Portuguese Chronicles', *The Medieval Chronicle*, 6 (2009), 91–104

Aquinas, St Thomas, *Summa Theologiae: A Concise Translation*, ed. Timothy McDermott (London: Eyre and Spottiswoode, 1989)

Barber, Richard, *Edward Prince of Wales and Aquitaine: A Biography of the Black Prince* (Woodbridge: Boydell Press, 1978)

Bellamy, J. G., *The Law of Treason in the Late Middle Ages* (Cambridge: Cambridge University Press, 1970)

Benedictow, Ole J., *The Black Death, 1346–1353: The Complete History* (Woodbridge: Boydell Press, 2004)

Bisson, T. N., *The Medieval Crown of Aragon: A Short History* (Oxford: Clarendon Press, 1991)

Black, Antony, *Political Thought in Europe* (Cambridge: Cambridge University Press, 1992)

Bloch, D., *Aristotle on Memory and Recollection: Text, Translation, Interpretation and Reception in Western Scholasticism* (Leiden: Brill, 2007)

Bothwell, J. S., *Falling from Grace: Reversal of Fortune and the English Nobility, 1075–1455* (Manchester: Manchester University Press, 2008)

Brandt, William J., *The Shape of Medieval History: Studies in Modes of Perception* (New Haven, CT: Yale University Press, 1966)

Caetano, Marcelo, 'As Cortes de 1385', *Revista Portuguesa de História*, 5:2 (1951), 5–86

Carr, E. H., *What is History?* (Harmondsworth: Penguin, 1964)

Castro, Filipe, 'In Search of Unique Iberian Ship Design Concepts', *Historical Archaeology*, 42:2 (2008), 63–87

Chandos Herald, *La vie du Prince Noir*, Beihefte Zur Zeitschrift Für Romanische Philologie, vol. 147, ed. Diana B. Tyson (Tübingen: Max Niemeyer, 1975)

Childs, Wendy, R., 'Anglo-Portuguese Relations in the Fourteenth Century', in James L. Gillespie (ed.), *The Age of Richard II* (New York/Stroud: St Martin's Press/Sutton Publishing Ltd, 1997), pp. 27–49

Coelho, António Borges, *A Revolução de 1383: tentativa de caracterização*, 3rd edn (Lisbon: Seara Nova, 1977)

Cohn, Norman, *The Pursuit of the Millennium: Revolutionary Messianism in Medieval and Reformation Europe and its Bearing on Modern Totalitarian Movements*, 2nd edn (London: Mercury Books, 1962)

Collingwood, R. G., *The Idea of History* (Oxford: Clarendon Press, 1946)

Cuttler, S. H., *The Law of Treason and Treason Trials in Later Medieval France* (Cambridge: Cambridge University Press, 1981)

Delachenal, R., *Charles V*, 5 vols (Paris: Picard, 1916), vol. 3

Deyermond, Alan, 'Historia universal e ideología nacional en Pablo de Santa María', in *Homenaje a Álvaro Galmés de Fuentes*, vol. 2 (Oviedo: University; Madrid: Gredos, 1985)

Estow, Clara, *Pedro the Cruel of Castile, 1350–1369* (Leiden: Brill, 1995)

——'Royal Madness in the *Crónica de Rey Don Pedro*', *Mediterranean Studies*, 6 (1996), 13–28

——'War and Peace in Medieval Iberia: Castilian–Granadan Relations in the Mid-Fourteenth Century', in *The Hundred Years War: A Wider Focus*, ed. L. J. Andrew Villalon and Donald Kagay (Leiden: Brill, 2005), pp. 151–75

Fernandes, Fátima Regina, 'Nobles and the Crown on the Eve of Portugal's Atlantic Discoveries', *Mediterranean Studies*, 9 (2000), 35–41

Ferro, M. José Pimenta, 'Para o Estudo da Numária de D. Dinis', *Do Tempo e da História*, 5 (1972), 201–28

Fowler, Kenneth, *Medieval Mercenaries: The Great Companies* (Oxford: Blackwell, 2001)

Friel, Ian, *The Good Ship: Ships, Shipbuilding and Technology in England, 1200–1520* (Baltimore, MD: The Johns Hopkins University Press, 1995)

Froissart, Jean *Chronicles*, trans. Geoffrey Brereton (Harmondsworth: Penguin, 1968)

Given-Wilson, Chris, *Chronicles: The Writing of History in Medieval England* (London and New York: Hambledon Continuum, 2004)

——'Official and Semi-Official History in the Later Middle Ages: The English Evidence in Context', *The Medieval Chronicle*, 5 (2008), 1–16

Gomes, Cristina Mota, *Money with History: Collection of the Bank of Portugal* (Lisbon: Banco de Portugal, 2006)

Gomes, Rita Costa, *The Making of a Court Society: Kings and Nobles in Late Medieval Portugal*, trans. Alison Aiken (Cambridge: Cambridge University Press, 2003)

González Paz, Carlos Andrés, 'The Role of Mercenary Troops in Spain in the Fourteenth Century: The Civil War', *Mercenaries and Paid Men: The Mercenary Identity in the Middle Ages*, rev. edn John France (Leiden: Brill, 2008), pp. 331–43

Green, David, *Edward the Black Prince: Power in Medieval Europe* (Harlow: Pearson Education, 2007)

——*The Hundred Years War: A People's History* (New Haven, CT and London: Yale University Press, 2014)

Kagay, Donald, 'Battle-Seeking Commanders in the Later Middle Ages: Phases of Generalship in the War of the Two Pedros', *The Hundred Years War (Part III): Further Considerations* (Leiden: Brill, 2013), pp. 63–84

——'The Defense of the Crown of Aragon during the War of the Two Pedros (1356–1366)', in L. J. Andrew Villalon and Donald Kagay (eds), *The Hundred Years War (Part II): Different Vistas* (Leiden: Brill, 2008), pp. 185–210

Kantorowicz, Ernst H., *The King's Two Bodies: A Study in Mediaeval Theology* (Princeton, NJ: Princeton University Press, 1981, reprint 1997)

Krynen, Jacques, *L'empire du roi: Idées et croyances politiques en France XIIIe–XVe siècle* (Paris: Gallimard-Jeunesse, 1993)

Landström, Björn, *The Ship* (London: Allen & Unwin, 1976)

Lapa, Manuel Rodrigues, *Lições de literatura portuguesa: época medieval*, 6th edn (Coimbra: Coimbra Editora, 1966)

Linehan, Peter, 'Castile, Navarre, and Portugal', in Michael Jones (ed.), *New Cambridge Medieval History VI c.1300–1415* (Cambridge: Cambridge University Press, 1999, 2000, 2004)

Livermore, H. V., *A New History of Portugal* (Cambridge: Cambridge University Press, 1966)

Lopes, Fernão, *Crónica de D. Pedro*, ed. Giuliano Macchi (Lisbon: Imprensa Nacional-Casa da Moeda, 2007)

—— *Crónica de D. Fernando*, ed. Giuliano Macchi (Lisbon: Imprensa Nacional-Casa da Moeda, 2004)

—— *Cronica del Rei Dom Joham I de boa memoria e dos Reis de Portugal o décimo, Parte primeira*, ed. Anselmo Braamcamp Freire (Lisbon: Imprensa Nacional-Casa da Moeda, 1977)

—— *Cronica del Rei Dom Joham I de boa memoria e dos reis de Portugal o décimo, Parte segunda*, ed. William J. Entwistle (Lisbon: Imprensa Nacional-Casa da Moeda, 1977)

——*Crónica de D. João I segundo o Códice no. 352 do Arquivo Nacional da Torre do Tombo, Parte I*, prefaced by António Sérgio (Oporto: Civilização, 1945)

——*The English in Portugal 1367–1387*, ed. and trans. D. W. Lomax and R. J. Oakley (Warminster: Aris & Phillips, 1988)

——*História de uma revolução: Primeira parte da 'Crónica de El-Rei D. João I de Boa Memória'*, ed. José Hermano Saraiva (Lisbon: Europa-América, 1977)

Lopes, Luís Seabra, 'Sistemas Legais de Medidas de Peso e Capacidade, do Condado Portucalense ao Século XVI', *Portugalia*, New Series, 24 (2003), pp. 116–64

López de Ayala, Pero, *Cronicas*, ed. José-Luis Martín (Barcelona: Editorial Planeta, 1991)

Macedo, Helder, 'Eight Centuries of Portuguese Literature', in S. C. Parkinson, Pazos Alonso, and T. Earle (eds), *A Companion to Portuguese Literature* (Woodbridge: Tamesis, 2009), pp. 1–24

MacKay, Angus *Spain in the Middle Ages: From Frontier to Empire, 1000–1500* (London: Macmillan, 1977)

Martins, Mário, *A Bíblia na literatura medieval portuguesa* (Lisbon: Instituto de Cultura Portuguesa, 1979)

——*Estudos de cultura medieval*, vol. 3 (Lisbon: Brotéria, 1983)

Mason, John W., 'Leonid Meteors and Comet 55P/Tempel-Tuttle', *British Astronomical Association*, 105:5 (1995), 219–35

Mattoso, José, '*In memoriam* de Teresa Amado', *Medievalista*, 15 (2014), 8–11 <https://journals.openedition.org/medievalista/257> [Accessed 2 February 2022].

O'Callaghan, Joseph F., *A History of Medieval Spain* (Ithaca, NY: Cornell University Press, 1975)

Ormrod, W. Mark, *Edward III* (New Haven, CT and London: Yale University Press, 2011)

Parkinson, Stephen, Cláudia Pazos Alonso and T. F. Earle (eds), *A Companion to Portuguese Literature* (Woodbridge: Tamesis, 2009)

Parkinson, Stephen, 'Fernão Lopes and Portuguese Prose Writing of the Middle Ages', in Stephen Parkinson, Cláudia Pazos Alonso and T.F. Earle (eds), *A Companion to Portuguese Literature* (Woodbridge: Tamesis, 2009), pp. 45–55

Passos, Maria Lúcia Perrone de Faro, *O herói na crónica de D. João I de Fernão Lopes* (Lisbon: Prelo, 1974)

Pérez de Guzmán, Fernán, *Generaciones y semblanzas*, ed. R. B. Tate (London: Tamesis, 1965)

Phillips, J. R. S. *The Medieval Expansion of Europe*, 2nd edn (Oxford: Clarendon Press, 1998)

Plöger, Karsten, *England and the Avignon Popes: The Practice of Diplomacy in Late Medieval Europe* (London: Legenda, 2005)

Rebelo, Luís de Sousa, *A Concepção do Poder em Fernão Lopes* (Lisbon: Horizonte, 1983)

——'The Idea of Kingship in the Chronicles of Fernão Lopes', in F. W. Hodcroft et al. (eds), *Mediaeval and Renaissance Studies on Spain and Portugal in Honour of P. E. Russell* (Oxford: Society for the Study of Medieval Languages and Literature, 1981), pp. 167–79

Renouard, Yves, *The Avignon Papacy, 1305–1403*, trans. D. Bethell (Hamden, CT: Archon Books, 1970)

Riquer, Martín de, *Resumen de literatura portuguesa* (Barcelona: Seix Barral, 1947)

Rose, Stanley L., 'Anecdotal Narrative in Fernão Lopes', *Crónica de D. Pedro I*, *Luso-Brazilian Review*, 8:1 (1971), 78–87

Round, Nicholas G., *The Greatest Man Uncrowned: A Study of the Fall of Don Álvaro de Luna* (London: Tamesis, 1986)

Ruiz, Juan, *Libro de Buen Amor*, ed. G. B. Gybbon-Monypenny (Madrid: Castalia, 1989)

Ruiz, Teofilo F., *Spain's Centuries of Crisis: 1300–1474* (Chichester: Blackwell Publishing, 2011)

Russell, P. E., *The English Intervention in Spain and Portugal in the Time of Edward III and Richard II* (Oxford: Clarendon, 1953)

——*Portugal, Spain and the African Atlantic, 1343–1490* (Aldershot: Variorum, 1995)

——'As fontes de Fernão Lopes', *Revista Portuguesa da História*, Colecção Universitas (Coimbra: Coimbra Editora, 1941); rev. and trans. as 'On the Sources of Fernão Lopes', in *Portugal, Spain and the African Atlantic,* II (Aldershot: Variorum, 1995), pp. 1–30

Rymer, Thomas, *Feodera, conventions, litterae etc*, rev. ed. A. Clarke, F. Holbrooke, and J. Coley, 4 vols in 7 parts (London: Record Commission, 1816–1869)

Serrão, Joaquim Veríssimo, *História de Portugal*, vol. 1, *Estado, Pátria e Nação (1080–1415)*, 2nd ed. (Lisbon: Verbo, 1978)

Serrão, Joel, *O carácter social da Revolução de 1383,* 3rd edn (Lisbon: Horizonte, 1976)

Smalley, Beryl, *Historians in the Middle Ages* (London: Thames and Hudson, 1974)

Spufford, Peter, Wendy Wilkinson, and Sarah Tolley, *Handbook of Medieval Exchange* (London: Offices of the Royal Historical Society, 1986)

Sumption, Jonathan, *The Hundred Years War, II: Trial by Fire* (Philadelphia: University of Pennsylvania Press, 1999)

——*The Hundred Years War III: Divided Houses* (London: Faber and Faber, 2009)

Vale, Malcolm, *The Origins of the Hundred Years War: The Angevin Legacy, 1250–1340* (Oxford: Clarendon Press, 1996)

Vernier, Richard, *The Flower of Chivalry: Bertrand du Guesclin and the Hundred Years War* (Woodbridge: Boydell Press, 2003),

——*Lord of the Pyrenees: Gaston Fébus, Count of Foix, 1331–1391* (Woodbridge: Boydell Press, 2008)

Villalon, L. J. Andrew, 'Spanish Involvement in the Hundred Years War and the Battle of Nájera', in L. J. Andrew Villalon and Donald Kagay (eds), *The Hundred Years War: A Wider Focus* (Leiden: Brill, 2005), pp. 3–74

CPSIA information can be obtained
at www.ICGtesting.com
Printed in the USA
JSHW061402180623
43011JS00003B/4

9 781855 663961